T0086193

FINDING
HIS STORY
IN HISTORY

MATT SOMERLOT

WESTBOW
PRESS®
A DIVISION OF THOMAS NELSON
& ZONDERVAN

WestBow Press books may be ordered through booksellers or by contacting:

WestBow Press
A Division of Thomas Nelson & Zondervan
1663 Liberty Drive
Bloomington, IN 47403
www.westbowpress.com
844-714-3454

Scripture quotations taken from The Holy Bible, New International Version® NIV® Copyright © 1973 1978 1984 2011 by Biblica, Inc. TM. Used by permission. All rights reserved worldwide.

ISBN: 978-1-9736-9822-7 (sc)
ISBN: 978-1-9736-9824-1 (hc)
ISBN: 978-1-9736-9823-4 (e)

Library of Congress Control Number: 2020913133

Print information available on the last page.

WestBow Press rev. date: 09/17/2020

DEDICATION

To Ruthie, Liz, and Joey who nudged me to follow Jesus in a way that fanned the flame of a love for scripture and trivia and helped me find a way to fuse them together for His kingdom.

And to Mom, Dad, and my treasured siblings for instilling in me an awareness of God's kingdom and His love.

FOREWORD

A little more than five years ago I had the privilege of leading a group of dedicated people in the planting of a new church. Matt Somerlot was one of the key volunteers on the launch team that set our new church into motion. I would say that Matt was my "right hand" man for the first few years – until he helped me develop other volunteers to take his place. I realized very quickly that Matt had an incredible heart for serving others and a unique gift of connecting with them. It became very apparent that Matt was a relational evangelist using the gift of hospitality. If you are unaware of the gift of hospitality, this is a gift of grace that draws people into a relationship.

I truly enjoyed getting to know Matt on a deeper level. Some of my favorite times in ministry at that church plant were the lunches shared with Matt at local greasy spoons. We loved searching out obscure restaurants and rating them. Honestly, Matt did all the research and I just followed along. Over lunch we would discuss the quality of the food we partook, but we also discussed the way in which God was feeding our souls and filling us up. In those lunch meetings I began to see Matt's passion and desire for ministry grow, especially the ministry of writing in a way that connects people with Jesus.

I encouraged Matt to begin ministering to our people through a weekly newsletter. People marveled at Matt's ability to use his God-given talent of writing. His Holy Spirit inspired creative use of words connected with people through quick wit and grace and truth. His writing style is a catchy way to present the gospel. Matt took a historical moment in time and drew that moment into scripture to bring about a relevant truth. I truly believe that Matt understands the value of time – how each day is a God-given historical moment that is to be relished. Over time he has taken these writings and added many more to create this book, Finding His Story in History. I must admit, it has been fun and encouraging to watch Matt and this book blossom.

Finding His Story in History will be a blessing to you. Read this book on a daily basis as a devotional or as a reminder of how every day is important and relevant in the eyes of God. Maybe you should get two copies and share one with a friend as a gift of hospitality.

In Christ,

Steven Brumbeloe

PREFACE

Author C.S. Lewis once said, "History is a story written by the finger of God." I love that quote because it illustrates this book's underpinning and the journey it took to get here.

I have always loved all kinds of history. I believe it is rooted in an appreciation for the mundane. It is recognition that throughout the Bible, we see God use regular, ordinary people and events to reveal his magnificence. But, what about someone's birth, the opening of a Broadway play, a speech, or an invention? If you look closely, you will find He is always there, and to bridge it back to His story, anchored in scripture, is to stir the dust that reveals fingerprints you had not seen at first glance. By writing this book, my preeminent hope is that eyes will begin to open to God's presence throughout history, and the here and now. It could help answer the question, "How can seeing what God has done in the past help me in the present?"

This book came into being out of a weekly newsletter email I was writing for my church. To retain readership, I was led by the Holy Spirit to introduce this concept to my captive audience. I still included the baptism announcements, pool parties, and other church events that go in a church newsletter, but it offered an opportunity to be bold for Christ and build on something stirring within my heart. I could preach the Gospel in my own unique way, introducing people to God in a brand new way. I called it *This Day In History, with a Biblical Slant*, and it was as simple as taking a historical event from each day of the year and tying it to a scriptural point of reference to create a relevant truth or life application. Some align incredibly well, and others, well, you tap into the creativity God grants you and let the Holy Spirit guide you! My sincere appreciation for trivia somehow seemed to help here!

With a foundation of weekly newsletter devotionals, I embarked on the full-year mission. I asked the Holy Spirit to highlight the event and scripture as I combed through the various happenings on each day of the year in preparation for this book. I sometimes found myself asking Him, "Is that really what you had in mind??" I learned oodles about how God can use historical events as a vessel for His message and there is no doubt I became a finer trivia player along the way!

Do you know who was born on your birthday, or what famous event may have happened on that same day in history? Frank Sinatra was born the same day as me, and Kenya gained its independence. The more insightful question is, how can finding God or understanding His role in history, tethered to scriptural references, help you develop, maintain, or deepen a relationship with Him in the present?

It is easy to find Him in the beauty of a symphony orchestra or piece of art. Likewise, I believe His story is also found in the history of the Oscar Meyer Weinermobile, or a flight where they milked a cow onboard and dropped milk cartons to folks on the ground. Yes, like manna from Heaven! When I began connecting God with historical events and random bits of trivia like this, I knew the Holy Spirit was leading me in an unconventional way. At that point, I knew that while my own acuity in this connection was intriguing, I simply had to share it.

Historical events are the river flowing beneath our very existence. Yet, we rarely acknowledge or associate a divine presence and guiding light to them, even the craziest, strangest, or most compelling events. This book is an opportunity to dig in and explore, finding God in a fun and meaningful way. Sure, each day is a box of chocolates, but it is also an opportunity to open your Bible. Throughout the book, as the connection between an event and scripture is made, you may not find the whole passage of scripture. That is intentional. I want you to use this daily devotional as a jumping-off point. I want to encourage you to dive into God's word and see for yourself that these relevant truths, ideas, principles, and teachings are all there. Don't take my word for it – open the finest history book of all time, the Bible, and see for yourself! I believe you will start making your own connections, thereby awakening a transformational awareness of the Kingdom of God. It will be completely unexpected, but I guarantee you will be filled with a joy that can only come from a relationship with the Holy Spirit that begins with scripture.

Each day is a gift. In the presence of this present, you have your own opportunity to make history and find that God's story, His story, is all around you.

When you seek God in history, you will find Him. After all, it is His story! Jeremiah 33:3 says, "Call to me and I will answer you and tell you great and unsearchable things you do not know." Read on and call out to God through prayer! Let Him answer through a bond formed between scripture and whimsical trivia. That is the place we will begin to *find His story in history!*

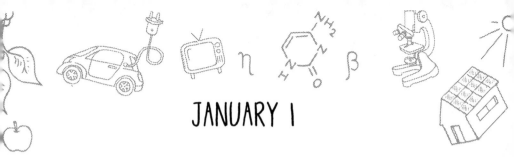

JANUARY 1

To the Ends of the Earth

Isaiah 45:22

On January 1, 1739, French explorer Jean Baptiste Bouvet de Lozier discovered the world's most remote island, Bouvet Island. That's certainly one way to ring in the New Year, huh? This uninhabited island is located between South Africa and Antarctica and is roughly 1400 miles away from the nearest humans.

What's His story? How close do you feel to God today? What does being close to God mean to you? Sometimes we may feel as far away from God as this island is from other people and landmasses. But His promise of grace, forgiveness, and the gift of the Holy Spirit draw us closer to Him. It includes those who might feel like they're on a lump of rock and ice in the middle of the ocean with only a few lichens and penguins for company. As we begin this journey together, and especially on a day on which self-improvement goals (i.e., resolutions) are professed, do not be dismayed that you are too far gone to be saved. As it says in Isaiah 45:22, "Turn to me and be saved, all you ends of the earth; for I am God and there is no other." Turn to God. You may feel completely alone, but as with the New Year's resolution you may have made today, we can do nothing apart from God! Remember, even the loneliest place on Earth, Bouvet Island, isn't too far for our God, but you might need to pack a parka. Are you closing the gap and turning to God? What needs to happen this year to make that happen?

JANUARY 2

The Slow Lane

Psalm 103:8

On January 2, 1974, United States President Richard Nixon signed a bill lowering the maximum United States speed limit to 55 mph to conserve gasoline.

What's His story? I am reminded of the Sammy Hagar song, "I Can't Drive 55!" Living in Atlanta, Georgia I don't believe I have ever seen someone driving 55 miles per hour on the highway unless they were eating a French-dip sandwich or reading a book – yes, I've seen both. When we are always in a hurry, we tend to miss things right before our eyes. This bill is a reminder to slow down and savor our surroundings. When we do that, our eyes are opened to the abounding love our Lord reveals all around us. It is ever-present in the Bible. The reminder in Psalm 103:8 that the Lord is compassionate and gracious, slow to anger, abounding in love is our assurance that it's okay to drive slowly and let people over even when they don't signal. In doing so, we acknowledge our desire to be patient, slow down, and absorb the glorious gift we repeatedly receive from our ever-patient Lord. Sometimes slow is the way to go, and you never know what you'll encounter when you deliberately take it easy. God can reveal plans, dreams, and encouragement to an open heart, but if we're speeding by, we can miss it. So even though speed limits are back up, the reminder and the gift remain. Don't go through life missing the signposts God has set in front of you! Slow down and enjoy it. You might be surprised by what you see.

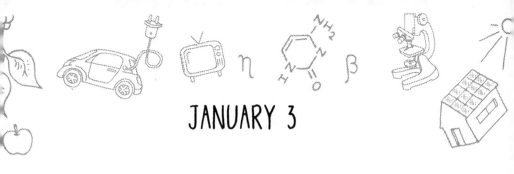

JANUARY 3

The Next Generation

Psalm 102:18

On January 3, 1938, The March of Dimes was founded by then-president Franklin D. Roosevelt, who was stricken by polio as a young adult. He created the organization after his own experience cultivated deep empathy for the disabled. Typically a childhood disease, Roosevelt understood the need for a vaccine and asked the public to help. During one such fundraiser, a singer asked folks to send dimes to the president, thus the coining of the name.

What's His story? Aside from the world events he endured as president, Roosevelt understood how important it was to take care of the generation to come. The fact that he was thirty-nine when he contracted polio may have impacted his view, but I believe God used Roosevelt as an example for others so the next generation would know. We have the same opportunity to share the good news of the Gospel with the next generation. In Psalm 102:18, it says, "Let this be written for a future generation, that a people not yet created may praise the Lord." Like many of the Psalms, this one is a lesson for handling affliction while still rejoicing in the Lord. This attitude should be consistent from generation to generation. Roosevelt's empathy for the disabled that led to the March of Dimes is parallel to our opportunity to care for the next generation's spiritual health. What do you think a transformational vaccine would be, and would you take it?

JANUARY 4

Perfect Perfection

1 John 3:5

On January 4, 1930, legendary Miami Dolphins head coach Don Shula was born. Shula is currently the only NFL coach to have led a team to a perfect season with no losses or ties. Legend has it that the remaining members of the 1972 Dolphins gather to toast each year when the last undefeated team of the current season loses a game, thus preserving their unique place in NFL history.

What's His story? When you think of perfection, what comes to mind for you? Is it a fresh blanket of snow with absolutely no footprints? Or perhaps a perfect score on a test or assignment? When we celebrate an occasion like a football team that doesn't lose, we have placed a high value on perfection, but do we genuinely comprehend its worth? I believe the answer is in 1 John 3:5. It says, "But you know that he appeared so that he might take away our sins. And in him is no sin." That last part is the kicker. No, I don't mean the Dolphins' kicker, although he might not have missed a field goal during that season. The last part of this scripture says that in Him, there is no sin, and this is an attestation to Jesus' perfection. Because of Jesus, we are wholly forgiven and look to eternal life with him. Through faith in Jesus, we are reconciled, and the reason to repent and turn to Him is as clear as day. Do you accept that Jesus has washed away your sins? He is the lamb that takes away the sins of the world! You don't have to be a Dolphins fan to appreciate their perfection that season, but understanding the perfection of Jesus is so much greater!!

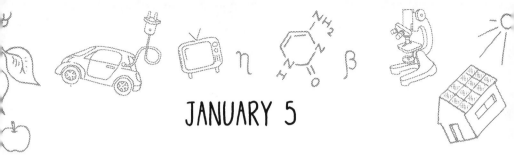

JANUARY 5

Bad Bounces

Matthew 17:16

On January 5, 1971, the Harlem Globetrotters lost to the New Jersey Reds in Martin, Tennessee, ending a 2,495 game winning streak! Yes, we have moved from perfection yesterday to almost perfection today! The Globetrotter games are a mix of entertainment and basketball. Between the Reds and the Washington Generals, over the years, the 'Trotters have won probably 13,000 games, so this was quite the upset. Apparently, the team was distracted while entertaining the crowd and lost track of the score. In the end, kids were crying, and fans were booing over the loss. I guess they came for the expected but got the unexpected.

What's His story? I would imagine the Globetrotters went into each game expecting to win, similar to the disciples who had been given power by Jesus to heal and drive out demons. They expected to be successful in all that they undertook. In Matthew 17:16, their winning streak hits a bit of a speed-bump when they were unable to drive the demons out of a young boy. Jesus comes to save the day, and in doing so, teaches us to remain humble and focused on him, for without him, we can do nothing. It's also a glorification of Jesus' power and an opportunity for Him to emphasize the importance of faith that can move mountains! Sometimes we put trust in the wrong things, assuming we are in our control. Jesus gives us perspective. The power of the Holy Spirit is within us. His teachings instill the importance of how and when as He equips us. So how do you react to the end of a 'win streak'? Do you refocus on the main thing, which is Jesus?

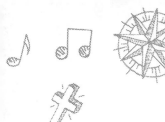

JANUARY 6

Buy a Vowel

Jeremiah 18:3

On January 6, 1975, the TV game show *Wheel of Fortune* premiered. I would call it a combination of a spinning prize wheel and hangman, where you spin the wheel and call out letters until you can solve the word or phrase to win money. I don't know about you, but I've always been a big fan! It is interesting to note that vowels have always cost $250, and co-host Vanna never wears the same outfit. I guess there is both a little stability and a little surprise in each episode.

What's His story? If you're like me, you have envisioned yourself up there, spinning the wheel and calling out letters. Do you also yell out letters or words towards the TV during the show? We sometimes just refer to the show as *Wheel*. There's another wheel in the Bible – the potter's wheel in Jeremiah 18:3. God tells Jeremiah to go to the potter and observe the potter at his wheel to see what he can do with a lump of clay. Just as the potter so skillfully makes a beautiful vessel out the clay, using only the wheel, his hands, and a bit of water, God applies the same skill to us. With His help, we become the vessel to carry His message and mission. The potter's workshop probably has many different types of vessels, and each is unique in its way. God establishes His sovereignty and reassures Jeremiah of the critical message he must deliver to Israel to turn back to God. Using the illustration of the potter's wheel and allowing God to mold us, we can create our Wheel of Fortune, but instead of prizes and money, we receive a much more vital gift by living faithfully in His principles. Are you a work in progress being molded by the expert craftsman? Or are you a beautiful vessel in action? Either way, the process itself can be as dynamic as a result, don't you agree?

JANUARY 7

Moving Pictures

Acts 11:4

On January 7, 1894, William Kennedy Dixon received his patent for a motion picture film camera or kinetograph. Using a viewer called a kinetoscope, a 50-foot section of the film was viewed at a time. From this, modern motion pictures were born.

What's His story? I'm sure you have a favorite movie. Perhaps it elicits and stirs such emotion in you that it transports you to another time, place, or feeling. Book adaptations are a recurring theme of movies. Think of the Bible and how many movies have been made out of the incredible stories within it. The Ten Commandments and The Passion of Christ are just two examples. Legendary director Cecil DeMille once said, "Give me any two pages of the Bible, and I'll give you a picture." Peter reveals his script in Acts 11:4 when he describes his vision in great detail, allowing us to form a vision along with him. It says, "Peter began and explained everything to them precisely as it had happened." When you read the Bible, does a motion picture of God's word form in your mind? When you think of how the Bible comes together as multiple authors across 66 books tell the story of God and his people, it reveals a picture of love, justice, grace, reconciliation, restoration, and salvation that is our life as believers. What scene are you directing in your heart today?

JANUARY 8

Not of This World War

Romans 12:2

On January 8, 1918, United States President Woodrow Wilson introduced his Fourteen Points plan. To end World War I, Wilson created this plan that he felt would make a long and lasting peace. Although much of his plan was scuttled in the final Treaty of Versailles, he received the 1919 Nobel Peace Prize for his efforts.

What's His story? You can argue that Wilson's religious convictions led his executive leadership style. He lived out Romans 12:2. It says, "Do not conform any longer to the pattern of this world, but be transformed by the renewing of your mind. Then you will be able to test and approve what God's will is – his good, pleasing, and perfect will." He was the only leader in WWI who presented a plan that set expectations and goals for peace. Even more than that, his Fourteen Points highlight Christian optimism and benevolence in a way that was not well received on the world stage. Through discernment and faith, he knew that it was the right thing, and he stuck to it. When we face the challenge of creating peace in our families or the workplace, we often do not know where to start. Maybe developing your own Fourteen Points is a beginning, but unless multiple nations are involved, you might be okay with just two or three points! Are you living confined and conformed to this world, or are you freed by the infinite points of God's grace?

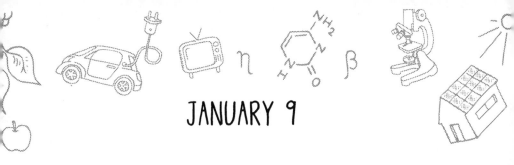

JANUARY 9

Guiding Light

John 8:12

On January 9, 1816, Sir Humphry Davy tested his safety lamp for miners. It was invented in 1815, tested on this date in 1816, and became known as the Davy lamp. It ultimately saved many lives. Methane gas in the mines and the flame from miner's lamps were an explosive combination before this lamp was invented. Davy's lamp separated the flame from the gas, thus creating a safe environment.

What's His story? As Jesus reminds us in John 8:12, "I am the Light of the World. Whoever follows me will never walk in darkness, but will have the light of life." In the case of miners using the Davy lamp, they obtained and followed the light of life. They trusted their lantern, just as we trust Jesus as the light in our life. We are following Jesus so that His divine light will diffuse over us in a pattern of joy, comfort, peace, and expectant hope every single day. We don't have to travel into a dangerous mine to experience this. The chance to demonstrate our devotion to Jesus and His light is out there everywhere we go. This world can often be as dark and pitch-black as a mine. Whose light are you following today? You'll be delighted to know the other option for this day was to expound on the fact that explorer Christopher Columbus, sailing on this day in 1493 near the Dominican Republic, confused manatees with mermaids, and supposedly said they were not as beautiful as depicted in art. I'm sticking with the Light, and you should choose it as well!

JANUARY 10

Where's the Beef?

Proverbs 15:17

On January 10, 1984, eighty-one-year-old Clara Peller first declared, "Where's the beef??" in that famous Wendy's hamburgers commercial. If you've never seen it, I'd say it's worth searching for it online. In the commercial, three ladies are standing by some marvelous-looking hamburger buns. When Clara picks up the bun and discovers a tiny patty of beef, she barks out her famous phrase. It was a very effective commercial and even found its way into the 1984 Presidential campaign.

What's His story? Have you ever examined your own life and explored areas of spirituality that need to be "beefed up"? Christ calls us to lead by example. Faith is often caught rather than taught. We can live a fluffy bun existence with little substance on the inside, or can we earnestly pray, and live in a way which says that I want to be in the kitchen with God co-creating a mega-stack burger that leads others to say, "There's the beef!!" Can it be a plant-based burger, since nobody can tell a difference today anyway? Yes! Proverbs 15:17 declares, "Better a meal of vegetables where there is love than a fattened calf with hatred." It sounds like an advertisement for a Christian vegan burger, but the point is that we have to include love in all that we do. And when we share and receive love, Christ is present. Are you inviting Him to our table, just as we have an open invitation to His? Who knew that Clara was just asking us to love fully? Are you living a life with no beef? Spiritual beef, that is.

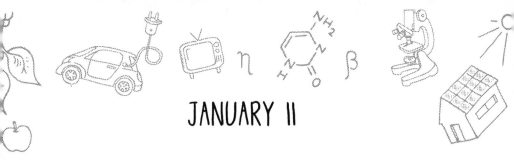

JANUARY 11

Happy Fluffy Clouds

Psalm 19:1

On January 11, 1983, the TV show *The Joy of Painting* with Bob Ross first aired. If you're not familiar with Bob, he is the one with the calm, gentle, pastoral voice creating masterpieces in literal seconds through brushstrokes and pallet knife technique. He teaches us to transform mistakes into happy little trees or squirrels. He was simply a maestro with the paintbrush, and we see many a Bob Ross reminder out there daily, including the Bob Ross Chia Pet that captures his trademark hair!

What's His story? There is magnificent beauty found in the creation all around us. Just look around you right now. It could be in a pattern in the carpet, or a building, or a natural expanse. God's hand in creativity is everywhere you look. Psalm 19:1 affirms, "The heavens declare the glory of God; the skies proclaim the work of his hands." Bob Ross' job, in which he took great pride and evoked great joy, was to teach us how to capture the grandeur before us. Whether as a cotton candy sunrise or a magenta sunset, the sky could be the backdrop for a more extraordinary display, but it also might be the star of the show. Either way, when we see the canvas before our eyes, God's glory comes to live within us. Just like the Psalmist, we should proclaim the work of His hands. Now, that's the joy of knowing God! What's on your canvas today? Where do you see God's hands working in it?

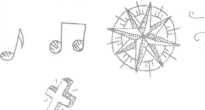

JANUARY 12

88 Keys to the Kingdom

James 1:17

On January 12, 1928, the very talented pianist Vladimir Horowitz debuted at Carnegie Hall in New York City. With his electrical temperament and talent, Horowitz brought an excitement to the piano like no other.

What's His story? While pianos come in different types like grand, baby grand, and upright, they almost all have 88 keys - 52 white and 36 black. Now, think about the Bible. And while there are different translations like the King James, NSV, NIV, it remains as a collection of God's word through 66 individual books of scripture - 39 Old Testament and 27 New Testament. As a talented pianist, Horowitz elevated the music produced by the collection of keys on any piano as he played with passion and exhilaration. As followers of Christ, we have an opportunity, and a requirement, to personally bring the words of each book of the Bible to life. As we delight in accepting God's grace, we can gain the same level of abundant vitality out of the Bible that you might be able to compare to Horowitz's passion for the piano. It's not the equipment or the words on a page, but it's how you use them. Your tools, combined with God-given talents, fan the flame, leading to the outwardly apparent love, joy, and happiness that shines out and transforms others. As James 1:17 says, every good and perfect gift is from above. What is your gift, and what is your outlet?

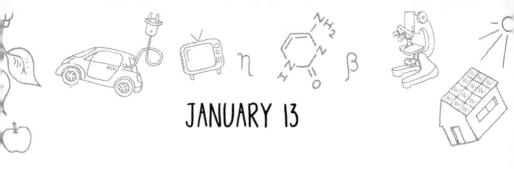

JANUARY 13

Ultimate Gospel

Matthew 28:19-20

On January 13, 1957, the Wham-O Company produced the first Frisbee. The Frisbee is a round plastic disc that looks like a flying saucer and can be thrown back and forth between players in a variety of ways. The creative inventor Fred Morrison and his wife loved to throw upside-down cake and pie pans to each other on the California beaches. Perhaps with safety in mind, he decided to create a plastic version. The word Frisbee came from the Frisbie Baking Company because their pie pans had the word Frisbie imprinted on each one. My older brother taught me how to throw one at a very young age and how not to get hurt by one. Thankfully ours were plastic and not metal!

What's His story? I believe that Frisbee is enjoyed best in a game called Ultimate Frisbee. Think of it as a cross between American football and Frisbee throwing. The critical rule is that once you catch it on the run, you can only take a few steps before you are required to throw it to someone else. Can't you just imagine Jesus playing Ultimate Frisbee with the disciples, maybe on a sandy field or beach? Our faith should be a lot like the game rule requiring you to throw to someone else. Instead of focusing solely on developing our faith, we should also be concerned with sharing it – distributing it across the field! Your faith can quickly grow when you share it with others. Matthew 28 is a reminder that we can confidently spread the word because He never leaves us. Therefore, we can joyfully and assuredly spread His message. How are you spreading a great message of hope today? Are you tossing your faith out for someone else to catch it?

JANUARY 14

A Beautiful Friendship

Philippians 3:21

On January 14, 1957, actor Humphrey Bogart died in Los Angeles, California. He began his acting career on Broadway and later moved to movies. Bogart starred in plenty of popular films like *The Maltese Falcon* and *The Caine Mutiny*. Still, his performance in a role opposite Ingrid Bergman in the movie *Casablanca* was his most memorable.

What's His story? The movie *Casablanca* itself is an absolute classic. Bogart plays a character named Rick, who goes through a transformation from a self-centered focus to one of selfless, sacrificial love. It is impressive to watch, and I believe we can all relate to it. We create belief systems that protect us after we've experienced pain and hurt. Control becomes a central desire. But I believe one line in the movie nails it when Rick tells Gracie, "..true yesterday, true today, and true tomorrow." Is there a better description of the truth of God's word? His word never changes. We are the ones who undergo a transformational change that occurs on the inside, yet manifests itself in outward appearance. Philippians 3:21 articulates this transformation from a lowly body to something like His glorious body in such a way that causes us to ask ourselves how are we showing that transformation to others. It is great if it is still a work in progress like me because that means God is still molding our hearts! Our relationship with God should be a beautiful friendship, shouldn't it?! Every day are you seeking a glorious transformation like Christ's resurrected body?

JANUARY 15

Preparation Makes Perfect

Proverbs 24:27

On January 15, 2009, US Airways pilot Chesley Sullenberger, III, also known as "Sully," was involved in an incident dubbed "The Miracle on the Hudson." One minute after taking off from New York's LaGuardia airport, Sully's plane flew through a flock of geese, resulting in multiple bird strikes and the total loss of the two main engines. Sully's calm, collected professionalism and skill as a pilot allowed him to land the plane on the Hudson River without any fatalities.

What's His story? The fact that a plane landed on a river with no loss of life is truly a miracle. Still, Sully's years of flying, preparation, attention to detail, and passion for learning put him into a position to accomplish his task. After the event, Sully wrote a book entitled *Highest Duty: My Search for What Really Matters*. The title itself puts things into perspective. Proverbs 24:27 also does this as it says, "Finish your outdoor work and get your fields ready; after that, build your house." It may sound like a to-do list, but it's sage advice for the proper order of how to carry out our work. Sully was very familiar with this through his extensive time training in a flight simulator, reading manuals, and all the things pilots do before actually flying. The preparation enabled him to handle any emergency calmly. The same is true for us. Through diligent biblical studies, engagement with other Christians, practicing being the hands and feet of the church, and establishing a Christian community prepares us for when things like natural disasters, pandemics, or other events test our faith. No matter where you are on the list, whether you are still finishing outdoor work or you are already building your house, look to God for guidance and discernment. Are you trying to build your house first? Will you miss out on harvesting for God if you never got your fields ready? Take the time to prepare so that you're able to land the plane, no matter where it might be!

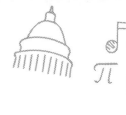

JANUARY 16

Lost Locks

Judges 16:19

On this day, January 16, 1939, the modern-day Superman comic was launched. You know, the guy who is faster than a speeding bullet and able to leap tall buildings in a single bound?

What's His story? Well, everyone loves a superhero, right? A superhero is someone who comes in and fights evil to save the day. Indeed, Jesus is our superhero from the Bible, and He had no weaknesses. While Superman had these extraordinary capabilities, his weakness was kryptonite. Mine is cheese and pickles... Whenever Superman was near kryptonite, his powers diminished. Whenever a deli tray of cheese and pickles is around, so do mine. When thinking about Superman and kryptonite, Samson is the one that comes to mind. In the story of Samson, something similar happens when Delilah tricks him, and the men cut off his hair. The incredible strength the Lord had granted Samson left him, but here's the key. God never left Samson. He heard Samson's prayer for one more boost of strength to help deliver the Israelites out of this dark period, and God listened. What's your kryptonite, and have you recognized that God is still with you? Have you asked him to help you deal with it?

JANUARY 17

The Persevering Pastor

Hebrews 12:1

On January 17, 1945, Gil Dodds retired from a competitive running career to pursue a career in ministry. At one time, he was the record holder for the indoor mile at just a hair over 4 minutes. He once won 21 straight races. You may be thinking Dodds made the right career choice. Or, more likely, you're thinking, how does one start a running career? What does the apprentice program look like, and is it even worth it?!

What's His story? Dodds' retirement was short-lived. He jumped back into running a few years later and believed he could do God's work better through his running. Dodds understood his gift and used it to spread the Gospel. He always included a Bible verse with each autograph and would never run on Sunday. He did earn some neat nicknames like "The Flying Parson" and "The Iron Deacon." I'm drawn to Hebrews 12:1, which reminds us to throw off all that weighs him down to persevere and runs our race, just like Dodds did. He ran the race that was his calling. He was able to set an example for Christ at each track meet and especially later in his career as a preacher. Even if you're not a runner, you can follow this biblical wisdom to embrace the freedom to run your race!

JANUARY 18

X-Ray Vision

1 Samuel 16:7

On January 18, 1896, the first demonstration of an x-ray machine took place in New York City. Strangely, in the 1940s and 1950s, the x-ray machine used to be a marketing tool to sell shoes! That is until they figured out the harmful effects of x-ray radiation. That put an end to it in that capacity. Today, it is still one of the most helpful diagnostic tools in healthcare.

What's His story? Well, consider what happens when you go to a doctor or hospital with an internal condition that requires a deeper investigation. If a broken bone is suspected, x-rays are usually the next step. It allows the doctor or nurse to get a picture of what's under the skin, hidden to the naked eye, but not to the power of the x-ray! In 1 Samuel, just before the anointing of King David, we read what we should already know about God being able to see our hearts. It says, "Man looks at the outward appearance, but the Lord looks at the heart." In this passage of Samuel, it's not just the picture that an x-ray might show, but also our almighty God's ability to see intention and the dirt of sin buried deep within, hidden from even the most potent and advanced x-ray machine. Thankfully, God is also able to cleanse and purify our hearts, leading us in the paths of righteousness for His name's sake. Release it to God, because His x-ray vision already knows your heart. And reside in the freedom of knowing that your chains have been broken through Christ's sacrifice for us. Have you thought about what a spiritual x-ray of your heart might look like to our heavenly radiologist?

JANUARY 19

Solid Rock

Psalm 62:6

On January 19, 1607, the San Augustin Church in Manila, Philippines, was completed. Construction for the church took nineteen years. After a mighty earthquake in 1863, the church remained the only public building that was left undamaged! It survived eight prior earthquakes and many more over the years. It still stands today.

What's His story? When we look to Psalm 62:6, we read: "He alone is my rock and my salvation; he is my fortress, I will not be shaken." Can you imagine the aftermath of the earthquake and seeing the church untouched? San Augustin Church served as a practical extension of God by providing help to those injured in the quake, and it was also a symbol of hope and assurance from God to those left to rebuild. It reminded them to make Jesus the cornerstone, using His words as the blueprint for construction. It was a reminder of the strength of the body of the church who, through the power of the Holy Spirit, will transform hearts of stones into living flesh to glorify His creation! Living temples to God can never be torn down! They must always be built on a firm foundation. Are you standing on solid rock?

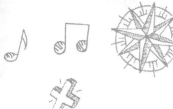

JANUARY 20

Roping Souls

Luke 5:27

On January 20, 1953, at his inauguration ceremony, United States President Dwight Eisenhower was lassoed by cowboy star Montie Montana. I am going to go ahead and assume he got this cleared first with the Secret Service. A few years ago, I was able to go on a Wild West adventure with some very dear friends. One of our stops was at the rodeo capital of the world in Cody, Wyoming, one hot 4th of July. Watching the roping and lassoing was captivating. I can see how Eisenhower loved the West!

What's His story? It takes significant skill to throw a rope with a loop at the end of it around something or someone. Cowboys can use a lasso to rescue a runaway calf or cow and bring them back to safety. In Luke 5:27, we find Jesus in the midst of lassoing his disciples, in this case, Levi. All Jesus had to say was, "follow me." What would it take for you to drop everything that you knew, the work you had done all of your life, to just follow someone out of pure obedience? It's a lot more complex than following someone on social media! Jesus was very adept at lassoing His messengers, the chosen twelve. Think about this, do you feel yourself wrapped in the rope of Jesus' love, or are you like the targeted animal running for the gate?!

JANUARY 21

The Watchtower

Isaiah 5:2

On January 21, 1968, guitarist Jimi Hendrix recorded Bob Dylan's song "All Along the Watchtower." Hendrix was without question one of the most talented electric guitar players of his time. And while his life was cut short, he certainly made an impact.

What's His story? This song is a driving, moving piece, and I believe some of the lyrics tie to the scriptural reference found in Isaiah 5:2. It says, "He dug it up and cleared it of stones and planted it with the choicest vines. He built a watchtower in it." The vineyard is mentioned both in scripture and the lyrics of the song. In the Bible, it is a representation of the kingdom of God. The watchtower could be the temple or merely a tower overlooking the vineyard. But when you think of a watchtower, it gives a sense of reassurance, safety, and fortification, doesn't it? When we decide to take up residence in the kingdom of the Lord, we are declaring ourselves to be present in the vineyard under the protection of the watchtower. You are the choicest vine, and God is watching over you to protect you, and He has cleared the field of stones to help you thrive. Are you responding with faith, because you no longer have to worry? Are you ready to grow?

JANUARY 22

Running Through Walls

James 1:2-3

On January 22, 1961, USA track star Wilma Rudolph set the 60-yard dash record with a time of 6.9 seconds! Rudolph was fresh off her triple gold medal performance at the 1960 Rome Olympics and had been named the Associated Press Woman Athlete of the Year for the second year in a row.

What's His story? Things did not always come easy for Wilma. She was one of twenty-two (wow!) children, but she also struggled throughout her youth with illnesses and disease. One of her struggles was polio, which left her with a brace on one leg. Through sheer determination and physical therapy, she was able to run again. In James 1:2-3, we find the words we don't always want to hear – that whenever you face trials, you should consider it pure joy because you know the testing of your faith produces perseverance. Why can't it just be like Staples and their "Easy Button?" Have you ever looked back on a particular trial or season and reflected on how your perseverance produced joy? James 1:12 sums up our reward, which is the crown of life! Wilma earned more than just medals, and so can you! It starts just like a race, putting one foot in front of the next. Are you ready to take your next step?

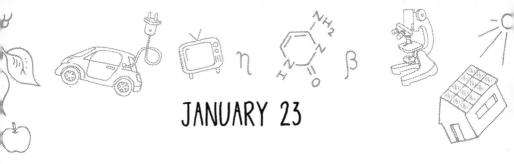

JANUARY 23

Deep and Wide

Psalm 36:6

On January 23, 1960, Navy Lt. Don Walsh and Swiss engineer Jacques Piccard descended to the deepest spot in the Pacific Ocean near the island of Guam. They were in a craft called the Trieste, designed to handle the pressure and stress of the deep descent. Ironically, it was designed and built by a man who made his name as a pioneering aeronaut, with several record-breaking balloon ascents in the 1930s!

What's His story? The deepest spot in the ocean is over 35,000 feet deep. The descent has only been repeated once since 1960. Film director James Cameron achieved this short-lived record in 2012. Yes, the Titanic movie guy! You know, "I'm the King of the World!" Ha! How about that for additional irony? The world-record for the descent no longer exists, but it is still a fantastic accomplishment. The incredible depth reminds me of the childhood Bible song "Deep and Wide," but more appropriately, the verse from Psalm 36:6, which declares God's righteousness like the highest mountains and the great deep. The depth of the Trieste's dive certainly qualifies as a great deep. The beautiful scriptural passage is a declaration of the sovereignty of our Lord, which is beyond our comprehension. Have you ever looked out upon the ocean and related it to God's sovereign power or His love? As for the Trieste, do your ears pop on the way down as they do on the way up? What have you seen that gives you a sense of how great and extensive His kingdom is?

JANUARY 24

Gold Rush

Mark 5:25-34

On January 24, 1848, James W. Marshall discovered a gold nugget at Sutter's Mill in Northern California, setting off The Gold Rush of 1849. Did you know this is where the San Francisco 49ers football team got their nickname?

What's His story? The settlers in the West were in the wilderness, wandering while trying to make a living, seeking fortune and a better life for themselves. There was a mad rush to an area when someone claimed to have found gold in them thar hills. Think about Jesus' time during his ministry. Throngs of people crowded around Him to hear Him preach. Whether it was because they wanted a better life or just wanted to be a part of a movement is hard to determine, but the stories make it known that Jesus changed lives back then just as He does now. But take, for example, the woman who reached out to touch only the tassel of Jesus' garment in Mark 5:25-34. It is one of my favorites, and you can compare it to the miners of California. All of them were thinking, "If I just find one nugget of gold, I will be better off than before." In this scripture, the woman with the bleeding problem had faith. Her healing occurred because of her faith. She knew that Jesus was her source of healing. My favorite part of the whole verse is picturing Jesus turning around to ask who touched Him because He felt power go out from Him! Her faith tugged on Him, and made Him feel her even though it was His garment she touched! What are you searching for today that you believe will solve your problems, and is your faith as strong as this woman? Look what it did for her! Seek Jesus and find the kingdom of Heaven, which is greater than any gold nugget ring ever made.

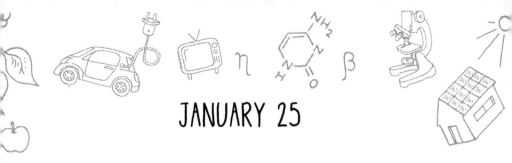

JANUARY 25

Fields of Gold

1 Corinthians 3:6-9

On January 25, 1799, the patent for the corn-planting seeding machine was granted to a man in Vermont named Eliakim Spooner. It was a machine that allowed a farmer to plant seeds more efficiently in his fields. They were dropped into the ground, evenly spaced by his instrument as the farmer walked.

What's His story? Indeed, there's the parable of the sower of seed in which it falls on different types of soil, representing the different ways in which we respond. However, I believe Paul's letter to the church of Corinth in 1 Corinthians 3:6-9 lays out the message in a way that makes us respond. As he says, I planted the seed, Apollos watered it, but God made it grow. God made it grow!! While we are fellow workers laboring and watering, it is through the Gospel that we realize that we are actually a seed in God's field. Are you planting the seed of the Gospel in others? And once you do so, do you trust in God that He will make it grow? Are you cultivating and producing fruit to be shared in a bountiful, never-ending harvest? What tools do you need to do your work in the field? God is better than a Home Depot or a Lowe's when it comes to gardening equipment because he already knows the exact mixture of nutrients we need, but also what others need. Trust in Him that he will provide for you and for your mission to spread His kingdom.

JANUARY 26

Flying for Others

2 Chronicles 15:7

On January 26, 1892, Bessie Coleman was born in Atlanta, Texas (not a typo!) She is well known for becoming the first woman of African American and Native American descent to obtain an international and a United States pilot's license. Determination and perseverance filled her life. As a child, she walked four miles each way to a segregated, one-room schoolhouse, where she excelled in reading and math. As a young woman, she became interested in flying, but could not get into flight school as a woman, so she found her way to Paris, France (not Texas) to get her license.

What's His story? If we look at 2 Chronicles 15:7, the context is about King Asa and the encouragement he received from God. It reads, "Now as for you, be strong and never be discouraged for your work has a reward." As Christians, the road to accepting God's rewarding grace can be challenging. In the New Testament, we find Christ, and the example He set in the face of constant adversity, was always focused on an eternal reward. In sacrificial love, He was doing this on our behalf. Similarly, Bessie was a pioneer on a tough road seeking ways to advance the careers of others like her. In Christian character, she was strong, courageous, and sacrificially focused on a reward that would benefit others more than her. In what ways are you helping others around you to stand tall and walk in Christ?

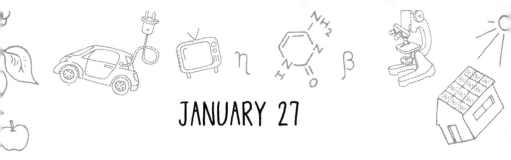

JANUARY 27

His Hands in Creation

Job 12:10

On January 27, 1888, the National Geographic Society, a global organization committed to exploring and protecting our planet, was founded. They accomplish their goals in many ways, but when I think about that trademark yellow square, the mind-blowing photography comes to mind.

What's His story? Through amazing content National Geographic helps us see God's creation in new and exciting ways, exposing us to the incredible wonders around us. The many pictures they have published of the Milky Way galaxy always fascinate me. I love photography, but until recently, I did not know that to see the Milky Way for yourself, you must get to a dark enough spot at the right time of year, with no moon, and no clouds, and look in the right direction in the sky. Those are a lot of conditions, right? And even if those conditions exist, when you look at the Milky Way with the naked eye, you will not see all of the color and detail unless you use a camera to take a long exposure picture. That's a long explanation to point out that even when we think all the conditions align, we may still miss the detail of what God is doing in our lives and how he is moving. Later, when we've been able to process and expose the details through prayer, spiritual focus, and improved spiritual eyesight, we are able to see the beauty and glory of His creation in and around us. Do you remember those great lyrics to the songs from vacation bible school? "He's got the whole world in his hands" is a perfect reminder. Job 12:7-10 spells it out and could be the motto of National Geographic. His fingerprints are everywhere, on every creature! Sometimes we can only see this after we step back and move into a position of contemplative awareness and reception. What can you do to improve your spiritual focus? How can you expose the details of God's creation in your life?

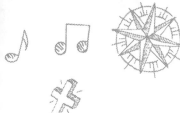

JANUARY 28

Building Blocks

Romans 12:5

On January 28, 1958, the Lego Company received its patent for its infamous interlocking plastic bricks, which some people have termed the toy of the century. Kids can unleash their creativity with the blocks to build whatever comes to mind, and of course, leave the spares in the carpet for you to step on in the dark! Others find their way into multiple plastic bins hidden throughout rooms and cubbies hidden away for rainy days.

What's His story? We should always abide by James 3:9-10 to guard our tongue when we step on Legos! But let's look deeper to gain a tremendous Christian perspective as we look closely at each brick. Romans 12:5 is a great place to start. "So in Christ we who are many form one body and each member belongs to the others." Each block can find a place to fit, color is insignificant, and the interlocking nature builds strength in numbers. It's the same for a church or community. We are each a unique piece masterfully created by God with a purpose, designed to fit into the body of Christ. Creativity, founded in Godly joy, makes Legos such great tools for kids and adults alike. Are you using your creativity to help you find your purpose in the masterpiece God is creating? Hint: the Bible is a great place to start!

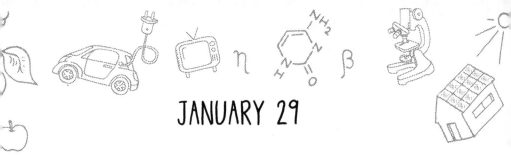

JANUARY 29

The Raven

1 Kings 17:6

On January 29, 1845, Edgar Allan Poe's "The Raven" was first published in the *New York Evening Mirror*. It is one of the most famous and recognizable poems and was a representation of Poe's macabre style of writing. It's not a very cheery piece, and you're probably already wondering where we are going with this reference from history.

What's His story? Growing up reading "The Raven" for school, it perhaps influenced my initial negative view of ravens. They seemed to be dark and menacing creatures. I have since changed my mind. When you look in the Bible and see the stories about ravens, it opens up a brilliant illustration of how a God view can change a worldview. In 1 Kings 17:6, the ravens are the ones who bring bread and meat to the prophet Elijah while he is hiding near the River Jordan, sustaining him and acting as messengers from God. They also make an appearance at the ark when Noah first sends a raven to see if the floodwaters have receded. In the case of Elijah, the ravens show God's power and ability to supply our every need, no matter what they are, and under any conditions or circumstances. Poe's raven is a dark, ghastly, ominous presence. In contrast, the raven of the Bible is a magnificent extension of God's provision. Ravens are smart, intelligent creations that can even mimic the human voice. Who knew? Is there a situation in your own life in which a worldview clouded a God view? Or is one of Poe's ravens tapping at your window to get your attention?

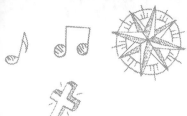

JANUARY 30

Hello Goodbye

Psalm 34:17-20

On January 30, 1951, musician Phil Collins was born in Chiswick, England. Collins was a part of the band Genesis. That's not His story here, but it could be! He's also been very successful in a solo career. Collins is unique in that he sings songs, but also plays the drums in his band! Have you ever tried to do both at the same time? It's incredibly tricky and illustrates that God honestly does give certain people talents beyond measure.

What's His story? One of Collins' songs is called "We Said Hello We Said Goodbye." If you take a read through the lyrics, you will find that it's a song about how life can be difficult, but there's a silver lining with every cloud, and life can get better with change. On a personal note, music is therapy to me, and this song was the first song I played after I got home from my dad's memorial service back in 1994. Life can indeed be difficult, and as Christians, we are not promised a life without strife. However, because God's presence gives us strength, we are equipped to deal with the challenges. When we trust in faith and rely on Him in earnest, inevitable change can take on positive meaning, imploring us to claim His divine guidance. Psalm 34:19-20 is an excellent example of this. I believe that in verse 20, it refers to Jesus' bones on the cross – not one was broken! How do you view change or a new direction? Do you see God in the details? What would it take to see him?

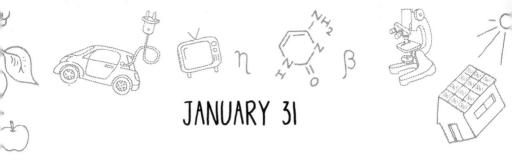

JANUARY 31

Child of God

Mark 9:37

On January 31, 1949, the soap opera *These Are My Children* aired for the first time on NBC. It is credited as the first televised soap opera. Soap operas were supposedly so-named because the soap manufacturers often sponsored them. This one only aired for about a month. That pales in comparison to *All My Children*, which aired for forty-one years! I guess the children got too numerous to count, so it became just a general hand reference to a gaggle of kids running around.

What's His story? Jesus talks a great deal about having a child-like faith and not childish faith. There is a big difference! I look at the title of the soap opera and imagine that as a good, good father, God refers to us that way. We ARE his children, and just like children, we sometimes think we know it all, or hold our breath when we don't get our way. God's infinitely tender love for us looks past our ineptitude and shows that His will is that no one should perish, but receive eternal life. What promise can you claim about the role you have as a child of God? What will that knowledge embody you to do today?

FEBRUARY 1

Being There

Genesis 28:15

On February 1, 1953, the TV show *You Are There*, hosted by Walter Cronkite, premiered. It was initially a radio show, and then made the transition to television. Cronkite went on to become a legendary TV news anchor, but this show was all about historical re-enactments, so of course, it had to be included in this devotional book! It was designed to place you at the scene of whichever historical event was being covered for the show, such as the Hindenburg Landing, the Gettysburg Address, etc.

What's His story? Focus for a moment on the title of the show - *You Are There*. I believe that refers to God's presence in our lives. Mainly, in Genesis 28:15, when He says to Jacob, "I am with you and will watch over you wherever you go and will bring you back to this land." It's just like the title of the TV show, except better. He is with us, and we are there, but the assurance that He never leaves allows us to live a life full of joy and fulfillment. We don't have to worry, and when we worry less, we do more! That's right; He never leaves us. How is He with us? It is through the Holy Spirit. The Spirit enables us to see, hear, and feel how God continues to put us in a place where we could say, "Yes, I am there!!" In His presence is the only place we need to be. Is there something you could change today that would lead to a more sweeping acknowledgment of God's presence in your life?

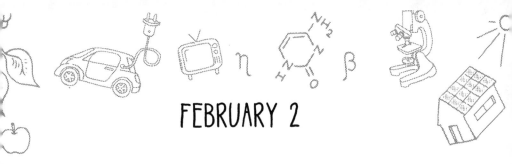

FEBRUARY 2

Oversized Squirrel

Romans 7:19

On February 2, 1887, in the town of Punxsutawney, Pennsylvania, the first Groundhog Day was observed. Now I don't know how many of you have seen the movie *Groundhog Day*, but it stars Bill Murray as a disenchanted and depressed newsman covering the "prediction of weather by an oversized squirrel," also known as Groundhog Day. In the movie, he experiences the same day over and over and over again.

What's His story? How many of us wake up each day to our own version of a spiritual Groundhog Day feeling like we have failed again? Like Murray's character in the movie, we may think our lives are insignificant and believe we can't make a difference, so we find ourselves in the same repeatable pattern every day. As we find in Romans 7:19, even the Apostle Paul struggled with these feelings. That pattern may take on different appearances like anger, resentment, sloth, etc. However, the answer remains the same. Jesus. We think we can overcome the pattern on our own. When we accept His grace and forgiveness and relinquish control to Him, we can hit the pause button on the Sonny and Cher song, thereby breaking out of the *Groundhog Day* cycle. What do you need to do to break the cycle? What is preventing you from living for Christ? How will you address it today?

FEBRUARY 3

A Perfect Shield of Freedoms

Psalm 18:30

On February 3, 1894, famed American artist Norman Rockwell was born in New York City. Rockwell is most known for his *Saturday Evening Post* covers that he illustrated for forty-seven years. His works captured the warmth of small-town America in a way that conveyed simple charm with many embedded elements of humor.

What's His story? Although Rockwell typically painted light-hearted subjects, in 1943, inspired by a speech by President Roosevelt, he painted a series of four paintings called "The Four Freedoms." The paintings represented the freedom of speech, freedom of religion, freedom from want, and freedom from fear. In the book of Psalm, you can quickly find verses to cover each of these. David and the other Psalmists wrote about fears and tribulations, but Psalm 18:30 says, "As for God, his way is perfect, the word of the Lord is flawless. He is a shield for all who take refuge in him." When we make God our refuge, we gain the freedoms Rockwell painted. What does it mean to make Him our refuge and sanctuary? It means to trust all things to Him. While it is not always easy to do, the beginning of the passage clarifies that his way is perfect and flawless, so why wouldn't we trust His way? Once we step in faith and trust, the perfection and excellent shield of God's refuge give us more comfort than a fireplace from one of Rockwell's 321 Evening Post covers! What step will you take today to accept His perfect and flawless way?

FEBRUARY 4

Solomon's Post

1 Kings 8:60

On February 4, 2004, the social network giant Facebook was launched. It began as a social media website launched at Harvard University by Mark Zuckerberg. In the first twenty-four hours of existence, over one thousand people signed up for the service. It now has over two billion active users!

What's His story? Do you remember that funny commercial where the lady has pictures of her friends taped on the wall of her house and says those are her Facebook friends? She's told quickly, "That's not how this works. That's not how any of this works." In her mind, THAT was social media! In 1 Kings 8:60, as King Solomon is finishing the Prayer of Dedication over the Temple in Jerusalem, he stands before the assembly of Israel and, in a loud voice, proclaims just as we would post on Facebook in ALL CAPITAL LETTERS. You've all seen those social media posts, you know, the ones in all caps for emphasis? Solomon's prayer is a proclamation that all the peoples of the earth may know that the Lord is God and that there is no other! Go back to 1 Kings 8:56 and imagine the entire prayer as a post on Solomon's Facebook account. How many likes and shares would he get? Now we just have to imagine what his profile picture might look like... and would he be posting photos of the Temple?? How are you using social media today to spread the kingdom of God?

FEBRUARY 5

Hammerin' Hank

Exodus 15:2

On February 5, 1934, baseball player Henry "Hank" Aaron was born in Mobile, Alabama. Aaron was the first to break Babe Ruth's all-time home run record when he hit his 715th home run in Atlanta, Georgia, in 1974. Aaron earned the nickname Hammerin' Hank for apparent reasons. He played for the Braves in two of their three franchise cities: Milwaukee and Atlanta.

What's His story? While Aaron was a capable baseball player, he realized at a young age that even he could not do it alone. He knew that he had been given a talent, but also the freedom to develop it. He believed that God was his strength and that he could depend on Him and didn't have to do it alone. Just as the Israelites sang the song of Moses and Miriam in Exodus 15:1-18 to celebrate God's victory as they were led out through parting waters of the Red Sea, we too can recognize the strength we have in God. Aaron relied on God for his strength. Do you see God in some of your talents? Are there areas with room for prayerful investment? Think of God as your first base and third base coach giving you discernment and wisdom to know your gift. Seek it out and start running your bases!

FEBRUARY 6

Wedding Scripture

1 Corinthians 13:13

On February 6, 1804, chemist Joseph Priestley died. He is credited with discovering the element of oxygen back in 1774. He did so by heating mercuric oxide. That detailed explanation is for the chemists, but can you imagine being credited with discovering….air?

What's His story? Oxygen is clearly one of the building blocks of life, along with carbon and hydrogen. Without oxygen, there would be no physical life, but to live is to love. In what I call the "Wedding Scripture," since this verse is read at almost every wedding, 1 Corinthians 13:13 sums up the building blocks of real love: faith, hope, and love. But the greatest of these is love. Physical life would cease without oxygen, and indeed spiritual life would stop without love. Plain and simply God is love. Therefore He is fundamentally the foundation of life!! The other thing to keep in mind is that love is not an emotion, but an action. What are you doing to make sure those around you receive affection and, in turn, make their own discovery of an essential building block of the spiritual life? The next time you are at a wedding and hear this scripture, think of Priestley as you take in a deep breath of oxygen and settle into the celebration of love.

FEBRUARY 7

Spice Island

Luke 14:34

On February 7, 1974, the small Caribbean island of Grenada received its independence from Britain. Grenada is known as the Spice Island, because of all of the spices found here such as cinnamon, nutmeg, ginger, mace, and vanilla. I suppose it could be called Pumpkin Spice Latte Island if only they grew pumpkins there, and had a few Starbucks coffee shops.

What's His story? In the Gospel of Luke 14:34, Jesus says, "Salt is good, but if it loses its saltiness, can it be made salty again?" When it comes to cooking and baking, salt is an important component. It can be used in savory dishes and in sweet dishes like desserts to help enhance some of the other spices such as those found on Grenada. But how can you make salt salty again? When my gravy is too salty, I can add a potato to make it less salty, but how do you do the opposite?? Jesus' point here is that true disciples are like good salt in the way that they conduct themselves and influence others to live a consistent Christ-like existence. Good salt is, therefore, not of the world but of God. Striving to be Godly is like throwing the potato out the window and embracing the salt of the Christian life. Being salty may now take on new meaning for you! How are you claiming your rightful position in God's spice rack?

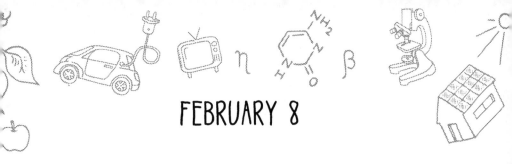

FEBRUARY 8

The Innocent Man

Luke 23:15

On February 8, 1955, American author John Grisham was born in Jonesboro, Arkansas. Grisham is famous for his legal thriller books, including *The Firm*, which was eventually turned into an excellent movie – even the Quaker Oats guy made an appearance. Spoiler alert, he turned out to be a bad guy.

What's His story? Grisham has written many books, and nine of them have been made into films. While Grisham typically wrote fiction, a book called *The Innocent Man* was his first foray into non-fiction. It's an intriguing story with all of the twists and turns found in his novels. However, it was based on a real crime from the 1970s in Oklahoma in which a disturbing and questionable legal process took place. It reminds us of the mock trial that Jesus endured before his crucifixion. In Luke 23:15, Pontius Pilate recognized that the charges against Jesus were not enough to warrant His death sentence. But the crowd declared His guilt, so he relented. There was no invocation of innocent until proven guilty. And although Jesus was tried six times, he was never convicted of a deserving crime death, yet that is what happened. Jesus was *The Innocent Man* of all mankind. How often do we find ourselves to be a member of the crowd declaring someone else's guilt before giving innocence a thought? How can Jesus help you today to summon the courage to stand up for what is right and just?

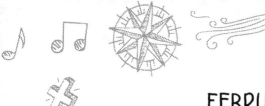

FEBRUARY 9

Tea Party

Deuteronomy 31:27

On February 9, 1775, the British Parliament declared the colony of Massachusetts to be in rebellion. What this meant for the colonists is that it permitted British soldiers to shoot suspected rebels on sight. Not all of the colonists at the time favored separation from British rule. Many colonists thought having a king would protect them from Parliament. But the acts of the ones who did favor separation probably led to this declaration.

What's His story? In many ways, we live in rebellion to God. We don't follow his commandments, we are sometimes a stiff-necked people just as the Israelites were in Deuteronomy 31:27, and we tend to desire control over faithful obedience. Frequently it is a result of adversity or a challenge that leaves us feeling abandoned. Still, the hardships we experience can work for good in our lives and truly become a testimony and example to others, so don't give up in rebellion! Repent and abide in the love, grace, and forgiveness offered through a relationship with Jesus. What kind of tea have you thrown in the bay as the rebellious colonists did in Boston? Even if it is chamomile or Earl Grey, you are never too far gone for God to rescue you.

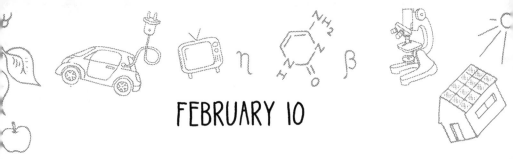

FEBRUARY 10

CheckMates on Pride

Proverbs 16:18

On February 10, 1996, Deep Blue, a chess-playing computer developed by IBM, beat human chess champion, Gary Kasparov, in a game for the first time. It marked the first time a computer had beaten a reigning world chess champion.

What's His story? We look to Proverbs 16:18 as it says, "Pride goes before destruction, a haughty spirit before a fall." Kasparov once said that life is a lot like chess. I believe he is right, and this passage from Proverbs affirms it. Often when playing chess or even checkers, we become fixated on a move our opponent has not seen. Perhaps it is an opportunity to exploit one of their blind spots. And when we achieve our goal, we sometimes leak out a smug, prideful smile. I know I have, but now my son can beat me at chess! Life is the same way. We often take a prideful stance, thinking we are better than, or greater than others. Life, just like chess, can be a teacher of humility if we allow it. Instead of focusing on other's weaknesses, we can focus on our own and with the help of God, restore and repair. As we go through this continual fixer upper process, we often realize that pride can hinder our relationship with God and with others. Kasparov, with his sage wisdom of how chess can emulate life and vice versa, probably went home to analyze his moves and how he could be better for the next round. Today, what is your next move, and how will it lead to a victory for the kingdom of God?

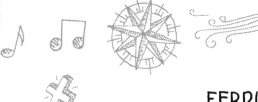

FEBRUARY 11

Behind Bars

2 Corinthians 4:9

On February 11, 1990, Nelson Mandela was released from prison in South Africa. Mandela accomplished some remarkable things in his lifetime, before AND after his time in prison. He was devoted to democracy, equality, and learning, never answering racism with racism. Because of his work against apartheid in South Africa, he was awarded the Nobel Peace Prize with South African President de Klerk in 1993. Even before he became South Africa's first democratically elected president, he was a warrior for justice.

What's His story? Mandela fought for justice and finally received his own after 27 years of incarceration. When you look at what he was able to accomplish behind bars, the example of the Apostle Paul comes to mind. Throughout all of his letters of encouragement, Paul reiterated the Gospel to spread the kingdom of Heaven. Behind bars, Paul trusted, obeyed, and moved others for the cause of Christ. 2 Corinthians 4:9 sums up Paul's attitude, which originated out of his knowledge and faith that one day his suffering would end, and he would gain God's rest. Persecuted, but not abandoned; struck down, but not destroyed. That mantra would not be a bad idea to put that on a sticky note for your mirror today (it would have made an excellent t-shirt for Paul back in the day.) What could your present situation reveal about how the death of Jesus leads to life in us, giving us hope and encouragement to overcome?

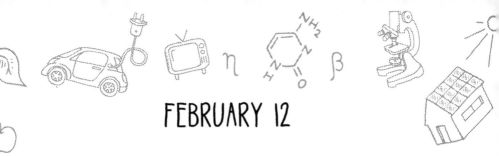

FEBRUARY 12

The Breakup

Acts 15:36-39

On February 12, 2004, a few days before Valentine's Day, toymaker Mattel announced the split between Barbie and Ken after forty-three years of dating. Who knew they were not married?? Either way, it was a sad day.

What's His story? Sure, you are thinking, how could you possibly find a way to find God here, right? Well, stay with me. When you think of splitsville in the Bible, not many couples come to mind, except for one, which would be Paul and Barnabas. In Acts 15:36-39, we learn of the break up between these two as they are planting and cultivating the church. Sadly, a disagreement between the two led to them going their separate ways. You would think that this could be detrimental to the mission of spreading the Gospel, but sometimes division can actually lead to multiplication! Both men were rooted in a foundation that allowed them to disagree without losing sight of the bigger picture. In doing so, their personal friendship was maintained. Barnabas was always a great encourager and came alongside Paul when he needed him, but as each man grew in faith, differences developed. That's not a bad thing. When we can recognize that the different perspectives and ways in which our faith guides us collectively contribute to a community of believers, differences become less of a divider and more of a multiplier. So while Barbie and Ken nipped it in the bud before Valentine's Day, Paul and Barnabas agreed in Christian love to go their own way, continuing the ministry that Jesus started. Can you identify some ways today in which division is actually a multiplier in your own life? Sometimes they are not easy to see!

FEBRUARY 13

Extracting Worry

1 Peter 5:7

On February 13, 1906, Alfred Einhorn was granted the patent for procaine, commonly known as Novocaine. While Lidocaine is a more popular analgesic or numbing agent, Novocaine is still widely used today, especially in dental applications. In full disclosure and apologies to any dental professionals reading this, I don't know anyone that loves going to the dentist. Still, I'm thankful for Einhorn and the chemical and molecular proficiency that allowed him to create such a remarkable substance that can so effectively numb pain.

What's His story? As mentioned, not many folks like to go to the dentist. Many of us, not naming names, will simply endure the pain and suffering of a toothache rather than have it taken care of at the dentist, even with Novocaine. In other words, we think the pain of a toothache does not always outweigh the pain of going to the dentist. It is similar to when we allow worry to rule, like when a decaying tooth is allowed to fester. It will only get worse and infect more of the surrounding area. Soon you are consumed by fear, and the infection could spread. I want you to think of God as the dentist. You may laugh, but we already know He is a gardener (John 15), so why not a dentist?! God can extract sin, worry, and everything else that compromises our spiritual health. His Novocaine is the Holy Spirit and the peace that comes through prayer and scripture. Peter reminds us in 1 Peter 5:7 to cast all of our anxiety on Him because He cares for us, so why not sit back, take in the soft, subtle Kenny G soundtrack, and let God extract the cavities of our life as only He can do.

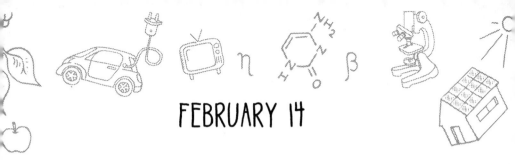

FEBRUARY 14

Fanning Flames

Acts 2:3

On February 14, 1886, the first trainload of oranges left Los Angeles, California, via the transcontinental railway.

What's His story? While I have not given you much on this historical event, let's focus on the orange. Have you ever taken a piece of orange peel, held it up to the light, and squeezed? (Do NOT do this near your eyes!) You see a spray of orange oil everywhere! That orange essence reminds me of what should be happening all around us. We should be spreading the good news of Jesus Christ and leaving the sweet-smelling aroma that is pleasing to God. Here's a science experiment to try. While carefully holding a candle or lighter, squeeze that orange peel nearby. There is oil in the orange peel called D-Limonene that is flammable! Oranges can spray fire! If you get nothing else from this book, you now know that oranges can shoot flames… Now let's connect the dots. If squeezing an orange peel is representative of spreading God's kingdom, and by doing so near a flame results in an explosive (it's actually quite tiny, but neat) reaction, then isn't that symbolic of using the Gospel to fan the flames of believers and non-believers everywhere? That's what happened in Acts 2:3 when the tongues of fire rested on the heads of the apostles. God's purifying flame is spreading the Gospel to the ends of the earth! Hopefully, the next time you eat an orange, you are reminded to spread the sweet aroma of Jesus!

FEBRUARY 15

Unity in Christ

Ephesians 1:10

On February 15, 1965, Canada adopted the maple leaf flag. It is one of the most recognizable flags in the entire world, and it practically screams, "Canada, eh?!!" in bold red and white! Personally, I like the flag, but perhaps the hockey stick would have been a more appropriate front-and-center symbol.

What's His story? A flag is a symbol of a nation's unity. It is designed to represent citizens without any additional distinctions like race or opinion. What are the symbols we think of as the earthly nation of Christians? The cross is a symbol of ultimate sacrifice for our sins, the dove represents the Holy Spirit and transformation, and colors like Red (Pentecost), Purple (Lent), and White (purity and resurrection) represent other aspects of Christianity. These few example symbols and colors are found throughout Christianity and bind us together under the flag of Christ. Ephesians 1:10 says, "to bring all things in heaven and on earth together under one head, even Christ." We can't all be united in our love of maple syrup, but we can under Christ! What symbolism resonates with you and reminds you of your kingdom citizenship?

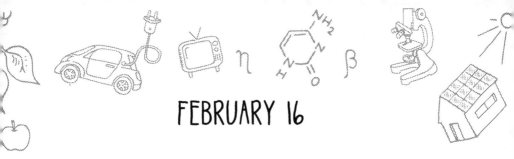

FEBRUARY 16

Hot Line

Psalm 91

On February 16, 1968, in Haleyville, Alabama, the first 9-1-1 emergency telephone service went into service. It was Alabama of all places and not New York City! The bright red phone used to make that first call is housed in a museum in Haleyville.

What's His story? This one is relatively obvious, quick, and to the point. Why do we call 9-1-1? We call when we need immediate help or assistance. It sometimes happens when you think you are adjusting the volume on your phone while cutting the grass…(I speak from experience, and that was rather embarrassing…), but almost always to contact police, fire, and ambulance resources for immediate aid. Jesus Christ remains our go-to in case of an emergency. We call out to Him in our time of need and angst. If we look to Psalm 91 for inspiration, we see that through it all, our Lord is there to protect us. And although there could be occasions that 9-1-1 must be dialed on your phone for physical help, our belief, acceptance, trust, and faith in Christ is our eternal emergency line to our Savior. By just adding another digit to Psalm 91, and it becomes our Psalm of rescue, doesn't it? Are you in need of immediate assistance from Jesus?

FEBRUARY 17

Red Skies

Matthew 16:3

On February 17, 1959, the first weather satellite Vanguard 2 was launched. The meteorological body carried two photocells to scan cloud cover over Earth during its orbit. This twenty-one pound object paved the way for how data is collected from space and had long-lasting impacts. Although its data is no longer used, it still orbits above us today!

What's His story? I am a weather nerd to the core, so this topic is intriguing. You don't have to love the weather to be affected by it. Often, we would really like to control the weather, or simply know what's going to happen. It wasn't that long ago that a three-day forecast was the norm. Now we can get twenty-day forecasts if we pay for the app's premium version on our phone. Do you get the sense that we are so busy trying to know or control outcomes like weather that we tend to miss the obvious signs? In Matthew 16:3, Jesus takes on the role of weather forecast observer for the Pharisees and Sadducees and points out that while they may be able to forecast the weather, they are unable to interpret the "signs of the times." Here he is talking about the fact that this is the time of the Messiah! It would be like getting a forecast for an inch of snow in the South and not buying any milk and bread. You have missed the point, y'all! As you look to the sky to determine whether you need an umbrella, what other observations can you make that might help reveal God to your heart and your eyes? Is there someone else in need of an umbrella, too?

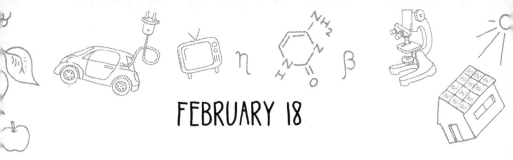

FEBRUARY 18

Flying Cows

Isaiah 11:7

On February 18, 1930, as a part of the International Air Exposition in St. Louis, Missouri, the first cow to ever take flight flew to Bismarck, Missouri, a distance of 72 miles. But there is more. This was not just any cow. This was Elm Farm's Ollie, who was also a Guernsey cow who could produce lots of milk. So not only was this the first cow to fly, but the first cow to be milked in mid-air. The cherry on top is that the captured milk was put into cartons and parachuted down to folks on the ground! Before the flight, her nickname was "Nellie Jay," but upon landing, it was "Sky Queen." That is a definite upgrade.

What's His story? You might be thinking there's no way there's one here. Remember, with God, all things are possible, including the opportunity to find His story in a flying milk cow. Isaiah 11 is a chapter full of prophecy concerning the Messiah. And in Isaiah 11:7, the peaceful nature of the coming kingdom is emphasized when it says that the cow will feed with the bear. Elm Farm's Ollie was selected for the flight because of her docile nature. Apparently, she was quietly living with purpose, just as Isaiah points out for us. What is the craziest thing you have heard or seen, and what did it reveal about how God is moving? Didn't see anything? Look closer, because it is not always as apparent as a cow in a Ford Tri-Motor airplane! By the way, the planet Pluto was discovered this same day, the same year. This was some kind of day and full of God!

FEBRUARY 19

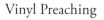

Vinyl Preaching

Numbers 24:4

On February 19, 1878, inventor Thomas Edison patented the phonograph. You might know it as a record player. It was a device that used large spinning cylinders with grooves, a needle, and a horn to produce sound. It really is an incredible invention when you look closely at a record.

What's His story? The phonograph cylinders were constructed initially of paper and then metal with a thin outer layer of tin, and then as they improved in manufacturing, wax was used. From 1925 to 1941, around one-hundred African American clergymen teamed up with some of the recording companies who had pioneered Edison's phonograph. They worked together to sell their sermons and distribute them widely. These phonograph preachers are the subject of a book by Lerone Martin *Preaching on Wax, The Phonograph and the Shaping of the Modern African American Religion*. The book tells the story of how they were able to get the message of hope and love out to so many people. They knew this message was important to share. Numbers 24:4 is a passage of scripture that emphasizes the power of hearing God's word. It is the third oracle of Balaam the Sorcerer as God has used him as a messenger, saying, "the oracle of one who hears the words of God, who sees a vision from the Almighty, who fall prostrate, and whose eyes are opened." In other words, the words of God have opened his eyes, and he has assumed the proper posture in response. These clergymen knew the power of God's word and wanted to leverage the invention of the phonograph to open eyes through the hearing of the Word! How are you using your platforms today to change the world around you?

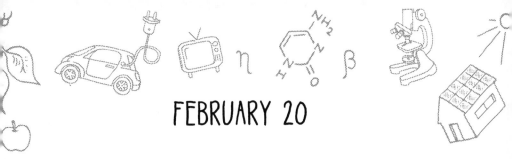

FEBRUARY 20

Fixer Upper

2 Corinthians 5:1

On February 20, 1979, the first episode of the show *This Old House* aired. These days we have an excess of home improvement shows on TV, from pools to trading spaces with your neighbors, to loving and listing. But back in 1979, this was a pioneering show. It also taught me as a Southerner how to speak "New Englander." It was a show that centered around one house and took several episodes to show the transformation. Coming from someone who is not particularly handy, this show was awe-inspiring!

What's His story? In Paul's second letter to the Corinthians (2 Cor 5:1), he talks about our heavenly dwelling. Not to dispel all of the work that Norm, Tom, and Kevin did on *This Old House*, but eventually, this earthly house we live in (our bodies) will be traded in for an eternal home in Heaven! And our eternal house will not be built by human hands, but by the hands of God. I don't know about you, but that sounds better than even the nicest bathroom or kitchen remodel. Can you imagine the inlay detail? Although a double oven is tempting, what our God promises is so much greater than this temporary habitation here on Earth. This passage of scripture can sometimes serve as reassurance or even a springboard when someone close dies. Think of how they are receiving and taking the keys to their new heavenly body and abode. How do you imagine your heavenly abode? It brings new meaning to living life as a fixer-upper because, in the end, God is the ultimate Norm. Only He can fix and repair you in a way for all eternity.

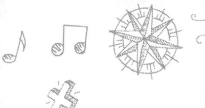

FEBRUARY 21

Spiritual White Pages

Psalm 23

On February 21, 1878, the first telephone directory was published in New Haven, Connecticut. I realize with the advent of the Internet, directories are no longer necessary, but this prompts me to wonder what people use for stools, paperweights, and booster seats these days, what did they use before the first directory? The telephone directory was a listing of names and numbers for everyone in a specific geographic area. As populations grew, so did the weight and size of the book!

What's His story? In the front or back of the book was the one thing all telephone directories had in common. There you found the numbers for the police department, fire department and poison control (you needed this last one if you had curious children who always wondered what things tasted like!) Similarly, there are scriptures in the Bible, which are the emergency verses for particular situations. This would be a passage of scripture in a time of urgent need. I believe Psalm 23 would be listed at the top of the list, and it covers a variety of situations, from fear and anxiety to thankfulness. It is one of the most well-known and delivers an important lesson we need to move through certain and uncertain situations. You may have a list of your own. If not, consider writing out your own scriptural directory. Will you create one today, even if it is a Rolodex of one? By the way, that is foreshadowing...

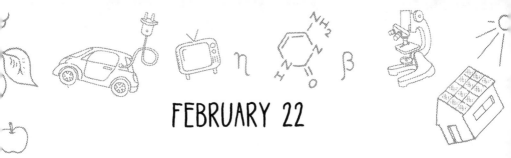

FEBRUARY 22

Miracle on Ice

Acts 5:12

On February 22, 1980, the "Miracle on Ice" took place. In the 1980 Winter Olympics, a scrappy United States ice hockey team took on the perennial powerhouse Soviet Union team in the semi-final and won 4-3. Since Cold War remnants remained and the United States was playing as an overwhelming underdog, this victory was underscored by many storylines. The United States team went on to beat Finland for the gold medal, and their place in the United States Winter Olympics history was cemented.

What's His story? As the final seconds ticked away in the game, announcer Al Michaels very poignantly said, "Do you believe in miracles...YES!" Finding His story is easy. Who is the source of the greatest miracles of all? Jesus! They are too numerous to name, and I would refer you to a book by Lee Strobel called *The Case for Miracles*. The book is a more in-depth review of why we should believe that miracles exist, but I like Acts 5:12. The Gospel is a message to the people. In Acts, the apostles performed miracles themselves, bringing thousands to become believers. Just as a group of scrappy hockey players on a chunk of ice in Lake Placid, NY prompted us to believe in sports miracles, the apostles after Jesus' crucifixion demonstrated the amazing power of our God, which led many to Christianity. What miracles have you seen in your own life? Are there situations you may not prescribe as miracles but really were?

FEBRUARY 23

Christian Warriors

2 Timothy 1:7

On February 23, 1778, Baron Friedrich von Steuben arrived at Valley Forge, Pennsylvania, to help train the Continental Army during the American Revolution. He had a significant impact on the outcome of the war through his training and tactics. His influence was evident in the United States military to the end of the War of 1812 and beyond. He published the *Blue Book*, which became the United States Army's first field manual. The techniques applied at Valley Forge were dedication, adaptability, enthusiasm, and discipline.

What's His story? If you look closely at what von Steuben taught the Continental Army at Valley Forge, these are the same things that we, as Christians, must also adapt. Look to 2 Timothy 1:7, "For God has not given us a spirit of timidity, but of power and love and discipline." Discipline was a foundation of von Steuben's principles, and it should also be at our foundation. It allows us to eliminate distractions and focus our core energy on glorifying God and giving thanks for His presence in our lives. What spiritual disciplines could you incorporate into your life today that might help you focus on growth?

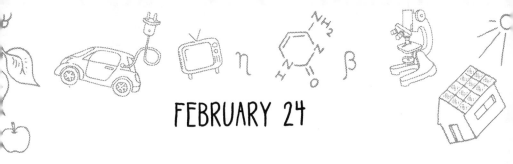

FEBRUARY 24

Tears in Heaven

Revelation 21:4

On February 24, 1993, the song "Tears in Heaven" by Eric Clapton won the best song award at the Grammy Awards. Clapton's song was written after the tragic accidental death of his son, Conor, and is a very moving song from one of the most talented guitarists on the planet.

What's His story? One snippet of the lyrics gives you a view of the pain that was in Clapton's heart as he wrote this song. They say, "Beyond the door, there's a peace I'm sure. And I know there'll be no more tears in Heaven." Just as we realized a few days ago with *This Old House*, when we get to Heaven, there will be no more pain and no more suffering. What a joy we have to look forward to joining with the angels in the eternal worship of God, lifting our heavenly voices in a sweet, sweet song of adoration. The pain of this world will be absolved, and we will be reunited with our Creator and Rescuer. So while songs like Clapton's express the pain we feel now, the joy we can look forward to will dry each and every tear. He makes everything new! Do you have extended grief that is difficult to release? Ask God to intercede and provide the salve of salvation.

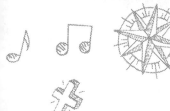

FEBRUARY 25

Passion of Christ

John 3:16

On February 25, 2004, director Mel Gibson released the film *Passion of the Christ*. This is the same guy that starred in *Mad Max* and the *Lethal Weapon* movies, but nonetheless, this film is incredibly powerful. It documents the last forty-four hours of Jesus' life and is a very moving film. I highly recommend it simply because it puts many things into perspective, including the suffering Jesus underwent on our behalf.

What's His story? The passion is the subject, and it is incredibly powerful. Most movies are usually an escape from reality, but this one is not, and yet it grossed millions more than some of the more popular titles that released around the same time. This movie prompts you to think about Jesus in a way that might lead you to understand John 3:16 in a whole new way. No longer is it just a scripture you see on a sign while watching an NFL game or under Tim Tebow's eyes. It takes on new meaning when we understand the sacrifice, as portrayed in scripture and on the big screen in the *Passion of the Christ*. I believe it is required Lenten viewing, but I'll leave that up to you. Whatever you choose, how do you acknowledge the sacrifice Jesus made for you and me? When you are behind the slow cashier or get the wrong order at a restaurant, are you thinking about this movie? That might seem like a stretch analogy, but it also might provide the necessary perspective! Christ went through so much agony, pain, and suffering for you and me. How do we remind ourselves of the passion that Christ also has for us?

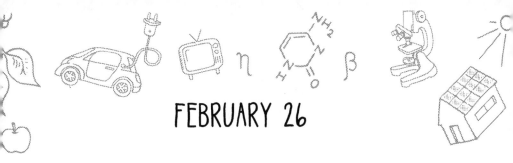

FEBRUARY 26

The Miserables

Matthew 25:40

On February 26, 1802, author Victor Hugo was born. He wrote the *Hunchback of Notre Dame* and *The Man Who Laughs* (could those be about the same man??), but his most famous work is *Les Miserables*. Translated from French, it could be written in English as The Miserables or The Poor Ones. The book examines the nature of law and grace, and the big screen and Broadway adaptions are equally adept at telling the story of life in Paris in the 1800s.

What's His story? In this story of redemption, one line sticks out. "To love someone is to see the face of God." With subplots around poverty, we are drawn to Matthew 25:40 in which Jesus says, "Whatever you did for the least of these brothers and sisters of mine, you did for me." This piece of scripture is widely used when referring to our obligation to the poor and underserved. When we serve them, we are serving Christ. It is a fantastic reminder that there are angels among us, and treating one another with respect, kindness, and love while providing basic needs is just one way in which we can live out our charge to live as Christ teaches us. *Les Miserables* reminds us to surround one another with a love that allows our soul to see God in the other person. It is an amazing and transformative experience when it happens. To take care of someone in need is to take care of Jesus. When it is presented that way, it is hard not to help. What are some ways you can do that today? The opportunities arise each and every day. Are you taking advantage?

FEBRUARY 27

Hold On

Proverbs 4:13

On February 27, 1990, the band Wilson Phillips released the song "Hold On." It is a great, cheesy song that epitomizes what songs sounded like in the late 1980s and early 1990s. Interestingly enough, it has been repurposed for a few more recent movies like *Bridesmaids* and *Harold and Kumar Go to White Castle*. Yes, those movies…

What's His story? When you hear a song, do you listen to the lyrics, just the beat, or a terrific guitar riff? In the case of "Hold On," it has to be the lyrics, but I guarantee if you find the song in a streaming service, you'll find yourself listening to the entire song - it's that catchy. What does it mean to hold on? Depending on the situation, it might mean to grasp tightly or to wait while someone answers another call on the other line. In Proverbs 4:13, we are encouraged to hold on to instruction. Instruction is wisdom. As we learn early in the same chapter of Proverbs, the beginning of wisdom is to gain understanding! Why should we hold on to it? It's simple. We should hold on because it places us on the path of righteousness. Are there songs reminding you of why you hold on and about what He is accomplishing in your life? Once we recognize the wisdom in something like a cheesy, sugary-sweet hit from the early 1990s, it takes song lyrics from an emotion to a deeper relationship with the God of scripture.

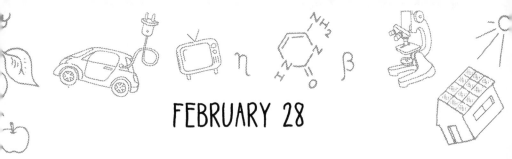

FEBRUARY 28

The Double Helix

Isaiah 43:7

On February 28, 1953, Cambridge University scientists James D. Watson and Francis Crick announced that they have discovered the double-helix structure of deoxyribonucleic acid, commonly referred to as DNA. Though DNA had already been found and studied, its role in genetics was not fully understood until Watson and Crick's discovery. Their subsequent mapping of genes gave life to many scientific discoveries.

What's His story? When you hear people talking about their DNA, they refer to it as their "make-up," and no, it is not the stuff you put on your face. DNA contains some of the basic blocks of your genetic structure, the parts that explain your unique features, even why you have two different shaped ears (yes, I do.) Isaiah 43:7 gives glory and honor to God as the source of our DNA as it says, "everyone who is called by my name, whom I created for my glory, whom I formed and made." God is the creator of the beautiful double-helix structure of DNA. As someone with a science background, I see God's fingerprints all over things like DNA, and the affirming words of scripture support and answer questions that remain when faith and science collide. He fearfully and wonderfully makes us, and we give thanks for things like DNA because these are the components that make us who we are. We are unique creatures formed and loved by God. What's in your DNA? Is it a love of God and his word? A double-helix sounds like a figure-skating move, but it is much more than that. It is the God-formed building block of our life and who we are as children of God!

FEBRUARY 29

Family Circus

John 1:46

On February 29, 1960, the comic strip series Family Circus first appeared. It was created by Bil Keane and is based loosely on his life as a suburban family of six. There are certainly some witty and dry comedic elements sprinkled throughout, and I highly recommend an archive search. Dolly is my favorite character. She's so very matter of fact about everything. I hold someone dear to my heart that is like that, with such an endearing quality.

What's His story? Bil Keane allowed his faith to permeate his gift of art and laughter. He shared the gift of Jesus in a way that warmed and engaged even those that do not know Him. He believed, "Jesus must have had a sense of humor. I like to think of Him as a guy who got people to listen to Him by leaving them laughing and chuckling with one another." There are numerous examples in the comic where religion and faith are presented directly. Keane provides an excellent model for us to follow regarding faith and vocation. One of my favorites is when Billy, based on Bil himself, asks at the dinner table, "When we say grace, are we supposed to look up at Heaven or down at the food?" Yes, is the answer! And yes, God does have a sense of humor. Just look at John 1:46 in which Nathanael, while referring to Jesus, asked, "Nazareth! Can anything good come from there?" I have literally written "LOL" in my Bible next to that one, but Jesus' response to Nathanael is even better. He simply says, "Stick around, and there's more where that came from." The passage of John 1:43-51 could easily be a Family Circus cartoon, or a comedy skit revealing God's sense of humor throughout, yet it still confirms the deity of his Son! Are you finding God in humor today? Look around! It is everywhere!

MARCH 1

Old Faithful

Psalm 145:17

On March 1, 1872, Yellowstone National Park was established. The park was the world's first national park and is comprised of over two million acres of beautiful bison-filled land in Montana, Idaho, and Wyoming. It also sits on top of an active volcano and is the world's largest caldera, which is code for the baddest, mack-daddiest volcano in existence. A recent visit to the park with dear friends, and a new friend Ranger Karl, reminded us of the power of nature.

What's His story? As an active volcano, Yellowstone has more than half of the world's geysers. There are over 500 in the park. A geyser is a hole in the ground that spews super-hot water into the air. None is more famous than Old Faithful, found in the southern part of the park. It is one of the most consistent geysers, erupting an average of seventeen times per day. Even with this consistency, folks still demand a schedule so they can be there right when it happens. Sound familiar? We tend to do that with God. Although He's faithful and never moves, we still expect him to accommodate our schedule, and our timetable to meet our demands. We get frustrated when we think He is not answering our prayers. Yet if we look through scripture, and especially Psalm 145:17-20, we see plenty of examples where patience paid off beyond imagination, and the righteousness of God reigns. As God helps us stretch our faithfulness, we start to grow and perhaps savor the time waiting for the big show! Are you willing to take a seat and wait for it?

MARCH 2

Green Eggs

Matthew 10:30

On March 2, 1904, Theodore Seuss Geisel was born in Springfield, Massachusetts. This is Dr. Seuss, famous for his quirky, yet lovable, children's books. I would argue that they are not always for children, because I still enjoy them. The rhythm and frequent tongue twisters are a good test of cognitive ability! Plus, when else can you make such funny noises and simply retort that you are just reading what is on the page?!

What's His Story? While it is hard to know for sure if Geisel's books had an intended biblical message, some had obvious themes. One obvious one comes from that lovable elephant, Horton. In the Dr. Seuss book *Horton Hears a Who*, we find an elephant who discovers Whoville, which is on a small speck of dust. Through ridicule and harassment, Horton protects and defends the Whos who live in Whoville, saying, "A person is a person, no matter how small." In Matthew 10:29-30, we get a clear understanding of Horton's wisdom through the providence of God, for if it extends to the smallest creatures on Earth, how much more will He care for you and me? What about you? Do you extend grace to all, big and tall, large and small? Be a Horton and protect just as God protects us, for no matter how small, if something is worthy of God's love, then unquestionably ours as well.

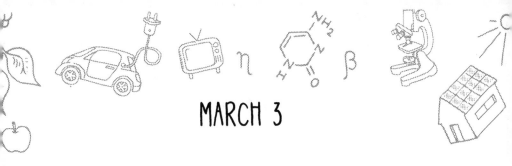

MARCH 3

Camel Hair

Matthew 3:4

On March 3, 1855, the United States Congress appropriated $30,000 to form the Camel Corps. You thought questionable government spending was something new? The Camel Corps was an experiment led by the United States Army to address the difficulty in the westward expansion. Because of the camel's characteristics such as large feet that can walk on sand without sinking, long protective eyelashes, nostrils that can block out sand, and ears covered in hair, it was an ideal candidate to face the harsh conditions out West.

What's His story? Abraham was known to have used camels, and there are other examples, but the one I like is found in Matthew 3:4. This passage refers to John the Baptist's clothes made of camel hair, along with a description of his unusual diet of locusts and honey. Camel hair, in keeping with some of the environmental characteristics, is coarse and gritty. We are not talking about the nice camel hair jackets that seem to pop up in the fall. We are talking about the rough, tufts of hair from the humps! That was a lot like John's personality; it suited his character and doctrine. John knew his place and his purpose as the precursor to the Messiah. It wasn't his dress that got the people's attention, but it is interesting to note how well his outfit fits his mission! It probably makes you itch a bit just thinking about wearing camel hair. However, when you look past the outer layer of clothing, your inner mission of servanthood comes to life. Do your clothes define you, or does your Savior?

MARCH 4

Four Seasons

Daniel 2:21

On March 4, 1678, musical composer Antonio Vivaldi was born in Venice, Italy. Vivaldi composed over 500 instrumental concertos and sacred choral works. He was also an ordained Roman Catholic priest, but the music was his focus since he was tasked with composing new musical works for each church feast. And we thought to have to bring a casserole and cornbread to a church potluck was a pain!

What's His story? Vivaldi's influence during the Baroque period was felt throughout Europe because he brought a bright, joyful sound, which was different from the darker aspects associated with this period. His most famous work, primarily ignored until around 1926, is the "Four Seasons." It is a string masterpiece full of violin, viola, and cello. In the Bible, as he is interpreting Nebuchadnezzar's dream, Daniel attributes the rightful power of timing and the seasons, stating that God has all power and prerogative. But frequently, we may find ourselves in a juxtaposition of seasons as we experience the highs and lows of life. Sometimes there is a palpable contrast between the cold, harsh winter, and other times it is more like a chilly, bright spring morning. As we navigate these seasons, it is essential to rely on God's timing. Just as one season offers a glimpse into the next, if we listen for God, we will move from a position of what is into what could be. That is where hope really does spring eternal. How do you approach the seasons of your own life? Like Vivaldi, how do you intertwine God's brightness and joy while acknowledging God's timing of the seasons themselves?

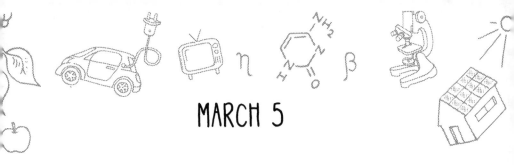

MARCH 5

Hula Hooping

Matthew 11:28-30

On March 5, 1963, the Hula Hoop was patented. A round wooden hoop used by Australian children in a gym class is what inspired Arthur Melin and Richard Knerr. The name Hula came from the dance you had to do to keep it going, which resembled the Hawaiian dance. You have already learned about the Frisbee, well, this was another Wham-O company invention. You would think I have stock in their company.

What's His story? Let's be honest; the Hula Hoop is probably the most-used toy by church youth groups for activities and spiritual lessons. It is for a good reason. One game is where everyone is holding hands in a large circle, and you must get the hoop all the way around without releasing hands. Talk about having to jump through hoops. And have you ever tried to keep just one hoop going? What about multiple? In Matthew 11:28-30, God isn't asking us to jump through hoops or even try to manage numerous hoops. He simply says, "Come to me." Keeping a hoop spinning requires core body strength, control, balance, and coordination. In contrast, in life, God can give us the energy to get things started and the momentum to keep things going. My yoke is easy, and my burden light. That sounds like good coaching for us, the weary hula-hoopers of this life. When we come to God and release our burdens to God, we are suddenly able to sway in a rhythm that keeps the essential hoops spinning. What hoops are you trying to jump through today? What can you release to God that will put you or your life in a better balance?

MARCH 6

Mother's Love

Isaiah 66:13

On March 6, 1475, brilliant and talented Italian Renaissance artist Michelangelo was born in Caprese, Italy. He grew up in Florence and studied under some well-known sculptors. Michelangelo also sculpted the renowned statue of David. And of course, there's the Sistine Chapel – more on that on a later date! It is still absurd to think about him painting it lying on his back. Spoiler alert, he wasn't on his back, but it works here.

What's His story? One of Michelangelo's earliest works, and actually the only sculpture he personally signed, is Pietra. It is a sculpture of the Virgin Mary holding Jesus' body after he has been crucified. The piece is powerfully representative of grief and sorrow through facial expressions and body positioning. In Isaiah 66:13, we find Isaiah comforting his nation as a mother would comfort a child. In Pietra, we find Mary comforting Jesus. The reversal will soon be true as the Messiah fulfills the prophecy. The love of a mother is special. It is warm, tender, and caring. She loves the child as part of herself. Fittingly, Pietra is carved out of a single piece of marble, fortifying the singularity we all have in Christ. Is there a particular work of art that speaks to you and makes you ponder our relationship with Christ?

MARCH 7

Jesus Joins the Call

Matthew 18:20

On March 7, 1876, Alexander Graham Bell patented the telephone. As a longtime telecommunications industry guy, this one is near and dear to my heart. When you think about the phone, and now the smartphone, we probably feel like we would be lost without Bell's invention.

What's His story? When it was first invented, people probably did not understand the telephone. They were used to face-to-face communication, or they wrote letters, but neither method is common today. Think of how the phone has changed your life and how you communicate with those around you. Some statistics show the highest phone use is on Mother's Day and Christmas Day. That does make sense. But as Matthew 18:20 says, "For where two or three come together in my name, there am I with them." That is like having the best, most important, star-of-the-show participant join your conference call, isn't it? The telephone is used to create and continue a community, isn't it? We sometimes take this for granted and do not realize how much of an impact a quick phone call packed with care and love can have on someone who needs it. This passage emphasizes the difference that just two people, filled with the Holy Spirit, can make in our world. The invention of the telephone allows us to reach one another in ways once never thought possible. Still, the gift of the Holy Spirit extends that reach in a way that joins us to him without having to fumble through adding a call, merging calls, or putting someone on hold. Pick up the phone and call someone today who needs a tender, caring voice. It may not be Mother's Day or Christmas, but every day is an opportunity to invite Jesus to join our call!

MARCH 8

Winning Team

Luke 5:11

On March 8, 1941, Hugh "Losing Pitcher" Mulcahy became the first Major League Baseball player to be drafted into World War II. Mulcahy, who played for the Phillies and Pirates, obtained the dubious nickname because he was frequently the losing pitcher. In fairness, there were other pitchers with worse records than him.

What's His story? Finding God here is fun, even if you do not like baseball. While Mulcahy was preparing for the upcoming 1941 baseball season, he was notified of his military service draft. He dropped everything and completed basic training, eventually deploying to the Philippines and the Pacific theater until his discharge in 1945. In Luke 5:11, as Jesus is calling the first disciples, it is one of the most astonishing verses in the Bible. After not catching anything, just like losing pitchers on the water, they bring in the biggest haul of all. They went from zero to hero. Then, the men haul their boats to shore, drop EVERYTHING, and follow Jesus. Mulcahy dropped everything as well, because he wanted to join a winning team. I have a feeling the disciples were moved to do the same. We should also want to be on that team. What would the disciples have as a team logo? You can draw your own team logo in the margin here! So whose team are you on? Are you waiting on the sidelines? Do not wait any longer. Join the team and play out a game that has already been won.

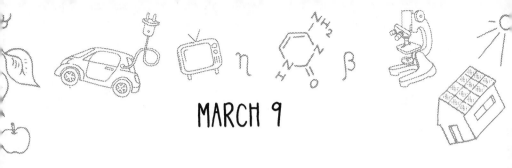

MARCH 9

No Littering

Ephesians 1:4-5

On March 9, 1985, the first Adopt-a-Highway sign went up in Tyler, Texas. Various groups adopt a two-mile stretch of road, pledging to keep it clean by picking up trash and debris.

What's His story? You have probably seen these bright blue signs along the roadway that tell you who adopted a particular stretch of road. Maybe you have seen a group busy with trash bags and fashionable vests of sweet-looking yellow and orange. Today I want you to focus on the adoption part here. When these groups adopt a stretch of highway, they are committing to its upkeep, well-being, and its general appearance by getting rid of the detracting and distracting trash that might give off the impression that no one cares. The road is to be treated as if it were a part of your own family. I point you to Ephesians 1:4-5 in which God has adopted us into His own family by bringing us to Himself through Jesus Christ. So, while you probably never thought of comparing yourself to a two-mile stretch of highway, the way in which we are adopted by God and kept clean by His renewing grace, and the way He takes pride in us is very similar indeed! I'll bet you will not look at another one of those signs the same. Let it be a reminder to reflect on your own adoption as a child of God! Just so you know, you don't look like a stretch of highway, but you do need to be adopted and cleaned up by the Most High.

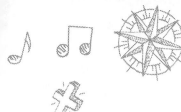

MARCH 10

Odd Couple

Ruth 1:16

On March 10, 1965, Neil Simon's play *The Odd Couple* opened on Broadway at the Plymouth Theatre in New York City. It starred Walter Matthau (think *Grumpier Old Men*, *Dennis the Menace*, etc.) as Oscar and Art Carney (think Ralph Kramden from *The Honeymooners*) as Felix. It is a story of two completely opposite individuals learning to live together. One was extremely neat, and the other incredibly messy.

What's His story? While there are plenty of odd couples in the Bible, the one that sticks out to me is the story of Ruth and Naomi. If someone said, tell me about your mother-in-law, you might hear something negative or perhaps a funny story. In my case, I have a truly wonderful one. Ruth also loved her mother-in-law, Naomi, and begged to stay with her. Naomi's life was a witness to God to which Ruth was drawn, and eventually, it led Ruth to Boaz. As a result, Ruth was then a part of the Messiah's family tree. How about that for the power of God working through an odd couple? The book of Ruth is short, but it is a compelling statement of how we can bring people to God, even in a time of crisis. It's a true story in the redeeming power of our Savior, and it reveals a God at work in the world around you. Look what He did with our Biblical odd couple of Naomi and Ruth. When we open our eyes to it, He can use you to bring family, friends, co-workers, and even strangers to Him. Are you open to it, or is something keeping you from relenting to the awesome craftsmanship of God's relational living? Like Naomi, is bitterness keeping you from experiencing the joy of His love? Let it be washed away in the redeeming power of His grace, and may the odd couple be yet another way in which Christ's love doesn't conform to the ways of this world!

MARCH 11

Don't Worry

Luke 12:25

On March 11, 1950, musician Bobby McFerrin was born. You might not immediately recognize the name, but if I gave you his most famous song from the 1990's you would. It is the song "Don't Worry, Be Happy." It is a very catchy tune and delivers a great message.

What's His story? This one is easy. Throughout the Bible, you'll find the phrase do not fear, or do not be afraid well over one hundred times. There is a reason for that. God is in charge. Therefore, we have nothing to fear, and every reason to give thanks and be joyful. Worry less; do more. We can even do this amid pain, confusion, or anguish. My go-to verse for perspective on worry is Luke 12:25, where Jesus pointedly asks, "Who of you by worrying can add a single hour to your life?" We can waste plenty of hours worrying. I believe McFerrin's song should be on everyone's heart because once we put our trust in God, His provision is revealed in His time. When we do so, we have no need to worry. It sounds impossible sometimes, but it is that single step forward in faith that plays the first note of a song titled "Don't Worry, Be Happy." Will you sing this song? It doesn't have to be karaoke, but it can be in your head as a reminder that Jesus asks us to be happy and joyful because of the Father's love for us!

MARCH 12

Fireside Parables

Matthew 13:10-17

On March 12, 1933, United States President Franklin D. Roosevelt, affectionately referred to as FDR, held the first of many "Fireside Chats." It was a new and adventurous way to reach the American people at one of the low points of the Great Depression and talk about the topics at hand for the nation. His first one was about the banking industry. It felt as if FDR was having a friendly conversation due to the informal and relaxed nature of the program. Journalist Robert Trout coined the phrase "fireside chat" to describe Roosevelt's radio addresses because the delivery style formed an image of someone sitting by a fire in a living room.

What's His story? Roosevelt wanted each chat to be easy to understand and consumable for all Americans, no matter their educational background. He used simple words and analogies to explain complex concepts or issues. Sounds familiar, doesn't it? When Jesus spoke, he often did so in parables that were relatable to His audience, but that also conveyed a complex message in simple terms. One day, probably after wondering how they could take Jesus' course titled Simple, Effective, and Persuasive Communication for Disciples, the disciples asked Jesus why he spoke in parables. Matthew 13:10-17 tells the story. Jesus' response was, "The knowledge of the secrets of the kingdom of heaven has been given to you, but not to them." You think the disciples in the back of the room might have been second-guessing themselves? Perhaps they were, but in less than twenty words, he has given them both assurance AND a mission with brilliant clarity. It is also the mission we have been given. So while it may not be by a crackling fire, God's message can be delivered quickly, simply, and powerfully. What's holding you back?

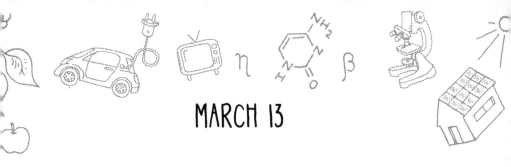

MARCH 13

Ear Muffs

Proverbs 18:13-15

On March 13, 1877, the patent for earmuffs was issued to one teenager, Chester Greenwood, from Farmingham, Maine. He was 15 at the time, and it was a patent for an improved version of earmuffs through a swivel hinge Greenwood developed that kept them tight on the ears. The town of Farmingham still celebrates his invention to this day.

What's His story? When you think of the purpose of earmuffs, it is usually to keep ears warm, but they can also be used to keep noise out. How often do we find ourselves closed off to hearing God's word because we have our own earmuffs on tightly? Ironically, a teenager was the inventor, but people of all ages are prone to close off hearing God's message. Many times, we predetermine our response before we have truly taken off the muffs and listened. Proverbs 18:13-15 provides great wisdom for how to listen intentionally. The passage encourages us to gather all of the information, reflect an openness to new ideas, and hear all sides before judging. In other words, take down any preconceived notions and listen with purpose. It is by doing this that discernment arrives. While earmuffs are great for cold weather, NASCAR, Monster Truck events, and fashion statements, they are no good when trying to gain wisdom that can help us live out God's dream over us. Besides, don't earmuffs always leave that hair dent across the top of your head? Are your ears free to listen to all that God has in store for you?

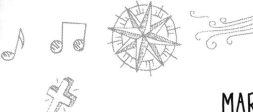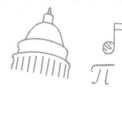

MARCH 14

Spirit Waltzing

2 Corinthians 13:14

On March 14, 1804, music composer Johann Strauss I, also known as the Elder, was born in Vienna, Austria. He is considered to be the principal composer of Viennese waltzes. His eldest son, Johan Strauss II, was also a composer who focused Viennese waltzes even though his father wanted him to follow a nonmusical profession. Strauss II composed the famous Blue Danube waltz. A waltz is a smooth, progressive dance (in ¾ time for you musically-inclined readers) characterized by long, flowing movements, with twirls incorporated throughout the piece. It is very rhythmic and melodic.

What's His story? Candidly, some days in history are easier than others. I'll admit that today's option took a while to develop, and was like learning a complex dance routine. When it came to me, it hit like the downbeat of a measure! When you watch a ballroom couple dance to a waltz, you really get soothed into the effortless flow of the rhythm. It's a bit like the interaction amongst the Trinity. The incarnation, divinity, and wholeness of God are illustrated through it. 2 Corinthians 13:14 thoroughly illuminates the interaction. Through the grace of Jesus, love of God, and the fellowship of the Holy Spirit, we are invited to participate in the dance. To join and move rhythmically in perfect peace with the Trinity is what our heart desires. The Father, Son, and the Holy Spirit are waltzing and asking us to join the perfect dance! Will you put down your punch and cookies and join in today?

MARCH 15

Casting Indoors

1 Peter 3:15

On March 15, 1897, the first indoor fly-casting tournament was held at Madison Square Garden in New York City. Fly-casting is fly-fishing using a very lightweight lure and specific casting techniques to land the lure right where you want it. The lures are designed to look like flying insects.

What's His story? You are probably wondering why they are holding this inside in an arena and not in a river somewhere you would expect to see fly-fishing. You are probably also dumbfounded that such a tournament even exists like I was. I have spent my share of time on rivers fly-fishing and understand the notion that some fishermen refer to the river as their church. As some will attest, you naturally feel closer to God in an environment that promotes reverence, conservation, solace, and humility. But an indoor tournament allows you to practice, compete, and develop your casting technique to the point that the correlation between hitting a target and catching a fish is tightly formed. Now transfer that concept to our evangelism of God's holy word. As 1 Peter 3:15 points out, we should be prepared to answer why we have hope, but do so with gentleness and respect. You just never know what might be on the other end. Where are you practicing your casting technique? Wherever you are, do not leave the rods in the closet to collect dust. Get out there and fish for followers!

MARCH 16

Soaring Passion for God

Psalm 84:2

On March 16, 1926, an American professor and inventor Robert Goddard launched the first liquid-propelled rocket. He is often referred to as the father of modern rocketry. His rocket was fueled by liquid oxygen and gasoline, and the first flight took place at his Aunt Effie's farm in Auburn, Massachusetts. She was obviously the fun aunt.

What's His story? Watching a rocket launch can be an awe-inspiring moment, feeling the rumble of the engines in your chest or seeing the glowing orange fire of propulsion is exciting and stunning wrapped up in one. The joy felt at lift-off is something spectacular. Think of the work and effort that went into that very moment! Many times we might refer to something as being our rocket fuel. It could be coffee, words of encouragement, or even closing a big business deal. Whatever it is, it gives us the energy to move beyond the inertia that is holding us back. As Christians, scripture should be our rocket fuel. We should have a passion for Christ that is so poised and strong that it ignites a fire powerful enough to push us beyond doubt, fear, and everything that creates an atmosphere of constraint. Psalm 84:2 pronounces what this looks like. My soul yearns, even faints, for the courts of the Lord; my heart and my flesh cry out for the living God. And just as the engineers know how much fuel the rocket needs, God knows the needs of your heart. Open it to Him. What do you need to rekindle and ignite your passion for God so you soar into the Heavens?

MARCH 17

Voyage of Life

Proverbs 22:6

On March 17, 1941, the National Gallery of Art in Washington, D.C. opened. At the time of its inception, it was the largest marble structure in the world. It houses some amazing and historic pieces of art dating from the Middle Ages to the present day.

What's His story? Even though today is known as St. Patrick's Day, this one is unrelated to leprechauns. There is no pot of gold on this day, but there is a really cool story about a piece of art in the National Gallery of Art. While there are thousands of prints in the National Gallery of Art, there is a series of four paintings that stood out and gave us our opportunity to find His story: *The Voyage of Life* (1842) by Thomas Cole. The series represents human life in the form of childhood, youth, manhood, and old age. Through these paintings, Cole sermonized about the way that we journey through life, but his inclusion of spiritual elements completes the allegory in a way that is moving and thoughtful. It requires us to think of our own life journey and the presence of God along the way. Like each painting in which the traveler is accompanied by a guardian angel, we should examine how God is a part of our own life journey. I invite you to Google this series by Cole and read about the symbolism found in each work. It is an extensive list and very intriguing. In keeping with the theme of the journey of life, Proverbs 22:6 reminds us, "train a child in the way he should go; and when he is old, he will not turn from it." Why would we want to depart from the peace and joy that comes from knowing and abiding in Christ?

MARCH 18

Lean in Love

Proverbs 3:5-6

On March 18, 1964, Olympic speed-skater Bonnie Blair was born in Cornwall, New York. Bonnie started speed-skating on the ice at age four and competed in the 1988, 1992, and 1994 Olympics, racking up five gold medals and one bronze medal. Her specialty was the sprint races, either 500m or 1000m. Do you know how fast these skaters go on the ice? They can reach speeds of around 30 mph!!!

What's His story? As we search and seek to find His story, we sometimes see a biblical slant, but in this case, it should be a biblical lean! To navigate the curves on the tight circular track, the skaters must lean until they are almost sideways on the ice. It is fascinating to watch, but even more impressive once you know how fast they are traveling. Did you ever contemplate that in our lives, we should actually try to emulate what the skaters do in the corners? Proverbs 3:5-6 gives great life-skating technical advice. It says, "Trust in the Lord with all your heart and lean not on your own understanding; in all your ways acknowledge him, and he will make your paths straight." We will be able to navigate the forces that are trying to push us out of pure form and into the wall if we lean into Him and trust Him instead of what we think with our infantile perspective. Blair's key to success was her rhythm and consistency, which allowed her to maintain momentum even after the tight curves. In other words, her paths were made straight! May our paths also be made straight as we develop a routine of scripture reading and learning to lean on Him. Are you going into the curves trying to do it yourself? What's one thing you can do today that will help you lean into Him?

MARCH 19

Just Say No

Romans 5:8

On March 19, 1983, First Lady Nancy Reagan appeared on the television show *Diff'rent Strokes* to promote her "Just Say No" to drugs campaign. The top-rated show from the 1980s starred Gary Coleman and followed the Drummond family as they learned various life lessons. During the presidency of Ronald Reagan, First Lady Nancy Reagan prioritized the big problem of illegal drugs and the impact it was having on the nation, especially children.

What's His story? Drug use can harm lives. It even warranted Nancy joining a sitcom to deliver a rather severe message to Arnold without him asking his trademark, "What are you talking about??" phrase! We can all see the physical harm it creates, but it also prevents us from loving and honoring God in a way deserving of Him. In Romans, the Apostle Paul is also very clear about sin and its effect on our ability to serve a loving God in a manner mirroring the honor and glory worthy of the Almighty. Yet in verse 5:8, the fantastic words we see "while we were still sinners" shows God's unconditional love, and by sending His son Jesus Christ, we gain assurance that we are not saved because we were good enough, but because He loved us. This alone should allow us to easily say, "Just say no to sin and yes to God!" We receive the gift and serve Him with whole hearts! Just today, how many opportunities do you have to say, "no?" Romans 5:8 should give you all the reason you need to go ahead and say it with confidence, turning towards God!

MARCH 20

Precious Blood of Rescue

Psalm 72:14

On March 20, 1852, Harriet Beecher Stowe's book, *Uncle Tom's Cabin* was published. It helped to focus light on the tragedy of slavery and placed it front and center. The book inscribed in the minds of readers a very personal understanding of the human casualties attributed to the horrendous nature of slavery.

What's His story? In her preface, Stowe makes reference to Psalm 72:14. It says, "But as for me, I will always have hope; I will praise you more and more." Why do you think Stowe selected this one? I believe it is because she knew, like we should know, that the hope referred to in this passage is one without disappointment. That is why we will praise God more and more. It is a suitable selection as the Psalmist ascribes that God will rescue the oppressed and reaffirms the credence of God's love for ALL who are made in His image. We are precious to Him, and our hope rests in Him. Therefore He deserves our praise! There are many more references to or evocations from the Bible throughout *Uncle Tom's Cabin*, supporting Stowe's affirmed place as an image carrier of God, and messenger of hope to others. While typically required reading in a high school literature class, I believe the book deserves a second or even third run to engage in that message of hope. It is also a reminder that we cannot ignore the plight of the oppressed or needy. Are you praising Him because of the hopeful expectation you have in Him? Would it change your mind if you knew you would never be disappointed?

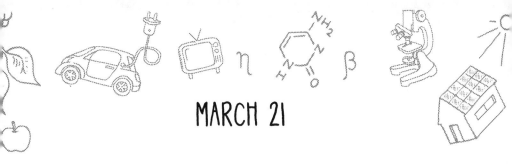

MARCH 21

The Hatfield – McCoy Feud

Romans 12:18

On March 21, 1891, a Hatfield married a McCoy, which did not end the long feud between the two families that spanned decades and geographically across the Tug Fork Tributary of the Big Sandy River watershed. Still, it did provide hope towards ending it. While the river formed the state boundary between Kentucky (McCoy) and West Virginia (Hatfield), and a physical border between the two families, the division itself, which started with an accusation of pig stealing, was deep, dark, and fiery.

What's His story? While the marriage was initially frowned upon, and violence escalated soon after, it provided a glimmer of hope for forgiveness and reconciliation. In Romans 12:18, Paul delivers a roadmap for how to serve as a living sacrifice just as Christ did. We are to live at peace with others. Interesting to note that relatives of the feuding families officially signed a truce much later, and even competed on the television game show Family Feud, how appropriate! The McCoy family won by $1, and a pig was also a part of the prize. Quite the story, but if we focus on the fact that reconciliation is forgiveness plus one, we see the role it should play in our lives every single day. It is forgiveness, plus restoral of the relationship. The Bible places no limits on forgiveness and even points out that it can sometimes be one-sided in favor of forgiveness. Isn't that love, sometimes? If we live as Paul guides us in Romans, the opportunity for reconciliation, in which both parties participate, is much more incredible. Do you have unresolved forgiveness, with a chance for reconciliation on the table? While it may not be as heated or fiery as the Hatfield – McCoy feud, what is holding you back from crossing the river of grace?

MARCH 22

Laser Focus

Acts 20:24

On March 22, 1960, Charles Townes and Arthur Schawlow were granted the patent for the optical maser, which today is called the laser. Lasers are used in many applications like surgery, cutting metal, and my favorite, laser light shows! One primary characteristic of a laser is the ability to focus the highly-charged and powerful light array onto a very narrow area.

What's His story? Some have certified the Stone Mountain Laser Show near Atlanta, Georgia, as a must-do experience. The perfectly synchronized lasers and music create an amazing show. When you look at lasers (actually don't do that – you'll need expensive safety glasses for that) and hear people refer to someone or something as being laser-focused, it means you are pinpointed on a single objective. We should be laser-focused on the message of the Gospel. Honing in on what matters most and to not be scattered by outside distractions allows us to act as the laser. Just as the situational use varies for a laser, our particular area of laser focus on the Gospel might vary. Once our laser is transfixed on the transformational words found in scripture, the power and impact will be as undeniably strong as a laser beam itself. Does that sound far-fetched? It's not. Staying in the word each day equips you with laser beams that will almost certainly come in handy later, plus you do not have to make that silly "pew-pew" sound as you're delivering laser beams of encouragement later. As Acts 20:24 reminds us, our AIM is to finish the race and complete the task the Lord Jesus has given me – the task of testifying to the good news of God's grace! So, where is your laser pointed?

MARCH 23

The Mullet

Psalm 13

On March 23, 1992, the song *Achy Breaky Heart* by Billy Ray Cyrus was released. With a perfectly coiffed mullet, Billy Ray shot to the top of the country and pop charts with this hit. Many of you have even line-danced to this song… I'm sure of it!

What's His story? You do not have to go far into the Bible to understand that our hearts are aptly described as being achy and breaky without God. Look at the Garden of Eden. In Psalm 13, we find a perfect example of pain and redemption. What's vital in this scripture is that in the beginning, the Psalmist believes that God has left him, when in actuality we know the opposite to be true, because God never moved; we do. By the end of this verse, we see that when he once again trusts in God's unfailing love, his heart rejoices in the salvation received through God. We can do the same thing. We sing His praise when we put our trust in God! Our achy-breaky hearts are then healed! What breaks your heart? Or, better yet, what are some ways in which you can mend a broken heart?

MARCH 24

Peaceful Rapids of Love

John 17:23

On March 24, 1834, American explorer and geologist John Wesley Powell was born in Mount Morris, New York. Powell's interest in geology, water conservation, and exploration of the American West led him to Wyoming and Colorado. He is best known for his research of the Colorado River and the long and winding pathway it takes through the Grand Canyon. In the late 1860s, Powell organized a few trips down the river, which at the time had not been mapped or charted. Keep in mind that these were some of the fiercest rapids in the entire West. Powell convinced a group to hop in a few boats and have at it! I hope he paid them.

What's His story? I don't know about you, but I tend to want to know what is ahead of me, whether it is traffic, weather, or some crazy rapids so that I will know how to prepare. Well, when Jesus gathered the disciples for the Last Supper, and that is what he was doing for them through His instruction. He was preparing them for what was to come and how they should handle it. Jesus was still speaking in parables, but in John 16, wrapping up His instruction, and packing spiritual provisions for them, delivers the ultimate life jacket. In John 17:23, like multiple rivers coming together, he says, "I in them and you in me. May they be brought to complete unity to let the world know that you sent me and have them even as you have loved me." In other words, because we are in unity with Jesus, and the Father loves Jesus, we are also loved by the Father! Jesus wanted the disciples to act as the body of the church, in unity, because He knew that's how they would be able to overcome the challenges ahead of them. We are no different. In accordance as a body of Christ, we can overcome as well, because He is in us, and we in Him! Think about Powell and the unchartered territory he was entering. It takes faith to step out, and with Jesus, we can step boldly and confidently so the world will know His name. Take the life jacket of the Father's love and enjoy the ride! Will you look at rapids on a river differently?

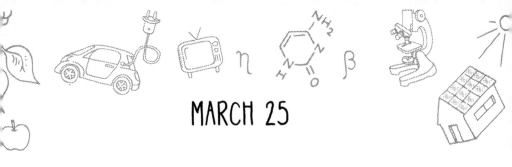

MARCH 25

During the Living Years

John 9:4-5

On March 25, 1989, the #1 hit song in the United States was *The Living Years* by a band called Mike and the Mechanics. The song is written from the standpoint of a child with a strained relationship with his father. It is only after his father dies that he realizes what a strong bond they really had, and he is remorseful that he did not say more while his dad was alive.

What's His story? The realization for the singer-songwriter, Mike Rutherford, was hard. He had put his musical career above all else, including a relationship with his father. How often do we find ourselves in the same position, but in this case with our Heavenly Father? While we are alive, we tend to go through life either through the motions or with a slightly self-centered focus. We are all guilty of this. However, maybe a song like *The Living Years* is a reminder, an alert, or a nudge to reposition what it is we see as a priority. We can then take advantage of the time we have to spread love to others we physically see while preparing for eternal adoration and worship of our father in heaven. John 9:4-5 is a stark reminder. While He is in the world, He is the light of the world. Let is be the same for us. How are you treating your living years? Are you living for Christ with no regret or remorse?

MARCH 26

The True Side Paradise

Luke 23:43

On March 26, 1920, the book *This Side of Paradise* by F. Scott Fitzgerald was published. Fitzgerald, named for his famous relative Francis Scott Key, who penned the words to the Star-Spangled Banner, is also the author of The Great Gatsby. He was able to draw on real-life experiences in both novels, as the Fitzgerald family was very affluent.

What's His story? *This Side of Paradise* is a book that explores the theme of love warped by greed and status-seeking. I am taken to Luke 23:43 in which Jesus is on the cross. In the scripture just prior, we learn the quick story of the two criminals who are also crucified at the same time as Jesus. One mockingly asks Jesus to prove he is the Messiah by saving all of them. At the same time, the other criminal selflessly admits that he is receiving his deserved sentence, also repudiating Jesus' punishment as unjustifiable. He further asks Jesus to remember him. Jesus brings this man into His side of paradise as He says, "Truly I tell you, today you will be with me in paradise." Now that's the right side of paradise, and Jesus offers us the opportunity to go there with Him. Which side of paradise attracts you today? Which of the condemned criminals resonates more with you today? Take the path to the right side of paradise. Today we have our own idea of what heaven will be and what we expect it to be. However, in reality, when we place a relationship with Jesus above all of that, the true picture of paradise comes into focus. And it will be more than palm trees, coconuts, and ukuleles!

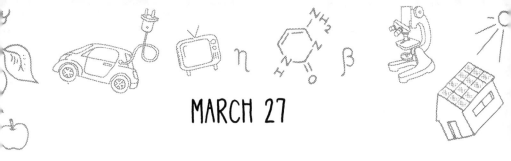

MARCH 27

Shaken Love

Matthew 27:51

On March 27, 1964, a devastating earthquake of magnitude 9.2 rocked the Prince William Sound region of Alaska. The event also triggered a major tsunami that caused damage and casualties all the way down to northern California. At the time of writing, it is still the largest earthquake in United States history.

What's His story? While some refer to it as the Great Alaska Earthquake and Tsunami, many simply refer to it as the Good Friday Earthquake, since it occurred on Good Friday. In Matthew 27:51, just as Jesus has given up His spirit and breathed His last on the cross, we find another story of a great earthquake. This earthquake occurs as the temple curtain is torn in two, the earth shook and rocks split. Christ's sacrifice for our sins has shattered and torn the barrier between God and humanity. This is an earthquake that cannot be measured on any scale, including the Richter. The timing of the Alaska quake is uncanny, but it is also a reminder of the magnitude of Christ's sacrifice and what it meant for the world. The separation between man and God was bridged by Christ on the cross. The very foundation of what men understood about the relationship with God to that point was shaken. At that moment, we became free to approach God because our sins were forgiven and our ability to approach God restored. All through an earth-shattering act, which gave all of mankind a gift we do not deserve. Are there monumental events in your life that serve as reminders of Christ's sacrifice and God's love?

MARCH 28

Parted Runway on the Sea

Exodus 14:21

On March 28, 1910, the first successful seaplane takeoff from water took place in Martinique, France. Its inventor, Henri Fabre, flew the seaplane. A fifty-horsepower engine powered the first flight over the water. The plane was nicknamed "Le Canard," which means "the duck" in French. Is it a boat, or is it a plane? I suppose it depends on whom you ask.

What's His story? The great thing about a seaplane is probably the freedom it grants a pilot. He can take off and land wherever there is water deep enough and wide enough, whereas a regular plane requires a concrete or grass runway typically designated for planes. In Exodus, I believe we find the best of both worlds. With God directing the way, Moses led the Israelites out of Egypt, acting as air traffic control, opening up a runway to a new life. Surely, Pharaoh wished that Le Canard was around back then, or that someone had invented sea chariots. In parting the Red Sea for the Israelites to cross, God opened up a solution for them, demonstrating His great power and love for His chosen people. So while a seaplane is a fantastic invention full of freedom to land anywhere on the water, it is not quite as amazing as the redeeming freedom offered through God as He parted the water to create His own runway for His people. Are you trying to land on choppy waters, or are you looking for solid ground prepared for you by God?

MARCH 29

A Part of the Royal Family

1 Peter 2:9

On March 29, 1951, the Rodgers and Hammerstein musical *The King and I* premiered at the St. James Theatre on Broadway in New York City. It ran until March of 1954, with a total of 1,246 performances. It is a musical adaptation of the book by Margaret Landon called *Anna and the King of Siam*.

What's His story? The title of the musical, The *King and I*, should describe our daily walk in the word. We should want to feel the presence of the King of our lives, the King of Kings. The title itself evokes imagery of a walk down a long and winding road hand-in-hand with the King as we claim our royal identity in Christ. As 1 Peter 2:9 reminds us, we are a part of a royal priesthood, and that He has called us out of darkness into the light. And as royalty, we are destined for a divine purpose that God has set out for us. By God's grace, we are born into this royal family. Are you walking with the King today? Is it the King and I, or just I?

MARCH 30

God's Humor

1 Samuel 5:1-4

On March 30, 1980, outside the Washington Hilton in Washington, DC, an assassination attempt was made on the President of the United States, Ronald Reagan. He was wounded, along with several others, including White House Press Secretary James Brady.

What's His story? Understanding that it is sometimes difficult to see the good in a tragic event like this, I draw you to Reagan's demeanor while in the hospital. First, he told his wife that he forgot to duck. Then he asked if the doctors were all Republicans, which was his political party. Reagan found a way to bring lighthearted laughter to a dire situation. Likewise, I believe that God has a sense of humor for us to see the fullness of his love – from sadness to laughter. As we are made in God's image, doesn't our desire to laugh come from Him? Now, I'll admit that what people perceive as humorous is sometimes debatable, but there are some great examples throughout the Bible, such as 1 Samuel 5:1-4. After the Israelites were using the Ark of the Covenant like a good-luck charm in battle, the Philistines stole it and put it in the temple of Dagon, which was their idol. When they came back the next morning, Dagon was found kneeling in front of the ark! The same thing happened the next day; only this time, the head and arms were broken! God demonstrated His power over idols and put Dagon in a position of submission. Can you imagine the looks on the faces of the Philistines? Priceless. Humor can direct, and it can also heal. How can humor help you see God moving in your life? Laughter really can be the best medicine!

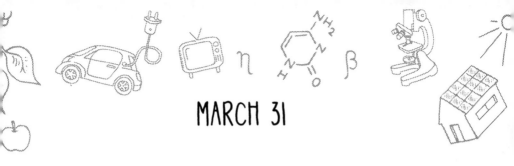

MARCH 31

The Blinding City Lights

Matthew 5:14

On March 31, 1880, the city of Wabash, Indiana, became the first electrically lit city in the world! We are not talking about just a few light bulbs. In fact, four electric arc "brush lights" were mounted atop the courthouse. The light could be seen from over a mile away. One of the original lights is still on display today in the Wabash County Court House.

What's His story? In Matthew 5:14, Jesus teaches, "You are the light of the world. A city on a hill cannot be hidden." Apparently, Wabash took this to heart and literally got out in front of it. Although the elevation of Wabash is only 712 feet above sea level, no hill is too small for us to be the light to the world. Being the light to others is allowing the reflection of the spirit within to overflow outwardly and illuminate the darkness. It could be a quick smile, or a kind act, or living a Christ-like existence when we think no one else is watching. Or, it could be lighting an entire city on a hill for others to see and understand how Christ's light bathes us perpetually. Either way, let your light shine so that others can see the joy you have in Christ! I wonder if the city motto for Wabash is "The city of this little light of mine." You might consider Bethlehem to be the original birthplace of The Light, but I love what Wabash did. How are you letting your light shine today? It can honestly start with a smile!

APRIL 1

Chewing Gum Full of Flavor

Proverbs 3:1-2

On April 1, 1891, in Chicago, Illinois, William Wrigley, Jr. founded the Wrigley Company. He started out as a soap salesman and added gum as a premium add-on. Eventually, his primary focus became the gum as it became more popular than the soap. You are probably familiar with Wrigley Spearmint or Doublemint, and there are those wacky people who love Juicy Fruit.

What's His story? The old slogan for Wrigley's gum and a central selling point was, "The Flavor Lasts." Think about gum for a minute, specifically bubble-gum. It can be rock hard or not very pliable at first, but the more you chew it, the softer and easier it becomes to transform it into something like a bubble. It is kind of like us when we are receptive to God's word, right? At first, we might resist and act hardened to it, but the more we get into it, the more pliable and receptive we are to His message, the easier it is to transform us. Now, think about flavor. Some gum, we will not name names (Zebra Stripe), just does not last very long. Wrigley's gum lived up to its slogan. Something else that does not lose flavor is God's word! It never loses its flavor or favor. We can chew into eternity, and it will still be as pleasant as when we first tasted it. Proverbs 3:1-2 reminds us not to forget God's word, as it will sustain us long into life, and long after the Zebra Stripe gum flavor has disappeared. Wrigley, and the field by the same name, is a soft spot for me, but that is a whole different book! How are you becoming soft and pliable to His word? Are you enjoying new and lasting flavor through God's word? Are you using all of your senses?

APRIL 2

Living Bread

John 6:35

On April 2, 1863, the Richmond Bread Revolt took place in Richmond, Virginia. This was during the United States Civil War. The revolt originated as a result of many factors related to the war. Ironically, and sadly, in a nation full of farmers, people were starving. Due to the war, fewer men were working the farms, and brutal fighting was destroying farmlands.

What's His story? In John 6:35, Jesus confirms that He is the bread of life. He has, and He gives life so that we shall never be hungry or thirsty. The satisfaction we attain through belief in Jesus replaces our constant hunger for stuff and our unquenchable thirst for things. Jesus' statement in John represents similar expressions of fulfillment. He is the bread of life and the living water to satisfy every need we have. As tragic and severe as the Bread Revolt was, it actually led to a more concerted effort to take care of the hungry and needy. How are you taking care of your own needs, but also the needs of others? What is your farm producing today to feed those around you? It can be both spiritual, as well as physical sustenance. How can you bring others to feast at the table with the Father, Son, and the Holy Spirit?

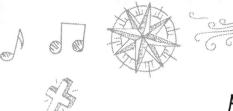

APRIL 3

Blessed Hooves

Exodus 20:8-11

On April 3, 1860, the Pony Express began. Founded as a quicker way to transport mail from the Missouri River westward, it utilized fifty riders, 500 horses, and 190 relay stations over almost 2,000 miles of untamed wilderness. It lasted a little over a year and laid the groundwork for additional communication efficiencies like the telegraph. The Pony Express riders did not have the luxury of GPS or Waze to avoid traffic or to find the quickest routes.

What's His story? One of the Pony Express founders, Alexander Majors, was a devout Christian and emphatically believed, as Exodus 20:8-11 tells us, that the Sabbath was holy and respected. Majors understood that the Sabbath is a day of rest and reflection. It is a recharge day for man, but also for a horse in this case. It is also a day set aside for worship. He insisted every rider do the same. As a way of encouraging other biblical principles, all Pony Express riders were given a Bible. Twelve such Bibles are still around today. Too often, we find ourselves looking past the sacred rest found in the Sabbath, believing that we are on a mission with no time to waste. But that mission is typically our own, with no reverence towards God on His day. So there you have it – on Sundays in 1860, as it is today, you will not be getting mail or a delightful chicken sandwich with waffle fries. It is because we should treat the Sabbath as holy. What is your Sabbath day like? Is it like any other day? If so, when and what do you set aside for God in worship?

APRIL 4

Free at Last

Deuteronomy 32:52

On April 4, 1968, civil rights activist and minister Dr. Martin Luther King, Jr. was assassinated at the Lorraine Motel in Memphis, Tennessee. Dr. King was in Memphis supporting a sanitation worker strike that day. News of his death sent shockwaves throughout the world. He was a gifted pastor with an ability to bridge divides like no other.

What's His story? Dr. King fought for justice. He fought for equality based on our status as image-bearers of Christ. He fought for a Promised Land that held these values in utmost esteem. His "I Have a Dream" speech is one of the most emotional and moving oratory symphonies you will hear from a man who achieved so much in his short time on Earth. But his speech the night before his death was eerily preeminent and equally moving. He recounts the end of Moses' life as he was led to the mountaintop to see the Promised Land. Like Moses in Deuteronomy 32:52, Dr. King somehow knew that he wouldn't enjoy this land of beautiful harmony. That did not stop his belief that eventually, we all would enter the new Promised Land in which we see one another as children of God with no regard for race or economic standing. Dr. King understood that he was leading the charge, but that it might not be his to realize. Even that knowledge did not detract or distract from his mission and message to love God and love your neighbor. A sniper's bullet could not stop this message. On this day, simply listen to any of Dr. King's sermons or speeches and reflect on his message of unity and love for one another.

APRIL 5

Ministry Veto

Mark 5: 18-20

On April 5, 1792, United States President George Washington exercises his authority to veto a bill. It was the first time this power was used in the United States. A veto is a constitutional right to reject a decision or proposal made by a law-making body. This veto was concerning the Apportionment Act of 1792, which set the number of congressional representatives in the House of Representatives of the United States Congress.

What's His story? Have you ever prayed for something earnestly and received a "no" or no answer at all? It feels like God is vetoing our plan. One key point is that God's silence is not evidence of His absence, and we often see the revised plan set before us. We know in trusting God that His plan is best, but initially, it sure does feel like we just received a veto. The story in Mark 5 is one of my favorites. Jesus has healed a man who had the demon who called himself Legion. Just the name gives the imagery of a snarled mess of issues. Upon his healing, the man was thrilled and wanted to join Jesus and His ministry to share his joy. But Jesus told him no! Jesus vetoed it!! It was because Jesus knew that the man's ministry would be more effective where he was, an area full of Gentiles and skeptics. But the man did not comprehend it until Jesus vetoed his request. Sometimes a veto is just what we need. Have you ever received a refusal or rejection and not understood why? Does the story from Mark give you renewed hope that God is still working in your life?

APRIL 6

Heavenly Medals

1 Corinthians 9:24-27

On April 6, 1896, in Athens, Greece, the opening of the first modern Olympic Games was celebrated. Eight nations participated in the games that year, with the host nation Greece winning the most medals. I would have to check, but that might also be the origin of the "home-field advantage!"

What's His story? Go to 1 Corinthians 9:24-27. In this passage, Paul is writing to the church in Corinth using the analogy of a runner – perhaps an Olympic marathon runner - to illustrate the dedication and training necessary to win a prize. We also learn that some prizes do not last. Have you ever practiced or trained for something and achieved or accomplished your goal? Did you reflect back on the hours and hours of preparation and training? The Christian journey is a lot like the marathon. It requires fitness, fighting uphill battles, and focus. But when you compare the finisher's medals, the difference becomes stark. Within this passage of scripture, we receive instruction about seeking the right prize. Just like an athlete in training, we also learn the importance of self-disciple. If we apply these principles in our Christian lives, we can earn the eternal prize, which is the crown that will last forever. Are you in training? Is it temporary or eternal?

APRIL 7

Spiritual Health

Matthew 9:12

On April 7, 1948, the WHO or the World Health Organization was established. The WHO, not the rock band, is an international health organization concerned with keeping the world's inhabitants, especially the vulnerable, healthy. They do this through training, care, and by watching for widespread illness or pandemics.

What's His story? There is physical health, and then there is spiritual health. God has equipped some of us, including doctors and nurses, to address our physical health, and we are thankful for that. Just like a medical team, we also need a spiritual team to partner with God for healing and wellness. Do you ever think about your spiritual health? As Jesus said in Matthew 9:12, "It is not the healthy who need a doctor, but the sick." It takes discipline and a desire to improve your spiritual health, and in doing so, we can then make a vitally important contribution to God's kingdom. In physical health, they say, "know your numbers." In spiritual health, I believe it's "know your Savior." When we have a relationship with Jesus, we walk in the ways that lead to eternal life, our pulse beats stronger for Him, and there is no treadmill. Did you go for a walk today? Was it a walk with your Savior? Sometimes if the weather is nice, you can do both!!

APRIL 8

Artistic Gifts

Exodus 31:3-4

On April 8, 1973, famed surrealist painter Pablo Picasso died. While my favorite Picasso is the dachshund (I've had dachshunds all my life), he painted some rather exciting and intriguing works. Do you have a favorite of his?

What's His story? Picasso was quoted as saying, "The meaning of life is to find your gift. The purpose of life is to give it away." We will not find artists listed in 1 Corinthians 12 and Romans 12, but that does not mean that art is not essential to the church. Picasso found his gift – art. Art is a beautiful gift from God, full of love and eager to form communication. Just as the Psalmist glorified God with his artistry of music, Picasso did so with his brush strokes. To be an artist is to be filled with the Holy Spirit. It even says so in Exodus 31:3-4 when the Lord is talking to Moses about Bezalel and Oholiab and the artistic skills God has bestowed upon them. The next time you find yourself filled with awe at a museum's painting, be in awe of the spirit-filled masterpiece in front of you. But do not discredit the macaroni ornament your child made for the Christmas tree. In each scenario, the artist has given away a piece of themselves as a gift to God. You will never look at a doodle or masterpiece the same way. What Gospel-inspired art are you making today?

APRIL 9

Fake Grass

Colossians 2:8

On April 9, 1965, the Houston Astrodome in Houston, Texas, was completed. Home of the Major League Baseball Houston Astros, it was baseball's first indoor, air-conditioned, domed stadium, and one monstrosity of a structure with seating for 70,000 fans. It is best remembered for its starring role in the movie *The Bad News Bears*. Just kidding. It did, however, have enough room to include a bowling alley and a chapel!

What's His story? One key characteristic of the Astrodome was its field surface, appropriately called Astroturf. It was fake grass. It looked just like the green weatherproof carpet you might see on somebody's screened porch. This may sound harsh, but unfortunately, we find fake worship within Christianity, and the Bible rightfully points this out to us. It is more of a warning to know what truth looks like. Paul's warning in Colossians 2:8 eloquently puts us on alert to understand that man-made solutions to life's problems are not the answer. Jesus Christ is the only answer for us. Everything else is as false as Astroturf when compared to rich, sweet, lush green grass. It really is that stark of a difference. Are there areas of your life needing to be ripped up and replaced with the authenticity of our Lord?

APRIL 10

The Little Ball Moved the Big Ball

Matthew 5:9

On April 10, 1971, "Ping-Pong Diplomacy" began when fifteen United States ping-pong players traveled to China. In a trip full of goodwill and sportsmanship across China that put politics and stalled diplomatic negotiations on the back-burner, the Cold War thawed at least for a bit. As Chinese president, Mao put it, "the little ball moved the Big Ball."

What's His story? Every church youth area seems to have a ping-pong table. I now ask you to rename them peacemaker tables. I am sure no one thought that a game like ping-pong could break down barriers between nations through the actions of just a few like it did back in the 1970s. But as Jesus points out in The Beatitudes and Matthew 5:9, blessed are the peacemakers for they will be called children of God. It all started as one player hopping on the Chinese team bus during the World Table Tennis Championships while they were in Japan. This act of friendship evolved out of love for God and a desire to do good towards all men, and it led to two of the largest nations in the world improving relations. As you go through your day today, observe just how many opportunities are presented for you to act as a peacemaker. It is probably more than you imagined. Call on the Holy Spirit for discernment and guidance for how to best become the peacemaker that God has called you to be.

APRIL 11

Heavenly Recovery Procedures

Psalm 59:16

On April 11, 1970, the NASA space mission Apollo 13 blasted off into space. This was another planned lunar landing mission. However, it was not to be. Not long in the trip, a problem occurred, which negated the lunar module's ability to land on the moon. It also put the safety of the three men on board in grim jeopardy. The movie remake by the mission name is an incredible re-enactment of the events and how the men handled it.

What's His story? This event is where we first heard that famous catchphrase, "Houston, we have a problem." It was the crew's way of notifying mission control that something serious was going wrong, and they needed instruction. The phrase is now used to sarcastically describe how we feel about receiving a bad grade, a flat tire, or the wrong order in the drive-thru line. Admit it – you have probably used it as well. In Psalm 59, through prayer and praise for God's saving help, we realize that God is our refuge and safety in this world full of trouble. The men of Apollo 13 needed very detailed instructions and procedures, which had to be executed in precise order to return home safely. Our guidance and procedures are found in the words of scripture. When we declare "Lord, we have a problem" to our God as mission control, He gives us the recovery procedure that leads us back into His loving embrace with all the warmth of a thousand rockets. Will you boldly declare your problems to God, trusting that He will provide you with heavenly provisioned precision to bring you home to Him?

APRIL 12

A 24-Hour Solid Rock

Isaiah 26:4

On April 12, 1954, Bill Haley and the Comets put their signature on rock and roll history with the song release of *"(We're Gonna) Rock Around the Clock."* The song became a hit when it was used in the opening credits of the movie *Blackboard Jungle.*

What's His story? This one is short, sweet, and to the point. GOD IS OUR ROCK AROUND THE CLOCK. As Isaiah 26:4 reminds us, "Trust in the Lord forever, for the Lord, the Lord, is the Rock eternal." Not only is there an emphasis on how God is our rock, but also through the repetition, it emphasizes who He is. He is eternal, or around the clock, watching over us in never-ending fashion. We can be assured that we are supported by the firm foundation of God's power and never-ending love. Even while we are sleeping, God remains our steadfast, immovable rock. There will be moments of darkness in which we think that God is not with us. It is because His answer does not match ours, or something else that allowed doubt to creep into your head? Stand firmly on the rock that is our Lord, who offers protection and love around the clock. Are your feet on the rock, or do you feel as though you stand on shifting sand? How can you take a step onto the solid bedrock that is available around the clock, both day and night?

APRIL 13

Handel's Messiah

Isaiah 53:5

On April 13, 1742, in a Dublin, Ireland concert hall, George Frideric Handel's *Messiah* was first performed.

What's His story? The *Messiah* is a three-part oratorio, which is a musical work for orchestra and voices. The first part includes lyrics that describe an extended reflection on Jesus as the Messiah. The second part contains the piece we are probably most familiar with - the Hallelujah chorus. We typically associate this song with Christmas, but this part of the oratorio is related to the final days of Christ on Earth, covering Palm Sunday through Easter! The third movement covers His resurrection and glorification in Heaven. In Isaiah, we find numerous references to the Messiah, which Jesus fulfills. Isaiah 53:5 unfolds the power of this work by Handel. The first part of this verse aligns directly with the Crucifixion. It describes the Messiah, who is to be pierced for our transgressions and crushed for our iniquities. However, it ends with "and by his wounds we are healed." If you've never heard this piece of music, I invite you to find a quiet moment and listen to the Hallelujah chorus in celebration of Christ's sacrifice and resurrection. Even better, I would suggest reading this passage of scripture from Isaiah as you are listening. We shall just call it reverent multi-tasking!

APRIL 14

Your Journey Journaling

Numbers 33:2

On April 14, 1860, the first Pony Express pouch of mail was delivered to San Francisco, California. Not only do you know precisely how long it took to get from Missouri to California (refer back to April 3!) but now you are going to know what was delivered! It contained forty-nine letters, five telegraphs, and some miscellaneous papers. I wonder if any of those papers were sales flyers for new gutters?

What's His story? You have already read about the Pony Express riders, the many relay stations along the route, and their observance of the Sabbath. As the Pony Express riders made it to each relay station, they reflected on their travel and adventure, hopefully feeling God's presence and protection. Buffalo Bill Cody was one rider who wrote about his experiences and exploits from Indian battles to being robbed along the route. In Numbers 33:2, God has asked Moses to record the stages of the Israelites journey, and the subsequent verses do so. Why do you think God did this? It was not for the local newspaper, so they would get the order right. It was so that an account might be preserved to record the good things that happened along the way, and where God's presence was made known. Too often, our memory focuses on the bad stuff, but have you noticed that when you journal a journey that the mercies and remarkable twists and turns with the Almighty's fingerprints suddenly spring to life like mountains rising from a distant plain? We are then keenly aware of how God is with us on our journey, not necessarily at our side, but rather out in front of us, preparing the way.

APRIL 15

Barrier Breaker

Titus 1:8-9

On April 15, 1947, baseball player Jackie Robinson made his Major League Baseball debut for the Brooklyn Dodgers. While Robinson broke the color barrier in baseball by becoming the first African American player, he fought for equal rights well before his baseball debut.

What's His story? Robinson once said, "A life is not important except in the impact it has on other lives." The impact that Robinson made cannot be summarized in a short paragraph, and the root of this quote shows how he lived his life as a brave example for others. In Paul's letter to Titus, we learn about what it means to be a Christian leader. Titus was a Greek believer and a living example for how Christ was working in the Gentile's lives, but it was not easy for him since it was so different from those around him. Paul's encouragement and leadership tips were what Titus needed. Titus 1:8-9 reflects Robinson's approach from the Christian perspective in the right order to set an example that encourages and leads others to Christ. Robinson overcame many obstacles. What are you doing today to set an example to lead others to Christ? Are you letting others out in traffic, or are you breaking down barriers with grace and strength? Any small act can be reflective of Christian living and will honor God.

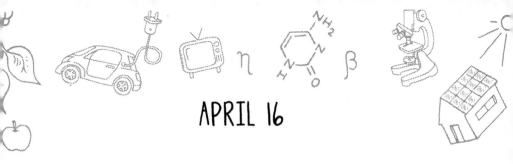

APRIL 16

Blown Chaff

Luke 3:17

On April 16, 1962, singer-songwriter Bob Dylan debuted his song "Blowin' in the Wind" at Gerde's Folk City in New York City. The song later appeared on Dylan's breakthrough album *The Freewheelin' Bob Dylan*. Dylan's singing style was what you might consider distinct, and resonated with the hippies of that era.

What's His story? The title of the song "Blowin' in the Wind" gives us a clue. When we look at Luke 3, we find a man who some might think is a hippie based on his dress, John the Baptist. John knew his place and calling, and urgently preached a message of repentance ahead of the coming Messiah. In Luke 3:17, John refers to Jesus as the holder of the winnowing fork, which would be used to clear the threshing floor. Harvesting the kernel of wheat was done by using a winnowing fork (think pitchfork) to toss the grains in the air. The heavier, more valuable kernel would fall to the ground, and the lighter, worthless chaff will be blown in the wind. If we don't repent, we are like chaff. Later in Luke, an unquenchable fire consumes the chaff, while the wheat is gathered in the barn. Which do you want to be? What are the ways in which you can allow Jesus to help you shed your chaff so that you might find peace in the barn? Don't want you blowin' in the wind…

APRIL 17

Luke & Laura

Jeremiah 17:14

On April 17, 2002, the 10,000th (wow!) episode of the soap opera General Hospital aired on ABC. I want you to think for a minute about how many scenes and lines of script that would be. And how many of those scenes involved arguably the most famous soap opera couple, Luke and Laura? Of course, I watched the show. I have two older sisters, after all!

What's His story? I spent a lot of time at hospitals, not in illness, but with my dad while he made rounds, and then later for work in the Microbiology lab. They are not always a happy place, but a hospital is a place of healing. The word hospital originates from the Latin hospes, meaning guest or stranger. The word patient comes from patior, which means to suffer. Etymologically, the hospital is a place where strangers who suffer come to be healed. To me, it sounds profoundly similar to a church or a Christian community. God's power knows no bounds. Therefore He is the ultimate healer. No matter if it is actually in a hospital or in a church, or whether the need is physical or spiritual healing, His touch can be felt, and healing begins. Sometimes the healing answer may not be what we have prayed for or expected, but God is able, in His way and His time, to reveal answers and His plan. Miracles happen, prayers are heard, and God is moving. Jeremiah 17:14 reminds us that we should praise God for healing. He is removing suffering just as a doctor might remove a bandage to reveal a scar that proves healing has occurred. A scar reminds us of God's continual faithfulness to our recovery. It may not improve the hospital cafeteria food, but when you consider it a place where suffering strangers come to be made whole again, the mystery meat is not so bad after all! Where have you seen healing take place?

APRIL 18

That's a Strange Diet

Romans 5:8

On April 18, 1521, Martin Luther went before the Diet of Worms. No, it was not a different way of saying Paleo or keto, and it was not a strict earthworm (no tapeworm, please) diet. A diet is another word for assembly. In this case, it was meeting in Worms, Germany, to discuss Luther's writings.

What's His story? Surprisingly, in my NIV Bible, the word worm actually shows up eight times, seven as a noun and one as a verb. Apparently, Timothy did need to hear it, but I digress. The diet assembled in Worms was called to address Luther's ninety-five theses. This long list of issues said that the church was selling forgiveness of sins instead of teaching that forgiveness is available through Christ alone and cannot be purchased or earned through our merits. Romans 6:23 is one of the most fantastic reminders of this. "The wages of sin is death, but the gift of God is eternal life in Christ Jesus our Lord." It is a gift that only God can provide, and it cannot be earned. Have you ever received a wonderful gift that you didn't ask for, but it was something you thought you desperately needed like a (fill in the blank, because I would probably put a pair of running shoes or something)? Now take that feeling of euphoria and pump it up thousands of times greater. That is how we should feel as we accept God's gift in thanksgiving. We rejoice in this very moment but also throughout your day. Do you accept the gift of eternal life in Christ Jesus? What is keeping you from doing so today? The other thing to ponder is how did the town of Worms get its name.

APRIL 19

Lightning Strikes Thrice

1 Peter 5:10

On April 19, 2018, while surfing in Hawaii, a young man named Dylan McWilliams was bitten by a shark.

What's His story? I know what you are thinking. That's it?? Nope. Hardly. It turns out Dylan is quite tasty to animals. In the span of thirty-six short months, he was bitten by the shark as mentioned above, mauled by a grizzly bear while camping, and bitten by a rattlesnake. I have to wonder whether Dylan's social media bio says something about loving the great outdoors. Obviously, Dylan survived each attack, so I believe where we find His story here is the courage he demonstrated in each attack and his subsequent positive attitude. In 1 Peter 5:10, Peter gave faithful Christians perspective on their suffering, with an eye on the fact that an eternal life with Christ means no sorrow. As it says, Christ will "restore you and make you strong, firm, and steadfast." Dylan could probably market a t-shirt with the verse above with a picture of the three animals and the words strong, firm, and steadfast. It is sometimes hard to see, but truthfully, our suffering is only temporary because of Him. Does your grief or sorrow sometimes feel like a pack of wild animals? Allow Peter's words to reassure you. Meanwhile, I would probably avoid hiking with Dylan or flying with Tom Hanks.

APRIL 20

Ballpark Churches & Chapels

Mark 8:21

On April 20, 1912, both historic baseball stadiums Fenway Park in Boston and Tiger Stadium in Detroit opened. While Fenway is still there, Tiger Stadium was torn down in 2008.

What's His story? Some baseball fans are rightfully called fanatics, and these historic stadiums are like churches to them. It is a place where reverence for tradition, acknowledgment of prior figures, and revivals like the bottom of the 9th comebacks have happened. Think of the unity created here and in how many ways it is similar to a church. There is out-of-tune singing, many desperate prayers, and usually a 7th inning stretch where you share the peace with your neighbor or a visitor. Strangers are welcomed, and troubles are left at the door. These old stadiums rekindle tradition, and longevity is something that draws us together. Unfortunately, the quote by former Giants player and Mets manager Wes Westrum is all too true, "Baseball is like church. Many attend, but few understand." We can get caught up in the production and completely miss the message. It's a lot like the disciples in Mark 8:14-21 when they forgot to bring the bread on the boat, and Jesus warned them against wrong teaching. Are you showing up to the stadium for the experience but missing the show? What are some ways you can examine your own worship to point it back to God? A life full of spiritual disciplines like prayer time, devotions, Bible-reading, and quiet time with God is the spring training you need to gain the understanding necessary to leverage the corporate worship experience of the church into something that lasts throughout the week!

APRIL 21

Empty Vaults

John 20:16

On April 21, 1986, the world watched as television journalist turned Indiana Jones, Geraldo Rivera, opened Al Capone's secret, hidden vault on live television. His goal was to see if the legend that the vault held treasure was true. I still remember watching it as a kid, riveted to the screen. Spoiler alert: the vault was empty!

What's His story? I never will forget the disappointment in Rivera's voice as he saw what we saw unfolding before his eyes and a live television audience. Utter despair and dismay is the only way to describe it. Mary had a similar reaction upon reaching the tomb where Jesus had been placed after the Crucifixion. In John 20:1-15, it is almost the exact same reaction Rivera had, but the pivotal moment occurs in verse 16, when Jesus calls to her, "Mary." At that instant, the Risen Lord is revealed to her, and she discovers an empty tomb is the greatest treasure of all. As we read this story, a mosaic is formed of the highs and lows associated with hope and expectation and a picture forms of the most beautiful sight – the face of our Lord, who has defeated death. All those years ago in the tomb provided by Joseph of Arimathea, the stone was rolled back to uncover an empty vault that could not hold the greatest treasure of our lives. Can you put yourself in the shoes of Rivera? What about Mary? How quickly despair can be transformed, but only Jesus' victory imparts an eternal treasure. And it all started with the original rolling stone, which was NOT Keith Richards.

APRIL 22

Earth Day

Nehemiah 9:6

On April 22, 1970, the first Earth Day was observed. It is an annual event that celebrates and demonstrates support for protecting Mother Earth and this delicate ecosystem.

What's His story? While one reference would be from Genesis in which Adam names the creatures, I believe the best one comes from Nehemiah 9:6. There we find acknowledgment that the Lord is the greatest of all things. He made the Heavens, Earth and all that is on it, and the seas and all that is in them. The Lord gives life to everything; with the multitudes of Heaven, we worship him. There is no better way to celebrate Earth Day than to thank the Creator for Creation, and in reverent acknowledgment, protect his creation. Every living thing is a part of God's creation. I believe that God uses Earth to alert us to Him and His sovereignty, as well as the vastness of His creativity. Look around you today. Pick up a leaf, a flower, or a blade of grass and purposely examine the details held within it. When we take a moment to soak in the details of our host planet, we slowly uncover the glory all around us. Think about those items again – the leaf, flower, or blade of grass. Have you ever used a magnifying glass to view the details? The word magnify means to show honor to God. How appropriate to use a *magnifying* glass to view His creation! Honor should then come naturally! How are you spending Earth Day? Celebrate with God as we savor creation.

APRIL 23

How-To Jesus Video

Matthew 13:33

On April 23, 2005, the very first video was uploaded to YouTube. It was an eighteen-second video entitled "Me at the zoo." Today almost 300 hours of video are uploaded to YouTube every minute, and over five billion videos are watched every day. There are more stunning facts and figures, but I do not want you to put this down to increase the numbers even more.

What's His story? Aside from all of the sermon videos, of course, YouTube is used for many, many reasons. I would say one of the top picks has to be the wide variety of how-to videos. You can learn how to do everything! For example, my kids and I found out how to make Rainbow Loom bracelets. If we look to scripture, I believe that Jesus' use of parables and Paul's letters are early YouTube how-to videos for giving step-by-step instructions on living a Christian life that honors and glorifies God. Some parables are short snippets, and others are long-winding tales. Either way, people were hungry for the truth and determined to pursue Jesus and subscribe to His channel. Even Paul was able to make "videos" from a jail cell. One of the shortest parables in the Bible is found in Matthew 13:33, "The kingdom of heaven is like yeast that a woman took and mixed into a large amount of flour until it worked all through the dough." I believe the yeast is symbolic of God's word as preached and heard all the way to the ends of the earth. This illustrates small beginnings with massively large results. I will take this twenty-word parable over an eighteen-second zoo video any day. Today, what how-to videos for how to live with Christlike wonder are you watching? Or is someone filming you as you set the example?

APRIL 24

The Living Book To Check Out Everyday

Hebrews 4:12

On April 24, 1800, the Library of Congress was established. It is the largest library in the world and contains millions of books, recordings, photographs, maps, and newspapers. It also houses the United States Copyright office. What began as a research library for the United States Congress is today a preservation institution.

What's His story? Of all of the books, recordings, photographs, maps, and newspapers found in the Library of Congress, there is only one book with the power to reform, redirect, and transform lives. Through God's word, revealed in the Bible, we are revived and awakened to the gift of the Advocate within us. No other book in this library or any other has the power to do that. None. As Hebrews 4:12 states, "For the word of God is living and active." Yes! The Bible is not just a collection of words and stories. It is alive and requires us to make decisions about how we let it shape our lives. Will you check it out of the library, allow it to collect dust on a shelf, or accumulate overdue fines? Or are you going to live and breathe the word of God, allowing it to penetrate your very being? Spend some time today in one of the most sweeping and transformative books available to us in all of history.

APRIL 25

One of a Kind Vanity Plates

1 Peter 4:10

On April 25, 1901, New York became the first state to require license plates on cars. As more and more cars were manufactured, it became necessary to identify vehicles. At first, the car owner's initials were shown on the handmade plates. Ironically, the first true metal plates were manufactured in Massachusetts. And later in 1903, New Yorkers made their own.

What's His story? License plates are a strange interest of mine, perhaps of yours as well. Whether it is playing a game on a long road trip or just taking in the design, it is fun to see the wide variation found here in the United States, let alone across the world. Some people still use their initials, and others use vanity plates. Some great vanity plate ideas are CGOD1ST, GODLVSU, or HE1SRZN. Okay, bring it back in…license plates are unique, and no two plates are the same. God's stamp on us is precisely the same. We are made unique, yet in His image. We find our identity, our license plate, so to speak, in what God has called us to be. 1 Peter 4:10 is a reminder of that unique identification, but it also calls us to put it into action through service to others. In doing so, we render and distribute God's grace in its various forms. It is an excellent call to action and better than any vanity plate. We know our fingerprint is unique, but what about the rest of our body and its making? There are many ways to pray and ask for discernment about the unique gift and calling God has dreamed over us. What are you doing to find your identity in a sea of white cars? And how are you serving others through it? Claim your identity in Christ and hold on for the most extraordinary ride of all.

APRIL 26

Free Bird

Matthew 6:26

On April 26, 1785, naturalist and ornithologist John Audubon was born in Les Cayes, Haiti. He is known for his paintings of birds of North America. The Audubon Society, which is named in his honor, carries on his legacy of interest and preservation of birds and bird habitats.

What's His story? Have you ever bird-watched? I mean, really bird-watched? Did you actually sit down with a pair of binoculars and watch a few birds in your yard or a park? They are active creatures that seemingly bounce from one area to the next in search of a worm or seed. For the most part (mockingbirds and birds of prey need not apply,) they are pleasant beings. I can understand how the remarkable coloration caught Audubon's interest. My sister, who lives in Australia, shares many pictures of the gorgeous and colorful birds found on the continent, and they are quite different. We can relate to Audubon. What about you? Matthew 6:26 serves as an exceptional illustration for us to live without worry as we observe the birds in the air, for they do not reap or sow, yet God still feeds them. Sure, sometimes we throw bread out to them, but you get the point. In comparison to the birds, the next verse reinforces God's ability to fulfill the things He promises to supply. Audubon's art served as a reminder of the beauty of God's creation, but the scripture serves as our reminder of God's ability to provide everything we need. Are you following the example of the birds, trusting in God to provide? Maybe you have a favorite bird? When you see a cardinal, my favorite bird, think of someone special.

APRIL 27

The True Role of the Appendix

John 1:3

On April 27, 1887, surgeon George Thomas Morton performed the first operation in the United States to remove an appendix, also called an appendectomy. You may not even have yours anymore, but it is a tiny little appendage that sits at the juncture of the large and small intestines. The appendix is like Rodney Dangerfield and doesn't get any respect. I will not bore you with the medical details, but suffice to say that it does some great work in the area of immunity.

What's His story? Many people think the appendix has no function, so you can survive when it is removed. But the same is true of your kidneys, part of your liver, etc. I told you I would not bore you with medical details. The point is every single part of your body serves a function. God has created you as a functioning human-being full of intricate systems working together for the greater good. As we see in John 1:3, "Through him all things were made; without him nothing was made that has been made." While this sounds as cryptic as the function of the appendix, God created the entire universe! How can anyone think something as small as an appendix could be bigger than Him? In that same vein (sorry, had to), there is no problem too big for Him, which is why we must acknowledge that our God is bigger than any problem we can even comprehend. Do you sometimes wonder if you are a part of something bigger? Wonder no more, because to God, you are loved and a part of Christ's body.

APRIL 28

Under the Lights

John 12:46

On April 28, 1930, in Independence, Kansas, the first official minor league baseball night game was played. Although a couple of games had already been held "under the lights," this was the first officially scored game.

What's His story? While several verses mention light in the Bible, this one from John 12:46 is particularly appropriate: "I have come into the world as a light so that no one who believes in me should stay in darkness." Obviously, that night in Kansas, no one in the stands stayed in the darkness, but believing in Him and having the light of Jesus within you is much greater than any light that allows you to play baseball at night. His light shines brightly in the night, but during the day as well. For that light to shine, we have to accept His invitation into a relationship so that light can genuinely shine, and others might enjoy His glory. He came to bring us out of our darkness, but we have to take that first step out of the shadow of sin, fear, and doubt. Are the lights turned on in the stadium of your life? Or do you feel like you are playing a game in the dark?

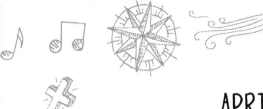

APRIL 29

Mood Indigo

Philippians 4:11-12

On April 29, 1899, talented American songwriter, composer, and musician Duke Ellington was born in Washington, D.C. Ellington is most certainly a pivotal figure in the history of jazz music. He produced and performed some absurdly good music.

What's His story? One of Ellington's biggest hits was a song called "Mood Indigo." Throughout his music, Duke was a great storyteller and described what this song was about - two young children, a boy and a girl who love to spend time together every day at the same time. Until one day, the boy does not show up. This song by Ellington describes her mood. Indigo, a shade of blue, represents sadness. In Philippians 4:11-12, just before the well-known 4:13 verse, Paul talks about being content in his circumstances. We often equate sadness with a lack of or a belief that we need something to complete us. Paul is teaching us to know because when we rely on God's promise to fulfill our needs, and Christ's power to remove unfounded desire, we will be content! We cannot rely on another person to complete us. I, too, know that line from the movie *Jerry McGuire*, but only the Holy Spirit and a relationship with Jesus can complete us! If we first acknowledge that we are incomplete, or in a mood indigo, then we can earnestly seek God's wholeness to provide true contentment and joy that surpasses the insatiable void of desire for worldly things. Do you recognize this void in your own life? How do you sometimes seek to fill it?

APRIL 30

A Hope That Doesn't Disappoint

Romans 5:1-5

On April 30, 1939, the World's Fair opened in New York City. The World's Fair is held in various cities all over the world. It is an opportunity for countries across the globe to highlight achievements and accomplishments. The host city entertains the international exposition for roughly three to six months. When I went in 1982, it was in Knoxville, Tennessee, and the theme was Energy Turns the World. I still have the pencil sharpener souvenir!

What's His story? The theme of the 1939 New York City World's Fair was Dawn of a New Day. The main purpose of the fair itself was to lift the spirits of those in the United States by hosting the largest international event since WWI and giving visitors a view into the world of tomorrow. In other words, it was to provide hope for the future. Little did people know they were on the cusp of another deep and dark period with WW II around the corner. In Romans 5:1-5, we find hope that does not disappoint. We can rejoice in the hope and glory of God. In this letter, Paul goes on to set the proper order in how we get to this hope. It is probably not the way we would expect, but it is the way of God. We rejoice in our sufferings, because it leads to perseverance, leading to character and, finally, hope. Was that the order you had in mind? Probably not, but because it is in this order, we can live in hopeful expectation for that "Dawn of a New Day," mainly because God has given us something that does not disappoint. I wonder how many of those exhibits at the World's Fair are even still around today? We know one thing that will never go away, and that is the peace we have in God through Jesus Christ. That is truly a hope that will not disappoint! What is your hope in the dawn of tomorrow?

MAY 1

Never-Ending Circles of Eternity

Ecclesiastes 3:11

On May 1, 1941, the breakfast cereal Cheerios was first introduced. This American cereal brand is known for its small circles of pulverized oats and the ability to wedge into seat cushions all over the world. For over thirty years, there was just the original flavor, but now there are more than fifteen varieties, including, you guessed it - Pumpkin Spice. My favorite, being from the Peach State, naturally has to be peach.

What's His story? I mentioned the shape of Cheerios. The cereal was first called CherriOats, but because they are in the form of an O, it makes sense that the name Cheerios must have won that round in the product marketing discussion! A circle, or ring, represents the symbol of eternity and never-ending existence. As Ecclesiastes 3:11 serves as a reminder that God has "made everything beautiful in its time. He has also set eternity in the human heart, yet no one can fathom what God has done from beginning to end." While we are limited to understanding God's mysterious and miraculous works, we also realize that with God, there is no end, just like the circle. Now every time you have a bowl of cereal goodness or clean out your car or couch cushions, you might receive a reminder that the kingdom of God is just like that circle, eternal in nature and in perfect symmetry with his creation. It does not matter if it is apple cinnamon, blueberry, peach, or pumpkin spice, the ring of truth of God's never-ending nature is known in the bowl and everywhere! Do you see ways in which symbolism reveals more and more about God's glorious kingdom, or do you see a round piece of pulverized oats? Representations of God's spiritual truths are all around.

MAY 2

Ships Don't Stay in Harbors

Psalm 96:3

On May 2, 1969, the luxury cruise ship *Queen Elizabeth II* made her maiden voyage. It was a trek from Southhampton, England, to New York City, and took just under five days to complete the trip. The ship was retired in 2008, sailing to Dubai for retrofitting to become a floating hotel!

What's His story? Have you ever watched a ship launched from the dry dock where it was being built? It is an enthralling sight, and I highly recommend watching a video of one. The vessel is guided down into the water and then lists back and forth until it is steady and sails out to sea. One sentence cannot do justice to the vigorous rocking back and forth that takes place. There must be a fair amount of fear for the shipbuilders as they watch. A ship is not built or made to stay on dry land, nor is it designed to stay in the harbor. It is designed to sail! Likewise, the joy we gain from learning about the Gospel is not to be held within us. God's word and the good news should be shared with others. It should be the wind that fills our sails and takes us on a journey of testimony. Psalm 96:3 "Declare his glory among the nations, his marvelous deeds among all peoples." As a ship sails from port to port, delivering goods, we should also carry praise for our great God to everyone we encounter. The joy that the Psalmist writes about should be our joy, our song, and we should want to share it because His word can keep our sails filled and motors running. We are meant to sail! You certainly do not want to become a floating hotel, do you? How well are you at docking and sharing the word? How are you on the open, sometimes rocky seas?

MAY 3

Wrenched Hip

Genesis 32:24

On May 3, 1956, the Judo World Championships were first held in Tokyo, Japan. Judo is a martial-arts sport that involves grab and throw techniques to defeat the opponent. Strikes, punches, and joint-locks are also used in Judo.

What's His story? In Genesis 32:24, we find the story of Jacob wrestling with the angel of God. However, at the time, he did not know it was an angel. They wrestled for a long time, and eventually, the angel touched the socket of Jacob's hip so that it was wrenched. I never knew I could associate the word wrench to the body until I turned forty, but now I do. He was in severe pain, yet Jacob kept fighting, probably using some Judo moves of his own. Finally, the match ends, and Jacob realizes he was wrestling with an angel of God. The angel blesses Jacob because he has wrestled with God and His people. Jacob triumphed because he was tenacious. Where in your spiritual life do you need to be more intentional, more persistent? We often start the match, but when we feel a twinge of disappointment or rejection, we retire early, fearful that we cannot go on any longer. God gives us the strength to carry on, for His name is power. Are you able to endure the struggle through tough and seemingly insurmountable odds? God has equipped you with the most remarkable spiritual Judo moves to tackle anything that comes your way.

MAY 4

The One That Got Away

Ephesians 2:8-9

On May 4, 1953, Ernest Hemingway was awarded the Pulitzer Prize for his novel *Old Man and the Sea*. It is a story about a fisherman named Santiago, who fights a giant marlin for three days and finally lands it. There was no hip wrenching taking place here! Back on the boat, the fish was so large he had to leave part of it hanging out of his tiny craft. Sharks end up eating most of it as the fisherman headed back to shore. The fisherman had longed to show the people back on land what he had done by catching the trophy fish, but he now had nothing left to show.

What's His story? This novel by Hemingway has been critiqued in many ways. However, it supports a very religious theme. One example is how Santiago is more concerned with showing off his prized catch than his own safety. He is obsessed with proving his worth. We sometimes try to do the same thing. But as we learn in Ephesians 2:8-9, we have been saved by God's grace and not by our own works. In many ways, we are like the fisherman in Hemingway's book, more focused on appearances than substance. How are you trying to prove your own worth instead of accepting the saving grace offered directly from God? Accept the gift of His salvation, and then in gratitude, seek to serve others. That is how we can show true thanksgiving for such a wonderful gift that really is a matter of life and death.

MAY 5

A Joyful Sound

Psalm 95:1-2

On May 5, 1891, Carnegie Hall, which was then called The Music Hall of New York, opened in New York City. Entrepreneur and philanthropist Andrew Carnegie, whom the hall was renamed for in 1894, opened to much fanfare with many famous musicians and composers participating. Tchaikovsky himself came and conducted his "Marche Solennelle."

What's His story? Music is just one beautiful way to worship God. It also creates fantastic stories. Carnegie built The Music Hall of New York for the Oratorio Society of New York, of which his wife Louise was a member. On their honeymoon cruise, Walter and Louise Damrosch met with Carnegie to discuss building a concert hall in New York. Walter just so happened to be the director of the Oratorio Society. Oh, and Carnegie Hall was built by an architect who had never before designed a concert hall! Perhaps you have seen firsthand the ways music can delight senses, raise spirits, and transform. It can be simple or complex, and there is no limit to musical potential. The notes and arrangements are boundless in possibility, just like God's kingdom. In strikingly similar ways, it is all around us. Psalm 95:1-2 instructs us to "sing for joy to the Lord and extol him with music and song." We can do this each day, either directly by playing an instrument or by being a physical instrument of God, allowing him to create sweet music. When we make music, even tapping on your steering wheel in traffic, we do it in joyful exultation to him! What music are you making today? We do not have to be in a fabulous concert hall to create or enjoy it!

MAY 6

Arduous Journeys

Deuteronomy 4:30

On May 6, 1940, author John Steinbeck was awarded the Pulitzer Prize for the book Grapes of Wrath. Written in 1939, *The Grapes of Wrath* is a story about the exodus of a family from the Oklahoma Dust Bowl to California. It describes the trials experienced along the way. Steinbeck was also awarded the Nobel Prize for Literature in 1962. You could say he was quite an author.

What's His story? *The Grapes of Wrath*, with the title alone, pulls imagery from Revelation 14:17-20, but we also see several biblical references throughout the novel. It starts out similar to the story of Job. The Joad family in the book lost everything back in Oklahoma and had to pack everything up for the long trek to California. Doesn't that sound a lot like Noah? They were seeking a land of opportunity, of fresh starts. This is similar to the Israelites in the wilderness, but also during exile in Babylon. Deuteronomy 4:30 is an appropriate reference verse because it reassures us that although we may experience tribulations, the road leads back to Him. He will never forsake us or leave us. Do you think the Joad family of Steinbeck's book may have realized this along the way? Recognize that the tribulations you may be enduring today are producing a hope that rests in a merciful and loving God. Hope is confident expectation in the goodness of God; that he will never leave you. What kind of trek are you on today? Is it comparable to what various figures in the Bible may have endured, and do you see a similar pathway leading back to the revelation of God's enabling grace in all of it? What prayer will you lift to God to ask for wisdom, discernment, and deliverance?

MAY 7

The Pearl

Matthew 13:45

On May 7, 1934, in the warm, blue waters of Palawan Island in the Philippines, the world's largest pearl was discovered. It was found in a Tridacna clam, which is the massive clam with the wavy opening you've probably seen in the cartoons. You know, where the Little Mermaid might sleep? The pearl weighed fourteen pounds and carried with it an astonishing tale of deceit and legend even after its record weight was surpassed when a gigantic seventy-five-pound pearl was found in 2006!

What's His story? A common interpretation for the parable of the pearl merchant in Matthew 13:45 is that the pearl represents Jesus. However, we cannot buy the kingdom of Heaven! I believe, to the contrary, that the pearl merchant is Jesus. Therefore, we, the body of the church, are the pearl, which He purchased at a great, great cost! He gave everything for us! To illustrate how we are the pearl, let us quickly review how a pearl is formed. A grain of sand or a similar irritant is introduced to the tender tissue inside the shell. This causes the oyster or clam to secrete the mother of pearl substance known as nacre. Layer upon layer is formed over the grain until a pearl is formed. Now think about the church. Are we not the same?! The church is one body, formed over time as God restores souls layer by layer until a great work is revealed! The true value of the pearl, an object of beauty to God, should not stay hidden in the deep, dark depths of the ocean. You have a luster and shine unique to you, and entirely given by God. Are you letting it shine in thanksgiving for the value God sees in you, and so others can see the great works He performs in all of us?

MAY 8

Triple Play

Isaiah 9:6

On May 8, 1878, the first unassisted triple play in big league history occurred in a game between the Providence Grays and the Boston Red Caps. Providence fielder Paul Hines caught a ball and ran to third base to get the other two outs. He recorded all three of the outs himself, which is an infrequent occurrence in baseball. Only fifteen have been recorded in the history of Major League Baseball.

What's His story? This is an incredible accomplishment and always really neat to see it happen during a game. Joey and I have not seen one in person, yet we will keep trying. Things have to happen exactly right, and the ball has to be hit hard and close to one of the bases. Fortunately, the ultimate triple play is already offered to us, and it is on endless replay. It is not unassisted; it is complete with assistance (Holy Spirit), grace (God), and incarnate glory (Jesus.) While the word trinity is not found in the Bible, or in this verse from Isaiah 9:6, it leaves no doubt. This passage is also a favorite at Christmas. It succinctly and perfectly describes the assistance we gain through a life devoted to God. I would say it is more amazing than Paul Hines' triple play to see the prophecy throughout the book of Isaiah hundreds of years before the birth of Jesus. Are you in the dugout or bullpen waiting to get in the game? What's holding you back?

MAY 9

A Special Day for Special Mothers

Proverbs 31:10-31

On May 9, 1914, United States President Woodrow Wilson signed a proclamation declaring the second Sunday of May as Mother's Day. Even though it had been observed as such for many years, this made it official.

What's His story? Proverbs is a book full of wisdom, beginning with an exhortation to absorb and embrace discernment, ending with an appropriately beautiful depiction of a woman of noble character. Wilson's declaration of a special day to honor mothers is fitting and apt, but the words of Proverbs 31:10-31 should be on every single card handed out on Mother's Day! It is the picture of a woman who fulfills the characteristics and qualities and inspires in many ways. Proverbs 31 is an example of the power of women who are equipped by God and strengthened in the knowledge of His word, but in the same breath, it should serve as an inspiration and not a measuring stick. You might read through this passage and wonder when she might have time for anything else. This passage is more of a celebration of the many beautiful and steadfast characteristics of women. As we mark each Mother's Day on the 2nd Sunday in May as Wilson proclaimed, we joyfully surround mothers and non-mothers alike with love and adoration! Do you receive these words in Proverbs as a gift, or does it feel like a test? Honor God by fearing Him and accepting the gift of wisdom.

MAY 10

The Eternal Giving Tree

1 John 4:19

On May 10, 1999, noted and award-winning children's book author, songwriter, and poet Shel Silverstein died. Silverstein wrote some very memorable books, including *Where the Sidewalk Ends, A Light in the Attic,* and *Who Wants a Cheap Rhinoceros?* That last one could make you ferret owners rethink your decision.

What's His story? While those books are great, one of Shel's all-time greatest has to be *The Giving Tree.* It is a story about a tree that gives and gives to a little boy. The generous tree gives apples, shade, and branches for swinging. As the boy grew, he wanted more and more, and the tree continued to provide. No spoiler alert here, but it is not the ending you might think. A poignant tale of the gift of giving and the capacity to love in return, it is a lot like our relationship with God. He gives and gives and gives, and we demand more until, finally, we realize the words of 1 John 4:19 - we love because He first loved us. We should be able to freely and endlessly give the gift of love because we have received it in abundance. This is one of my favorite verses in the Bible. It prompts us to be the first to smile, the first to forgive, the first to extend a hand, the first to lend a hand, and so on. Because of the message in 1 John, our reaction to His action should be one of love, because God has loved us first. In all of our ugliness, dinginess, and sagging branches lacking any spiritual fruit, He still loved us first. What is one way that you can be a giving tree? Extend your branches today around someone and outwardly lavish an armful of the spiritual fruits that live within you!

MAY 11

Good to the Last Drop

Ephesians 3:20

On May 11, 1926, Maxwell House Coffee's "Good to the last drop" slogan became a registered trademark. This slogan has been around for almost one-hundred years. It was once thought to have been attributed to United States President Teddy Roosevelt. I am not sure if it was because he needed the caffeine or loved the coffee. It is a reference to drinking every last bit of coffee, I guess because it tastes so good.

What's His story? Think about why people drink coffee. Unlike me, who drinks decaf, most people drink it for the caffeine and energy boost. Let us look to Ephesians 3:20, "Now to him who can do immeasurably more than all we ask or imagine, according to his power that is at work within us." We may think it is the caffeine, but it is the glory of the Holy Spirit at work that gives us the energy to expand His kingdom and reach others in a way that transforms our communities. When you have the spirit of Jesus within you, life takes on new meaning. The old is cast off, and the new set you free to enjoy life in Christ to the last drop! Are there ways that you can savor the last drop just a little bit more?

MAY 12

Ready to Pair

Ecclesiastes 4:12

On May 12, 2015, Dutch researcher and inventor Jaap Haartsen is inducted into the National Inventors Hall of Fame. Before I tell you what he invented, who knew there was an inventors' Hall of Fame? I wonder if they have a pinball hall or a robot hall…they do! I digress. Haartsen established the foundations for what we know as Bluetooth!

What's His story? Bluetooth is a technology intended to unite various other technologies allowing them to work seamlessly together. Plain and simple, it will enable us to operate different devices without wires and across different types of technologies. Bluetooth is named for a 10th-century king of Denmark and Norway, who was known for uniting warring tribes. For us, God's word is the unifying "technology." When you think about how you can use scripture to find commonality around which you can build relationships, friendships, and bonds that transform lives, the verse found in Ecclesiastes 4:12 comes to mind. We are meant to live in community, working with one another, because as the verse points out, a cord of three strands is not quickly broken. We cannot live self-centered lives. If we live in unity, with God's word as our bond to create a tightly woven rope, walls can be scaled, and distant sides are brought together. If you're like me, Bluetooth is still a mystery (why is pairing devices so hard?), but the story behind the name and concept should encourage you to seek community and form your own united ropes of God's word with others.

MAY 13

God's Mountains

2 Chronicles 20:15

On May 13, 1995, British mountaineer Allison Harbreaves ascended Mt. Everest without the assistance of oxygen or Sherpa support. She was on a mission to climb the three tallest mountains in the world in a single year. This had never been done before, and unfortunately, she tragically died near the summit of K2, failing to complete the feat.

What's His story? As Harbreaves scaled that last portion of Everest, she famously declined cups of tea, which were offered to her as she passed by the tents of other climbers. Stunning that a Brit would refuse tea, but what a fantastic accomplishment to reach the summit, tea, or no tea! Does it sometimes feel like you are climbing your own mountain, scaling it without feeling like you are clipped in, and sometimes gasping for oxygen in the thin air of confusion and distress? God can provide relief. Watching climbing documentaries about Everest, it becomes apparent how much the mountain climbers rely on the Sherpas and oxygen tanks to survive. Shouldn't it be that way with us as we navigate our own mountains, which are sometimes actually just molehills? We should rely on and trust God as our lifeline for survival as He answers prayers in His way and reveals answers and helps to assure us that He knows best. Although our control mechanism likes to take over and we charge past without stopping to sip some tea, He patiently waits for us, for He never moves. In 2 Chronicles 20:15, as the enemy bore down on Judah, they were reminded, "For the battle is not yours, but God's." Take heart and find your spiritual Sherpa and seek God's guidance. What mountains do you have to climb today?

MAY 14

Sliced In Half

1 Kings 3:16-28

On May 14, 1998, the very last episode of the comedy series *Seinfeld* aired on NBC. It was a show that had a very distinct style of humor, and yet was typically about a show about "nothing." Comedian Jerry Seinfeld, who created the show, knew how to draw humor from some of life's most uncomfortable and awkward moments. And boy, were there some memorable moments on this show.

What's His story? Even if you have never seen the show, you would appreciate how the writers could weave everyday events and occurrences into something relatable. One memorable episode comes to mind and ties directly to 1 Kings 3:16-28. Newman, the mailman, was playing the role of a judge to settle an argument between Elaine and Kramer, both friends of Jerry. They were arguing over the ownership of a bicycle. Just as King Solomon suggests cutting the child in half in 1 Kings, Newman tells them to just cut the bike in half to settle the dispute! In other words, wisdom is sometimes instilled in a jolting, jarring sort of way instead of gently proposing a solution. The solution is not always the answer; instead, it is designed to elicit a way of thinking that leads to greater wisdom. In Solomon's case, it demonstrated to the people that God had given him great understanding. This wisdom is ours, but we must apply it, asking God for a discerning heart full of prudence and perception. Are there situations in which you desire discernment? Solomon didn't ask for things or power from God. He asked for wisdom and insight. We should ask for the same!

MAY 15

Big Apple Crusade

Matthew 7:24

On May 15, 1957, the Reverend Billy Graham began his New York City crusade in Madison Square Garden. By the time it finished in September, Graham would be known as one of the most influential evangelists in the United States.

What's His story? Sure, this one is relatively obvious, but I want you to stop and think for a moment about what Billy Graham accomplished over a hot summer in the Big Apple. Graham had been preaching for many years before this, but the summer crusade in 1957 was clearly his biggest endeavor, not to mention longest-running. It was initially planned to run six weeks, but was extended three times and ran until September 1st of that year. Can you imagine the vast number of people he reached? In a metropolis of New York City, Graham knew there was a significant non-churched population, and they needed to hear the Gospel, and so he met them where they were. It didn't hurt that the flyers mentioned the air-conditioning of Madison Square Garden, too! In his first sermon of the crusade, he told the crowd, "Listen with your soul, tonight; your heart also has ears." Did you ever think of your heart having ears? What about when words break down or encourage? How does that affect your soul? That proves that your heart does indeed have ears! Matthew 7:24 says that whoever hears the words of Jesus and puts them into practice is like the wise man who built his house on the rock. Graham knew that this crusade was not about elevating his star status, but rather about giving thanks to God for the opportunity to preach and reach so many. While no one is expecting you to jump off into a crusade like Graham, how are you trying to reach the unchurched or those that earnestly need the word of God?

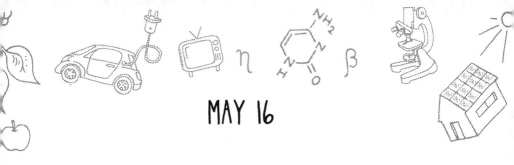

MAY 16

Old Made New

2 Corinthians 5:17

On May 16, 1949, a man by the name of Frank Zamboni applied for a patent on a machine he called, appropriately, the Zamboni! If you do not know, the Zamboni is a machine used on ice rinks to keep the surface smooth and pristine after it has been gouged up, cut, and gashed by the sharp blades of ice skates. You cannot skate when the surface feels more like chunky snow.

What's His story? There are a few things people will just sit and mindlessly observe, like a crackling fire, a babbling brook or stream, and a Zamboni. You know you have done it! I will not go into the details of the process but suffice to say the Zamboni scrapes away the old ice and replaces it with a clean new sheet. The cross is our spiritual Zamboni! Our sins are given a clean, fresh start through Jesus's sacrifice on the cross. Our sins, and the gouged, cut, gashed lives we live are smoothed over like brand new ice. As 2 Corinthians 5:17 tells us, "the old has gone, the new is come!" If you are having trouble visualizing Jesus cruising around a rink on a Zamboni sponsored by the local attorney, I get it. But for a minute focus on the finished product, which is the fresh, clean slate we are given through His sacrificial love for us. I would argue that it is more mesmerizing to watch the spiritual Zamboni clean up the rink of your life by washing away our sins through the sacrifice on the cross. Are you trying to skate on chunky snow? I do not even skate, and it does not sound fun, but neither does living without the refining and cleansing grace of God.

MAY 17

Miracle at SouthFork Ranch

John 11:25

On May 17, 1985, the character of Bobby Ewing on the evening soap opera series *Dallas* died in the season finale. Yes, this was J.R. Ewing's brother for all of you out there who remember the show and the characters.

What's His story? Well, Bobby returned the following season. Apparently, soap opera writers are very creative and figured out a way to "bring him back to life." In John 11, we get the story of Lazarus. It's one of my favorites for several reasons, but John 11:25 is the key verse. Jesus said to her (Martha), "I am the resurrection and the life. He who believes in me will live even though he dies, and whoever lives and believes in me will never die. Do you believe this?" Wow. Indeed this is not what a bunch of soap opera scriptwriters had in mind with Bobby Ewing on ol' Southfork Ranch, but as Jesus shows through the raising of Lazarus from the dead, He has the power over life and death. When we realize the blessed assurance we have in our Lord, the words "Because I live, you also will live" absolutely take on new meaning. Writing a character back into a script is one thing, but the eternal life we have in Jesus is another. Why would we want anything else?

MAY 18

Breaking Barriers

Psalm 29:3

On May 18, 1953, American pilot Jacqueline Cochran became the first woman to break the sound barrier! She did it in a jet borrowed from the Royal Canadian Air Force.

What's His story? When planes or other objects break the sound barrier, which means it has managed to outrun the speed of sound, a sonic boom is heard. If you have ever heard a sonic boom before, it is a brief rumble that can rattle windows and shake houses. In Psalm 29:3, we read: "The voice of the Lord is over the waters; the God of glory thunders, the Lord thunders over the mighty waters." This bit of scripture by David reaffirms our belief that the Lord is sovereign over everything, but it is also a stark reminder that no matter how hard or fast we try to outrun something, including His voice, we cannot. The voice of the Lord will not lead us to cower in fear from the noise of thunder, but delivers confident knowledge to remain steadfast in His glory! Therefore in the middle of a storm, we are rest assured that He is with us. Did I mention that Jacqueline was also the first woman to land and take off from an aircraft carrier, fly the Goodyear Blimp, and land a plane blind with no instruments? She was a busy lady in the air and paved the way for female aviation. Are you trying to outfly and outrun your problems, or are you coming home to God?

MAY 19

Dark Days

Isaiah 9:2

On May 19, 1780, the northeast region of the United States experienced what became known as New England's "Dark Day." This was not just a total eclipse kind of darkness, but darker. It was enough that the night songbirds added to the melancholy of the atmosphere.

What's His Story? This May day in New England started like any other late spring day might with a mix of rain and fog. As the morning went on, the sky grew darker and darker until midday was like midnight. It turns out that it was a perfect mix of fog, smoke from forest fires, and cloud cover that created the darkness. Panic set in, and overreaction began. Everyone reacts. Differently, I suppose. Half of the people went to church to confess sins and pray, while the other half went to party it up in town. Some things have not changed, have they? If we look to Mark 15:33, we see an example from the Bible in which darkness really did come over the land, and it was as Jesus was nearing the end of His life in human form on Earth. It must have been frightening to experience, but isn't it interesting that Jesus, even in death, is the source of the light. Even in Isaiah 9:2, we find the prophecy that describes the people in New England in the late 1700s, but also this very day. For it says, "The people walking in darkness have seen a great light, on those living the land of the shadow of death a light has dawned." Even the darkness of death cannot defeat Him! Are you in darkness today? How can the word of God strike the match to light your way?

MAY 20

Spirit of God

Genesis 1:2

On May 20, 1927, on a small airfield on Long Island, New York, pilot and pioneer Charles Lindbergh took off in a plane named *The Spirit of St. Louis*. It was Lindbergh's attempt at the first solo flight from New York to Paris, France.

What's His story? It starts with the name of the plane. It was named *The Spirit of St. Louis* in honor of the supporters from the town of St. Louis, Missouri. It might have been called The Spirit of the Moose had he named it for his own hometown in Minnesota. In naming the plane, he was acknowledging their support to accomplish the monumental feat of crossing the Atlantic Ocean on this solo flight. As Lindbergh flew across the vast dark waters, I cannot help but go to Genesis 1:2. It says, "Now the earth was formless and empty, darkness was over the surface of the deep, and the Spirit of God was hovering over the waters." It is said that Lindbergh would bring his plane down close to the water to feel the sea spray to wake him up while he suffered from a lack of sleep. And just as those supporters from St. Louis were accredited with supporting Lindbergh, and in essence "flying" with him, the image of the Spirit of God hovering over the waters yields a loving, caring, supporting father who is active in creation then, now, and forever. Are you flying with the Spirit of God today?

MAY 21

Perennial Runner-Up

Job 42:2

On May 21, 1999, soap opera star Susan Lucci finally won the Daytime Emmy Award for her role as Erica Kane on ABC's *All My Children*. You may not know Lucci, her character, or even the show (gasp), but here is the kicker. She won after being nominated eighteen straight years!

What's His story? Imagine being nominated that many years in a row and not winning. Around year eight, I might just start showing up in my sweatpants, or not showing up at all. In all honesty, what Lucci showed was grit and resolution by performing her craft to a level worthy of admiration and accolades each year. When you think of faith being tested in the Bible, Job comes to mind. Indeed, others were tested and persevered, but the book of Job is an excellent example of going through a period of doubt while questioning God. Job's friends gave him horrible advice, however, Job 42:2 reveals the faith Job had in God. Now I don't know Lucci's friends and fellow actors and the direction they were giving her, but I do know Job's patience is rewarded through God's mercy, and everything he lost was restored, and then some. Job's story can be our story as we learn to trust God's plans as bigger and better than anything we could ever dream. As we endure loss or trying time, we must look past the immediate disappointment of the plan that God has for our lives. Sometimes, do you feel like Susan Lucci when you are passed over for something you wanted or thought you needed? How can we learn to lean into God's plan for our life so that we can take the stage and accept from Him the award of eternal life?

MAY 22

The Ultimate Procrastinator

Joel 2:12

On May 22, 337 (yes, that is the correct year…), the emperor Constantine I was baptized on his deathbed. He waited until the very last minute to receive this holy sacrament and blessing.

What's His story? While historical, this was a common practice to receive baptism this close to death. The lesson for us is stark. There is no time like the present to turn to God. In the book of Joel, we find the prophet Joel urging others to repent of their sins and return to the Lord. Urging provides the connotation of something that needs to be done right away, and in Joel 2:12, God told the people to turn to Him while there was still time. It goes on to say, "Return to the Lord for he is gracious and compassionate, slow to anger and abounding in love." Why wait? While our lives are on Earth are yet a vapor, we should not let anything hold us back from loving God fully and wholly, accepting forgiveness as we repent of our sins. His compassion and love await us. Apparently, it sounded like Constantine I was a pro-level procrastinator when it came to accepting God's gift. The good news is that you do not have to follow that lead. Return to the Lord today. Are you fully turned towards God, or are there still some degrees left in that angle? Although it is never too late to come to God, why wait?

MAY 23

A Great Green Expanse in a Concrete Jungle

Zechariah 8:4-5

On May 23, 1963, Central Park, located in New York City, was designated as a National Historic Landmark. Frederick Law Olmsted and Calvert Vaux designed it in the mid-1800s. This expanse of lush green fields, bridges, walking paths, and ponds has been featured in many movies and is a must-see in the Big Apple. The stark contrast between the concrete jungle of the city and the green space of Central Park is incredible and transformative.

What's His story? Back in 2010, the United States Census recorded that twenty-five people gave Central Park as their permanent residence. Daily, these twenty-five people entertain thousands in this green expanse they call their home! People young and old use the park for exercise, play, solitude, and retreat. In the Old Testament book of Zechariah, we find a description of another place that could be described as a park. In fact, in some Bible translations, Zechariah 8:4-5 uses the word parks instead of streets. Either way, the depiction of the New Jerusalem during the Messiah's new reign is one of old men and women with canes sitting in the streets/parks and these same streets/parks filled with children playing. While Central Park is one of the most famous parks in the world, it could be anywhere, and this verse is a reminder of the peace and beauty of God's creation all around us. With birds chirping and flowers blooming, we can find God. God is present in the redundant click-click of an elderly person's cane or the joyful glee of a child's squeal. Do you need a majestic, magnificent enormity like Central Park, or can you find evidence of God's creation in your own backyard or neighborhood park?

MAY 24

God's Morse Code

Numbers 23:23

On May 24, 1844, inventor Samuel Morse sent the first telegraph message. The telegraph enabled communication over long distances by transmitting electrical signals over strands of wires. Morse invented a system, which was a coded series of short (dots) and long (dashes) taps representing different letters of the alphabet, which could be used to spell out words and phrases. Years later, the telegraph would be replaced by newer technology like the telephone, eventually the fax machine, and then ultimately by texting your loved one who is upstairs in the same house.

What's His story? The first message Morse sent was between Baltimore, Maryland, and Washington, D.C. The message read, "What hath God wrought!" It was taken from Numbers 23:23. The NIV translation is, "See what God has done!" It is the story of Balaam, who was a sorcerer, or one who would look for signs or omens to be able to tell the future. We often try to look forward, missing the gift of the presence, but this serves as a reminder that we do not need to look for signs or omens. It is also an admonition for us to open our eyes to God's goodness without any additional conditions. Can you see what God has done in your life? Or do you need to tap out an SOS (three dots, three dashes, three dots) to God? He will hear you! We have a direct telegraph wire to Him.

MAY 25

Star Wars

Ephesians 1:7

On May 25, 1977, the movie Star Wars was released in theaters. This was the original! Please do not hold it against me. I have only seen a handful in the entire series of Star Wars movies, but this was one of them. It was a hot summer in Atlanta that year, and we did not yet have air-conditioning in our house, so off to the cool theater we went!

What's His story? I know some of you may not be Star Wars fans (members of my family...no names...) and have never seen the movie. Even if you are not a fan, if you look closely, there are plenty of biblical themes in this release, and indeed through the entire series. Sure there is the good vs. evil theme, but also an overall theme of redemption. Many of the characters experience transformative moments that bleed into other installments of the Star Wars saga. When we look at the Bible and our salvation, it is clear that it comes through Christ. Ephesians 1:7 is one of the most unmistakable reminders of this. It reads, "In him we have redemption through his blood, the forgiveness for our trespasses, according to the riches of his grace." A whole lot is packed up in just a short sentence. This saving grace wins the greatest battle of all time, and in Christ, we are on the winning side! There is no death star here!

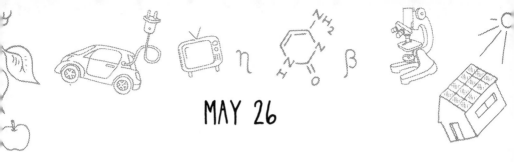

MAY 26

The Duke

Psalm 119:62

On May 26, 1907, in Winterset, Iowa, a man named Marion Mitchell Morrison was born. Regardless that this man had the easiest monogram of anyone, he was actually known by another name, John Wayne. Yes, he was The Duke, but not the mayonnaise brand. Wait, so he has three names? Wayne was famously known for his cowboy roles in movies like *True Grit, Rio Bravo,* and *Red River.*

What's His story? Correlating multiple names was tempting, but I believe one of Wayne's quotes is even better! He said, "Tomorrow is the most important thing in life. It comes into us at midnight very clean. It is perfect when it arrives and puts itself in our hands. It hopes we've learned something from yesterday." Psalm 119:62 says, "At midnight I rise to give you thanks for your righteous laws." The Psalmist was not awake at the midnight hour fretting. First, he was awake, praising God. If we look at Wayne's quote about the cleanliness of midnight, we soon realize that if we look at it the same way as the Psalmist, then we too, ring in the newness of the day with the appropriate spiritual posture towards God. It is right to give Him thanks and praise each and every hour, but especially in the first hour of the day. Each day is truly a gift from God, a clean slate and a new beginning. For you insomniacs out there, this is reinforcement that if you are up, why not pray to God in thanksgiving? And may the "something" we learned from yesterday be a glorifying and magnifying force for today!

MAY 27

Firm Foundation

Matthew 7:24-27

On May 27, 1933, Disney released an eight-minute short cartoon called "The Three Little Pigs." This was the story of those crafty, handy, and clearly domesticated pigs that were pursued by the big bad wolf that came to blow their house down. The first pig built a house of straw that was no match for the wolf. The second pig built a house of sticks, and again, no match for a wolf disguised as a sheep. But the third pig built a house of brick, which was able to withstand the huffing-and-puffing of the big bad wolf and kept his brother pigs Fifer and Fiddler safe. By the way, the pig that built this solid house was named Practical – no message here, right?

What's His story? In the Gospel of Matthew 7:24-27, Jesus teaches about the importance of building on a solid foundation. Like the two pigs in the Disney cartoon, who used materials that would not stand up to the storms of life, Jesus talks about the man who foolishly built on shifting sand. But remember the third pig? He made a sturdy house on a firm foundation that thwarted the wolf. To build on the rock of a firm Christian foundation means to hear and respond to scripture in obedience to God. False teachings or superficial knowledge of God's word, leave you with no anchors into the solid foundation to help you withstand the wind and the waves, or the wolves at the door. Challenges to the integrity of your building will come in many forms. Just as in the story of the three pigs, when your firm foundation protects you, in Christian love, you are fully equipped to help those who have not prepared or responded to God's word. How are you being Practical today? There is double-meaning in that name for sure! Are your feet on the rock?

MAY 28

Bridge of Humanity

Luke 4:21

On May 28, 1937, The Golden Gate Bridge in San Francisco was officially opened. By now, you are probably at the point where you read the first sentence and try to guess where we might find His story before reading ahead. Is this one about the Golden Gate? Not this time. The bridge is actually a rusty red. The bridge is so-named because it spans the Golden Gate Strait, a narrow waterway connecting San Francisco Bay with the mighty Pacific Ocean.

What's His story? Let's talk about bridges and the greatest, grandest bridge of all time, now and forever. I love bridges, and there are some fantastic ones out there like the Golden Gate, but none greater than Jesus. He is the bridge between man and God. Completely divine, yet completely human, Jesus' perfection and acceptance of our sin on the cross bridged the gap and saved us from eternal separation from God. Also, through the fulfillment of the Old Testament's prophecy, He bridges the Old and New Testament together. Luke 4:21 is an excellent example in which Jesus is in the synagogue reading from Isaiah 61, and lets everyone know that "the bridge is now open." He cuts the ribbon by saying, "Today, this scripture is fulfilled in your hearing." But even the most remarkable bridge of all time was not accepted as a prophet in His own hometown. The next bridge you drive over should give you pause. What are the ways Jesus had built a bridge in your life when you thought you would never get to the other side? Open your eyes, and you will see Him do it again!

MAY 29

Liberty or Death

Colossians 3:2

On May 29, 1736, attorney and great speech deliverer Patrick Henry was born in Studley, Virginia. Henry, one of the Founding Fathers of the United States, is best known for his speech in 1775 in which he declared, "Give me liberty or give me death!"

What's His story? There is no doubt that Patrick Henry was a gifted orator. His famous line declaring his desire for freedom was delivered just a few weeks before the beginning of the American Revolutionary War. What we found in his will after his death in 1799 reveals where we find His story. After a long dissertation in which Henry addressed property and possessions, he wrote, "This is all the inheritance I can give to my dear family. The religion of Christ can give them one which will make them rich indeed." In other words, Henry understood that earthly possessions are precisely that – worldly. What Christ offers is a different kind of wealth. It is something that can be passed down through a legacy to the next generation. Henry recognized that the focus should be on the eternal, not temporal, just as we see in Colossians 3:2. His will leaves no doubt about his priorities, but also serves as an urging, an imploring, to focus on the things that will genuinely make one wealthy in eternity. And it offers us liberty that frees us from death!! Would you say this is easy or difficult to do? Why or why not?

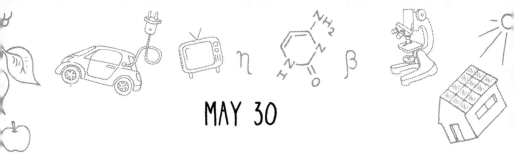

MAY 30

Shipwrecked Healing

Acts 28:8

On May 30, 1991, Joanne Lagatta, a thirteen-year-old student from Clintonville, Wisconsin, won the 64th annual United States National Spelling Bee. If you are not familiar, a spelling bee is a contest in which a word is verbally pronounced by a proctor, and the contestant must correctly spell the word.

What's His story? First of all, watching these kids spell in the spelling bee is an incredible and exciting experience. I am always blown away by how well they perform under pressure. What was the word that clinched the win for Joanne? The word was antipyretic. Part of knowing how to spell the word is knowledge of what it means. I knew this definition, but only because I was a biology major in college! Its definition is fever-reducer. When you have a fever, the aches, fatigue, and general malaise prevents you from doing anything productive. There is the story of Jesus healing Simon's mother-in-law in Luke. Still, I like the way the story in Acts 28:8 inverts the fever of sickness and turns it into a spiritual fever of desire for a relationship with the Lord that glorifies God. In this passage, Paul, on his way to Rome, is shipwrecked on Malta. Then he is bitten by a viper. Since he does not die, this scares the islanders who think he is now a murderer! Later, Paul places his hands on and heals Publius, who is the chief official of the island, who had been stricken with, you guessed it, a fever. In the end, the islanders honored Paul and the agape love he shared while in his own condition. Is your ability to care for others shipwrecked? Allow the salve of Jesus to cure your fever and turn it into an unquenchable thirst for His word!

MAY 31

Rooster Crows

John 13:38

On May 31, 1859, Big Ben rang out for the first time. While the iconic landmark in London, England, is known as Big Ben, the structure itself is simply The Clock Tower. The nickname refers to the largest bell in the clock tower. Big Ben keeps watch over Parliament and is known for its accuracy and precision. Between the four clock faces and chimes every 15 minutes, Londoners have no excuse for tardiness, except that they were looking down at their phone and had ear-buds in their ears!

What's His story? Back in Jesus' time, there were no clock towers. So what did people use for alarm clocks? Probably the same thing farmers could use today – roosters! Have you ever been to the country and heard the crow of a rooster early in the morning? In each of the four Gospels, we find the story of Peter and the rooster. It is an all-too-relatable story in which, after His mock trial, Jesus tells Peter that he will deny Him three times before the rooster crows. This happens just as Jesus says, and Peter denies Him the third time and then hears the rooster crow. How deeply that must have wounded Peter. Just as Big Ben rings out to remind us to stay on time, this story from the Gospels reminds us to be watchful and awake, shunning worldly bravado for spiritual humility. While scars can remind us of previous failures, this is also a story of forgiveness for Peter and the restoration he experienced as he went on to preach of the hope that Christ extends to sinners everywhere. Is your rooster crowing to remind you of your lack of faith? Or have you asked Christ for forgiveness?

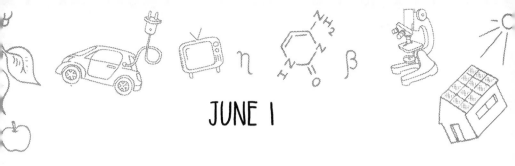

JUNE 1

Eephus Pitch

Luke 21:36

On June 1, 1943, Pittsburgh Pirates pitcher Truett "Rip" Sewell threw a pitch called an eephus pitch in a baseball game. The eephus pitch is an extremely slow, high arcing pitch that looks like a rainbow as it leaves the pitcher's hand and crosses over home plate. The word eephus might originate from the Hebrew word for "nothing." The pitch is often referred to as a nothing pitch or junk pitch because it is so rare and strange in appearance.

What's His story? The eephus pitch is designed to catch the hitter off-guard. Imagine you are at bat, and all of the previous pitches were coming at you as fast as a car travels on the highway. Then all of a sudden, a ball going half as fast and arcing high in the air comes toward you. It is a knee-buckling change of pace. How often does this happen in life? Events can sometimes turn life on its end. Good for us that in Luke 21:36, like a baseball hitting coach, Jesus tells us how to remain watchful and prepare. We prepare for Christ's coming again, and in doing so, we get ourselves spiritually fit to be able to move when God asks us to go and swing when He tells us to swing. We do not let the anxieties of life distract us from that, just as a batter does not allow the hotdog guy to distract him at the plate. In this verse, Jesus' instructions are very much akin to a batter at the plate and help us crush the curveballs and eephus pitches that life sometimes throws our way. By staying in scripture, obeying God's commandments, and loving as Jesus loved, we will be ready for any pitch – even a "nothing" pitch! Are you prepared to step into the batter's box of life and swing with focus and earnest?

JUNE 2

The Mighty Oaks of Righteousness

Isaiah 61:3

On June 2, 1981, talented TV personality and skilled interviewer Barbara Walters asked actress Katharine Hepburn the famous "what kind of tree?" question. Walters became known in the 1980s for her interviewing style, which was intriguing and probing all wrapped up in a tenacious package of never backing down, but always treating subjects with respect.

What's His story? During the interview, while providing insight into her health and stamina, Hepburn said that she was like a strong, old tree. Walters, in true character, asked, "What kind of tree?" Hepburn replied that she was like an oak tree. Living in the south, we can sometimes take oak trees for granted, but their splendor cannot be understated. In Isaiah 61:3, we dig deep into the ground for our story. In this verse, God chooses the oak tree to represent the people of Israel. It reads, "They will be called oaks of righteousness, a planting of the Lord for the display of his splendor." How well does an oak tree capture God's splendor? Think of the sturdiness and strength of the branches as they spread broadly. Several times the phrase, under an oak tree, is mentioned in the Bible for a good reason. Its majestic stature is not only a comforting shelter, but an inviting place of rest. We can be a mirror of the welcoming, open arms He wraps around us as His children. Whether Hepburn intended it or not, her answer gave glory to God through the affirmation of the oak as a symbol of strength and stamina to grow and produce spiritual fruit. Are you spreading your beautiful oak branches, or do you feel like the T-Rex oak with very stubby arms?

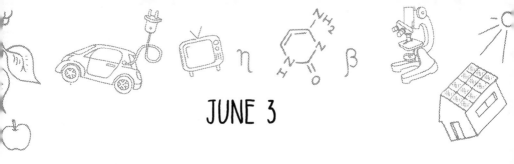

JUNE 3

Pilgrims of the Air

Matthew 19:27

On June 3, 1925, the Goodyear Blimp flew for the first time in Akron, Ohio. You have probably seen this famous blimp over a sporting event on television at some point. In fact, the Goodyear Blimp is the only non-player or coach inducted into the College Football Hall of Fame. Blimps, or dirigibles, are giant oblong balloons filled with a lighter-than-air gas, allowing them to float. A small cabin is typically located on the underbelly, and an engine is used to slowly propel it in the sky.

What's His story? Each Goodyear Blimp receives a name, and the first one that flew was named *Pilgrim*. After this initial flight, blimps were filled with helium instead of hydrogen, which was safer. Helium is not explosive or flammable. The name of the ship, *Pilgrim*, is particularly interesting. To be a pilgrim is to head out on a journey. To be sure, we are on the journey of life from the cradle to the grave – and thankfully beyond the grave! As a pilgrim or sojourner, the trek starts with a step in faithful obedience to God. The pilgrims who left England to come to America are a great example. In Matthew 19:27, we find another instance in Peter's statement to Jesus, "We have left everything to follow you!" Stepping out in faith as a pilgrim will often require sacrifice, but as we find in the rest of this verse, Jesus reassures the disciples that anyone who gives up something valuable for His name's sake will be repaid many times. We can also rest in this assurance. The next time you see a Goodyear Blimp, think of the first one, and the journey we are all on as pilgrims, journeying for Christ. Sometimes it feels as slow as a blimp, right? It is all in God's time.

JUNE 4

Crumbs Under the Table

Matthew 15:27

On June 4, 1895, an inventor from Boston, Massachusetts, named Joseph Lee, was issued a patent for his breadcrumb machine. This device automated the tearing, crumbling, and grinding of the larger pieces of bread into crumbs. Lee invented the breadcrumb machine to address the food waste that was occurring when day-old bread was being thrown out instead of being used in food preparation. This frustrated Lee, and he came up with a solution that became widely accepted.

What's His story? In Matthew 15:21-28, the woman whose daughter has been possessed by a demon has approached Jesus in hopes that He will heal her. Here we find what might be a mixed message as Jesus tells her, "It is not right to take the children's bread and toss it to their dogs." This does not contradict that Jesus' message is for all. While initially, the message is first directed to the Jewish people, it is then delivered to the Gentiles, which is what she was. Therefore, her response, "yes, Lord, but even the dogs eat the crumbs that fall from their master's table," demonstrates a great faith showing that even the smallest crumb is vitally important. Jesus then heals her daughter. Joseph Lee felt similarly regarding breadcrumbs because he was also able to see the bigger picture and highlighted the intrinsic value of the crumbs instead of wasting the entire piece of bread. Sometimes we may feel like crumbs are all we have, but as the woman in the passage points out, salvation can come when we recognize the blessing of Jesus. Where are you today at the table? Join the feast, and may you never lose sight of the value held in even just a crumb.

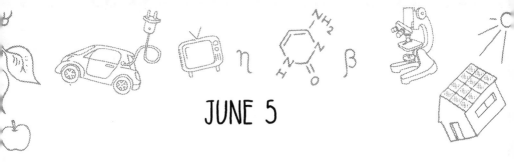

JUNE 5

When Dinner Bites Back

Matthew 7:5

On June 5, 1977, heavy metal singer Alice Cooper's pet boa constrictor died from an infection it received after being bitten by a rat it was trying to eat. I will let that sentence sink in for a second. Also, did you know the heavy metal rocker credits Christianity with saving him from the dangers of addiction? For now, let's focus on a snake whose dinner gains the ultimate revenge.

What's His story? You would probably assume that a snake eating a live rat will be aware of the inherent occupational hazards associated with its dining choices. Still, one could not be expected to see it going down this way, right? Sometimes things are not always as they appear. In processing the unfortunate demise of Cooper's snake, and turning the tables, we are taken to Jesus' teaching about judging others in Matthew 7:1-6. This is where Jesus asks why we are so concerned about the speck of sawdust in our brother's eye while we miss the plank of wood in our own. In other words, how can we magnify our brothers' faults when we are also guilty? It is habitually easier to point out the inadequacies or imperfections of others. Yet, Jesus asks us to look internally and remove the plank from our own eye so that we may see clearly again. You may not like Alice Cooper's music or style, and very few folks want to cuddle up to snakes. However, the message in this is not to assume or judge others lest we first judge ourselves. Do you find it easy to judge others? Do you need to remove the plank from your eye?

JUNE 6

Summoning Courage Against All Odds

Luke 22:43

On June 6, 1944, Operation Overlord, also known as the D-Day Invasion of Normandy, took place during World War II on the beaches of Normandy, France. This was the largest amphibious landing in history and was a turning point in the war against Germany, thwarting the Third Reich's expansion throughout Europe.

What's His story? Saving Private Ryan is one of the best movie depictions of what took place that day and pays homage to the courage and bravery exhibited by all involved. In the Bible, there are many, many examples of individuals who summoned mettle and courage when necessary to overcome an unconquerable obstacle. I believe the best model to be Jesus when He was in the Garden of Gethsemane on the Mount of Olives. In Luke 22:39-44, Jesus was in such anguish over the total separation from God, He was soon to face during the crucifixion and death for the world's sins. He was in such agony that He even sweats blood, but He does not stop fighting. An angel of the Lord strengthened Him. The men of D-day were also bolstered by their band of brothers to their right and to their left. Jesus completed the mission as He had been directed; similarly, those brave men on those Higgins boats had to do the same thing in the early morning hours in 1944. We can summon the resolve to face seemingly impossible odds because of the examples that have been set for us, but we do not have to do it alone. Courage is found in faith, and even as Jesus lay bare His anxiety in the Garden. Today we can call on it through the companionship of the Rescuer – the Holy Spirit. Are you struggling to attain or maintain courage? Call on Jesus in prayer, be guided by the Holy Spirit, and be delivered.

JUNE 7

The Cross As a Reminder

1 Corinthians 1:18

On June 7, 1993, the musical artist from Minnesota, Prince Rogers Nelson, became The Artist Formerly Known As Prince and changed his name to a symbol. It was a unique and hard to replicate symbol and was often referred to as a love symbol. He was a very talented musician and really, really loved the color purple.

What's His story? Symbols have been used throughout history. A symbol is, by definition, a mark or character that represents or stands for something else. While it is a rapid transition to go from D-day to Prince, finding His story in history presents an opportunity to expound this day on the greatest symbol of all - the cross. The cross is the main symbol of Christianity and represents the cross on which Jesus was crucified. 1 Corinthians 1:18 is a reminder of the Passion of Christ and the suffering He endured and the redeeming grace He offered through it so that we might have eternal life. It reminds us of the hopeful expectation of His presence in our lives and is representative of the faith we have in the truth. It is a symbol of the power of God. Look around you today. Where do you see crosses? Do you see them in the sky via airplane contrails, on signs, or tree branches? The list goes on and on, but the one true cross on which our Savior died remains. That is the symbol above all symbols. Today, I want you to find at least one cross, the magnificent instrument representing the power of God, and being reminded of his gift to all!

JUNE 8

White As Snow

Isaiah 1:18

On June 8, 1824, Noah Cushing patented the washing machine. While his invention made washing clothes easier, you still had to operate it manually via a crank handle.

What's His story? Yes, I could have gone with the name – Noah. Nah doing that would be too easy. Let's think more about a washing machine. You used to have to hand scrub clothes to get them clean, and it was tough laborious work. A washing machine takes away all, or most, of the labor involved in cleaning. You put something in that is dirty, and if you add a little detergent, it magically comes out clean. Some of you are now mortified, because I have not talked about sorting the clothes by color, selecting the appropriate water temperature, and adding the right amount of detergent. You can relax; I finally learned that clothes do need to be sorted. But seriously, the need for a cleansing action holds true for us. When we succumb to the ways of this world, we become dirty, dingy, and stained by sin and deceit. But Isaiah 1:18 says, "Though your sins are like scarlet, they shall be as white as snow." How are they made white as snow? Through the redeeming and cleansing power of our Savior, Jesus Christ, and the action of love He took on the cross. He takes the dirt, the dinge, and the stains full of pain and removes them. He does this for our sake. Through His sacrifice, He has made us clean. We become cleaner than any washing machine could ever make any clothes. OxiClean cannot even touch this, but it sure does come to mind when you read about Jesus's transfiguration! When we choose to follow Him, trust Him, and have faith in Him, we are cleansed in living water. The only requirement is that you put the washing machine on the Grace Cycle!

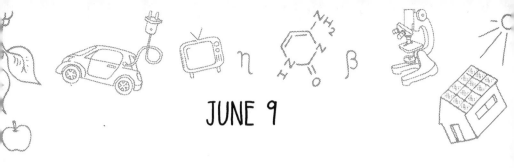

JUNE 9

Lazy Duck

2 Thessalonians 3:10

On June 9, 1934, the cartoon character Donald Duck made his first appearance in a short feature called "The Wise Little Hen." It was a story about a mother hen who was planting corn and needed some help. She asked Peter Pig and Donald Duck, but they faked bellyaches, so they would not have to work. In the end, the hen planted and harvested corn and offered some to Donald and Peter, who readily accepted. Little did they know she had also added castor oil to cure their "belly-aches"! And thus started the career of one Donald Duck.

What's His story? While Donald and Peter wanted the end results of someone else's work, they were unwilling to put in the hard work themselves. In 2 Thessalonians 3:10-12, Paul delivers wisdom comparable to the Wise Little Hen and her approach with one lazy duck and one lazy pig. He says, "If a man will not work, he shall not eat." Work can come in many forms, but he goes on in the next verse to clarify and urge those 'busybodies' to get to work for the Lord and earn the bread – literally. Every now and then, we might find ourselves idle, and the point is not that we should not enjoy a state of idleness every now and then. The Sabbath reinforces God's plan for us to rest. Instead, what Paul is advocating here is a love that teaches responsibility. How ironic that a cartoon from the 1930s could do precisely the same thing! What are the ways you stave off idleness that could develop into an unappealing habit? Make God a part of that plan, and you are sure to avoid the need for castor oil!

JUNE 10

Affirmed in God

2 Corinthians 1:21-22

On June 10, 1978, the chestnut Thoroughbred horse named Affirmed won the Belmont Stakes, thus becoming the 11th horse to win the Triple Crown. This meant winning the Kentucky Derby, the Preakness Stakes, and the Belmont Stakes races.

What's His story? This majestic animal's name is the eye-catcher. Affirmed. What does it mean to be affirmed? The word itself means to validate, confirm, or support the value of someone or something. Now that we are grounded in that, let's take off from the starting gate and walk through exactly how God has affirmed us. He first affirms us by drawing us out of the clay and breathing life into our lungs. He then makes us in His divine image, giving us domain over all living creatures and free will to come to Him with a whole heart. As we head into the backstretch, we find that God affirms us still by coming to live among us, to feel our pain and temptation. Down the homestretch we go, as Jesus then conquers death, affirming us worthy of eternal life, and free of the bondage of sin. And as we cross the line the affirmation of the Great Counselor, the Holy Spirit is sent to guide us. Finally, as the crown of victory is placed upon us, the words of 2 Corinthians 1:21-22 affirms us, "Now it is God who makes both us and you stand firm in Christ. He anointed us, set his seal of ownership on us, and put his Spirit in our hearts as a deposit, guaranteeing what is to come." Amen to that! Are you still running around the track, or do you stand affirmed as a worthy, valuable child of God?

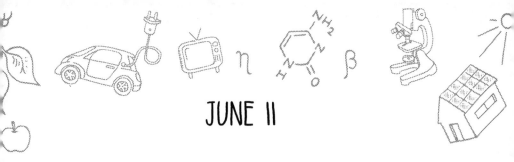

JUNE 11

Chariots of Fire

1 Samuel 2:30

On June 11, 1924, British runner Eric Liddell won the 400m race in the 1924 Olympic Games held in Paris, France. You may know Liddell from the 1981 movie *Chariots of Fire*. It is an inspirational movie based on his life. Liddell was actually considered to be better in the 100m events, but scheduling prevented him from running.

What's His story? Liddell didn't run the 100m events in the Paris Olympics, because the preliminary heats took place on a Sunday, and like Chick-fil-A, Liddell respected the Sabbath as a day of reset and reverence to God, so he backed out of the event. Liddell believed he ran for the glory of God. Before the 400m event on June 11th, a note was slipped to him. On it was a scripture from 1 Samuel 2:30, "Those who honor me, I will honor." This scripture is found in a section of verses delivering a harsh prophecy against Eli, but it is a reminder to all of us to honor God first. Liddell famously described his race plan as, "The secret of my success over the 400m is that I run the first 200m as fast as I can. Then, for the second 200m, with God's help, I run faster." His quote is a reflection of the scripture, in the sense that we are involved in co-creationism with God when we honor Him, and it becomes a partnership that God creates. Are you honoring God and running with Him? I get it; most folks do not like to run. How about, are you partnering with God, praising Him every step of the way?

JUNE 12

Living Water

John 7:38

On June 12, 1969, Niagara Falls ran dry! These famous falls at the Canadian border near Buffalo, New York, carry about six million cubic feet of water every minute. To shut off the proverbial faucet was a big deal. Niagara Falls is really three waterfalls located in close proximity, comprised of American Falls, Bridal Veil Falls, and Horseshoe Falls. In 1969, scientists made American Falls run dry to study the effects of the water flow on the rocks at the base.

What's His story? We can all agree that Moses and the parting of the Red Sea is a great story that would connect, but let's dig deeper. Look to John 7:38: "Whoever believes in me, as the Scripture has said, streams of living water will flow from within him." When we trust and believe in Christ and invite the Holy Spirit to truly become our Advocate, something amazing happens. The ever-flowing rivers of living water will flow, unable to be stopped by the paralysis of our fear, doubt, or anxiety that comes with our human condition. This living water that is eternal life can transform us. What is your shutoff valve that keeps your living water from flowing? What do you have bottled up inside of you? Put it in a barrel, send it over the edge, release it to Him, and restart the living waters within you! Do you think the falls are more beautiful with water flowing? Well, so are you.

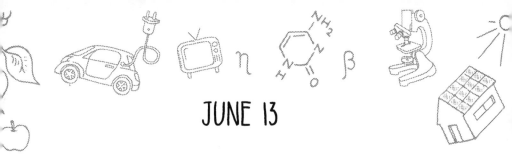

JUNE 13

Hiccups and Sand

Psalm 139:17-19

On June 13, 1922, the longest recorded episode of the hiccups began for an Iowa man named Charlie Osborne. Before we get to just how long, let me ask you something. What is the longest bout you have ever had with the hiccups? You probably have a go-to remedy to make them stop. Apparently, none of Charlie's remedies worked, because his episode lasted until February 19th of ….1990!!! That is an estimated 425 MILLION hiccups!

What's His story? I can't imagine having to live with the hiccups for fifty-eight years! All of Charlie's hiccups remind us of Psalm 139. It is one with a theme of a God that is all-seeing, all-knowing, all-powerful, yet He knows us personally and intimately. And our gift is to know Him. But the expanse of His love is found in Psalm 139:17-19, "How precious to me are your thoughts, O God! How vast is the sum of them! Were I to count them, they would outnumber the grains of sand. When I awake, I am still with you." I have so many questions about Charlie. Did he hiccup in his sleep? How loud were they? But one thing we do not have to question is whether we are ever too far from God. The answer is a resounding NO! Do you know the love your Savior has for you and how numerous the ways His dream is made for you? This passage of scripture provides a perspective on just how many ways God loves us. Known remedies to cure hiccups are to put a spoonful of sugar under your tongue, drink a glass of water upside down, or have someone scare you. Spending just a few minutes reflecting on just how big, yet intimate, God's love is for you will make hiccups an afterthought. I wonder how long he waited on that last day to see if they really were gone…

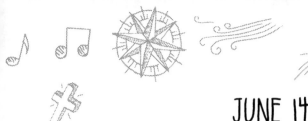

JUNE 14

The Great Carpenter

Matthew 18:21-22

On June 14, 1834, the first sandpaper patents were issued to Isaac Fisher, Jr. of Springfield, Vermont. The first use of sandpaper was recorded in 13th century China, and was made of crushed shells, seeds, and sand bonded to parchment paper using natural gum. Affixing a thin layer of sand to a piece of paper by an adhesive is how today's sandpaper is made. The varying coarseness of the grains of sand accounts for the texture, and subsequent use, of sandpaper.

What's His story? Sandpaper is used in a variety of ways, but especially in carpentry. Who is the most famous carpenter of all time? No, it's not Ty Pennington from Extreme Makeover: Home Edition or even Bob Villa. The most distinguished carpenter we know as Jesus! And as Jesus moved from carpentry into ministry, He never put away His great toolkit. Within it, you might find a hammer, which He used to hammer home points through parables. But, you would also find sandpaper. Not only would Jesus have used this in carpentry to smooth rough pieces of wood, but in Matthew 18:21-22, He uses it to instruct Peter regarding forgiveness. Sandpaper can rub us the wrong way. It feels rough in our hands. Forgiveness can also feel like sandpaper, but our master carpenter knows how to use the essence of forgiveness to smooth rough edges of our persona, so we understand that we do not forgive seven times, but instead seventy times seven! Are you using sandpaper this way today, or does the texture displease you? Think of how Jesus used it, and how you can also use it to create something beautiful!

JUNE 15

Blood of the Lamb

Hebrews 9:14

On June 15, 1667, Dr. Jean-Baptiste Denys performed the first documented blood transfusion on a fifteen-year-old boy in France. Now even if you are queasy about all things medical, keep reading, because it gets better!

What's His story? A blood transfusion is a process by which a batch of the same type of blood is introduced into the human body. This new blood can help the body recover from illness or disease. Blood is vital to life because it carries life-sustaining oxygen, nutrients, and minerals to all areas of the body, among other tasks. This particular transfusion was unique because Dr. Denys used sheep's blood for part of it! John the Baptist has already told us in John 1:29 that Jesus is the Lamb of God, who takes away the sin of the world. In Hebrews 9:11-15, the perfection of Christ's sacrifice is revealed for us as the author says, "How much more, then, will the blood of Christ, who through the eternal Spirit offered himself unblemished to God, cleanse our consciences from acts that lead to death." Ironically, the patient of the first blood transfusion needed it because he was suffering from blood loss related to a blood-letting practice thought to promote good health! As Hebrews illustrates, only the blood of Christ is enough for us. For this patient to live, he needed the blood of a sheep. For us to live, we also need the blood of a lamb – the Lamb of God! The good news is all you have to do is accept His sacrifice for you since using sheep's blood for transfusions has stopped! Did you know animals do not need to be sacrificed on the altar, because the blood of the Lamb took our sins away? Do you accept the blood of the new covenant? Take it, and all of the life it delivers.

JUNE 16

Lifted Up for God

Psalm 134:2

On June 16, 1884, on Coney Island, New York, the first roller coaster began operating. Do you like coasters? The thrill and speed can be exhilarating. Coney Island is considered to be the birthplace of coasters.

What's His story? Most roller coasters start with a colossal uphill climb, followed by a stomach-churning drop to gain speed and momentum for the rest of the ride. Some coasters have loops or tight turns, but almost all have peaks and valleys. Either way, we always feel a mix of fear and anticipation as we ride them. It is a metaphor for life, right? What I always found interesting was when thrill-seekers hop on a roller coaster, they raise both arms in joy through all of the ups and downs or twists and turns. Psalm 134:2 is the middle verse of a short three-verse Psalm, but it describes our roller coaster ride aptly. It says, "Lift up your hands in the sanctuary and praise the Lord." Everywhere is a sanctuary for God, including a roller coaster! It does not matter what you do in church during worship music (See author Jon Acuff for hand-positioning charts.) The folks that are worshipping in beautiful, joyful, reckless abandon towards the most deserving and most holy are doing it correctly!! We raise our arms in thanksgiving for the blessings He pours out on us. With pure love and joy, we trust in God and pray in thanksgiving for each hill and valley along the way. Are you willing to raise your hands to the air in prayerful thanksgiving, or is it just a little uncomfortable? Ride the roller coaster of life with God, and eventually, I would imagine getting to the "watermelon-truck" stage of hand-raising would not be hard at all!

JUNE 17

Lady Liberty

Exodus 23:9

On June 17, 1885, the Statue of Liberty arrived from France. It came across the Atlantic packed in 200 crates on the French frigate *Isere*. Lady Liberty was then reconstructed in New York Harbor in New York City, where a plaque at her base was later installed. On it was a poem written by Emma Lazarus.

What's His story? The poem Emma wrote was entitled *"The Colossus."* The poem serves as a reinforcement of Lady Liberty's symbol as a shining and welcoming light to those seeking freedom, democracy, and a better life. The section reads, "Give me your tired, your poor / Your huddled masses yearning to breathe free / The wretched refuse of your teeming shore / Send these, the homeless, tempest-tost to me / I lift my lamp beside the golden door!" Exodus 23:9 says, "Do not oppress an alien, you yourselves know how it feels to be aliens, because you were aliens in Egypt." Just as the Statue of Liberty declares, we should extend humanity and compassion to foreigners, or anyone for that matter, because we know what it is like to be a stranger. We have seen the fear and anxiety that comes from being a stranger. Lazarus' poem is an appeal to kindness, and a petition to be a shining example of unconditional love. God set the example for us in unconditional love, for He loves us as we fit every single description in Exodus, but also in *"The Colossus."* Are you living the Godly example of unconditional love? What is stopping you? Let the enduring symbol in New York remind you.

JUNE 18

Brave Women

Esther 4:16

On June 18, 1983, scientist and astronaut Sally Ride became the first female American to take a ride in outer space on the Space Shuttle *Challenger*. During the six-day space mission, Ride became the first female to operate Challenger's robotic arm to assist with a satellite retrieval mission.

What's His story? Through her bravery as an astronaut, Ride became an inspiration and role model for generations by encouraging girls to participate in science and technology. While there are many examples of female figures in the Bible who exhibit similar characteristics, Queen Esther comes to mind today. In the book of Esther, she and her older cousin Mordecai are involved in a situation that will require Esther's full resolve, courage, and a deep trust in God. She must be brave to confront King Xerxes and ultimately save the Jewish people. She had some bold choices to make, such as appearing to the King unsummoned, or confessing deception of the King, which may have cost her life. But through it all, Esther placed the greater good of her people above her own life. In her letter to Mordecai in Esther 4:16, she states, "And if I perish, I perish." That was her way of saying she was open to God's will. She placed her trust in God. If He had brought her this far, He certainly would not leave her now. Do you have Esther's courage to do the uncomfortable, or Ride's bravery to explore God's blanket of stars? Even small decisions sometimes take courage and trust in God, but the best first step is to just try. Take the first step. Are you ready?

JUNE 19

Lasagna Lover

Daniel 1:12

On June 19, 1978, Garfield Arbuckle, also known as Garfield the Cat, made his first appearance in a cartoon comic strip. Garfield was that lovable orange cat with his usual prank victims Odie the dog, and his owner Jon. If Garfield had his way, he would spend his days relaxing and eating lasagna, which was his favorite dish.

What's His story? Because of his love of lasagna, and food in general, Garfield often had to go on diets. It remained a common theme for Garfield, who, in return, was always plotting ways to sabotage Jon's plans for him to cut a few pounds and get back on the pathway to a healthy lifestyle. In Daniel 1:12, we find Daniel doing almost the exact opposite of Garfield, but it still centered around a diet. Exiled in Babylon and as a servant to King Nebuchadnezzar, Daniel found a way to honor God while in a culture that did not have the same values. He did it through a diet of vegetables and water, asking the King to compare his appearance at the end of the diet with those who ate the royal diet. It showed that he could still honor God and treat his body as a temple, even in the Babylonian culture. We can always seek out creative ways to continue our allegiance to the one true king, just as Daniel did. Garfield was always looking for ways to get back to his lasagna, rejecting the fruits and veggies he truly needed to stay healthy. How are you improving your health? What about your spiritual health? It is easy to become lazy like Garfield, but God's word in Daniel is an excellent example of how it can be done.

JUNE 20

Life-Saving Love

John 15:13

On June 20, 1874, Lucian Clemons received the very first Gold Medal for Lifesaving. The United States Coast Guard issues this honor. He was stationed at one of the many life-saving stations set up in coastal states for shipwreck victims. In his heroic mission, Clemons set out in a lifeboat to save members of the *Consuelo* crew after it capsized in a storm.

What's His story? When Congress set aside money to establish these life-saving stations, it acknowledged the need for a permanently crewed station to give aid to those in distress. In John 15:13, Jesus tells us, "Greater love has no one than this, that he lay down his life for his friends." In this case, Clemons' heroics were for a stranger, but Jesus' instructions were not meant to specify friends or strangers. We are to love each other as He loved us. Jesus loved us so much that He was willing to give His life for us. Remember, Jesus even laid down His life for His enemies, too!! We may not have to give our own life, as Lucian was willing to do, because sometimes the deep and sacrificial love that Jesus is calling us to extend is exactly the life-saving sustenance that the other person needs. Are you ready to do so? How do you love by listening, encouraging, and uplifting? Can you love someone even deeper today so that they are lifted to live again? In this passage from John 15, Jesus invites us to abide in Him. In our willingness to set aside our needs, we genuinely are accepting that invitation, just as Lucian Clemons did on this day so long ago.

JUNE 21

Italian Week Continues

Romans 12:9

On June 21, 1985, Ettore "Hector" Boiardi died in Parma, Ohio. You may not know him as Uncle Hector as his family did, but you might as Chef Boyardee! After it emigrated from Italy to Ohio, the Boiardi family's successful Italian restaurant venture led to the founding of his company in 1928. The restaurant was so successful that many patrons wanted to know how they could learn to cook Italian dishes at home. That led to selling the jarred, then canned pasta, and the rest, as they say, is history!

What's His story? Most have experienced the beautiful family atmosphere of an Italian restaurant. It is authentic, warming, and genuine. Trying to capture that essence and put it into a can is nearly impossible. The authenticity and loving sincerity an Italian chef puts into food simply cannot be replicated. Preservatives get in the way, right? In many ways, we can be like that can of pasta. Are you trying to duplicate what you think is a good example? All you really need to do is become a more accurate reflection of Jesus. In Romans 12:9, Paul tells us what it means to exhibit the sincere love Christ displayed. It says, "Love must be sincere. Hate what is evil; cling to what is good." What does it mean to be sincere? It requires work, faithful endurance, and always patience. It sounds like a good Italian meal, too. A few days ago it was lasagna with Garfield, now it is Chef Boyardee. Apparently, Italian week is here. Are you honoring God through sincere love by putting others first through acts of loving sacrifice? What is one small way you could do that today? Hopefully, the Spaghetti-O's at the store will now serve as a reminder!

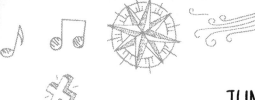

JUNE 22

River of Fire

Daniel 7:10

June 22, 1969, the Cuyahoga River caught on fire in Cleveland, Ohio. I know, I thought the same thing. Some things could only happen in Cleveland...

What's His story? A river of fire...it was not uncommon in Cleveland due to the amount of industrial waste and sewage. The 1969 Cuyahoga River event drew even more attention to water pollution and played a part in the Clean Water Act and the Environmental Protection Agency. Now let's get more biblical. How? Go to Daniel 7:10 and the river of fire representing God's sovereign presence, power, and judgment. Fire is also used throughout the Bible to describe and symbolize His cleansing, purifying work. The reason for the river of fire in Ohio was pollution. Just as we are dirty and polluted with sin and the things of this world, His grace, forgiveness, and love purifies and cleanses our soul so that we might serve and glorify Him. Fire is a purifying tool, removing impurities and trash that tarnishes the perfection of the material you are treating. In the case of the Cuyahoga, the fire purified it in a sense, because it led to stricter environmental regulations. And in doing so, a polluted river of fire transforms back into a river of living water. Maybe it is not fire, but perhaps the fire of the Lord's word is the purification you and I need. Go to the Lord in prayer and be cleansed!

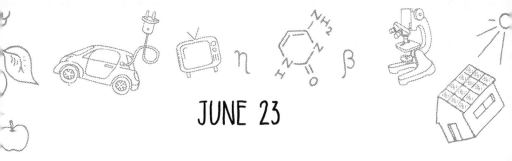

JUNE 23

Underwater Symphony

Psalm 148:7

On June 23, 1938, the first oceanarium in the United States opened in Jacksonville, Florida. Now known as Marineland, it began as Marine Studios and was designed by a couple of film industry veterans who used it to shoot underwater footage for movies and newsreels. The 1954 film *Creature from the Black Lagoon* was filmed at this location!

What's His story? An oceanarium is really just a large aquarium that mimics a part of the ocean and includes habitats that contain numerous and sometimes countless species of fish, mammals, and water creatures. Watching the interaction of all of the different types of fish can be mesmerizing. No wonder aquariums are stress relievers...except for the cleaning part. When you think of the abundant creatures in the ocean, do you imagine the multitude praising God? The Psalmist in Psalm 148:7 does as he writes, "Praise the Lord from the earth, you great sea creatures and all ocean depths." This passage tells us that all creation sings in harmony like a triumphant and wonderful underwater symphony making a joyful noise to our Lord. You may already know that whales and dolphins make noises, but did you know that even crabs produce their own kind of music? God is worthy of joyful praise, and as the sea creatures at Marineland sing, are you, the Landlubber, taking your place in this choir? And you do not have to don a wetsuit to sing His praises. Thank goodness.

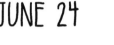

JUNE 24

Manna & The Marathon Match

Numbers 11:4-6

On June 24, 2010, tennis players John Isner of the United States and Nicolas Mahut of France completed the longest professional tennis match at the Wimbledon Tennis Tournament in England. They played this match for eleven hours and five minutes over two days at the All-England club. Isner won. I hope Mahut at least got a consolation prize for his efforts, but I think all he got was a handshake and some extra bananas.

What's His story? When you think of the marathon match these two players endured, the plight of the Israelites in the desert and wilderness on the way to the Promised Land comes to mind. I am sure Isner and Mahut had their moments of doubt, along with a desire to just retire or quit and go back to the comfort of the locker room, just as the Israelites wanted to go back to the melons, leeks, cucumbers, and garlic of Egypt. Ironically, in Numbers 11:4-6, even though God is providing everything they need, they are tired of manna and want something else. I'm sure the fans in the stands that were watching the Isner and Mahut match also wanted something other than another deuce point! In other words, somebody break this tie! Discontent or disappointment in our daily lives can sometimes cause us to turn our grateful gaze away from God towards even the most minuscule misgivings. We forget the big picture of God's provisions in our lives and find ourselves looking back into the rearview mirror when we should be looking ahead. Are you worried about the lack of cream with your strawberries (a Wimbledon tradition), or are you content with what God has already provided?

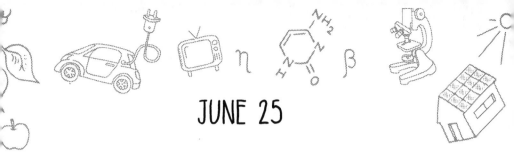

JUNE 25

Hidden Love

2 Peter 3:10-13

On June 25, 1947, the book *The Secret Annex* was released. This was the diary of Anne Frank. Anne Frank was a teenage Jewish girl who wrote in her diary while she and her family hid from the Nazis in an Amsterdam, Netherlands attic during World War II. They were eventually discovered and sent to concentration camps where Anne died in 1945.

What's His story? While it is incredibly hard to read, knowing the end result, the diary of Anne Frank gives a beautiful insight into the core beliefs of this young lady under brutal persecution. Her father, Otto, published the book. He was the only member of the family to survive, and he wanted to share his daughter's story of hope and emotional growth in a time of extreme adversity. In her diary, Anne wrote, "In spite of everything, I still believe people are good at heart." Clearly, she was mature beyond her years. While she lived in a time of uncertainty, fear, and anxiety, her attitude was like that found in 2 Peter 3:10-13. She knew that the day of the Lord was coming. The promise of a new Heaven and a new Earth was enough for her to see the goodness in people's hearts. That included those who might have revealed the Frank family's hiding place. We, too, can look forward to the restoration of God's world in joyful enthusiasm. Look around you today, evil seems rampant, but rest assured, goodness exists and will soon rule the earth once again. Do you seek out the goodness in the hearts of all people? Or are you quick to dismiss even the possibility? Leave the hard work to God, and love in hopeful expectation just as Anne did.

JUNE 26

Clean Teeth, Cleaner Heart

Joshua 1:8

On June 26, 1498, the bristle toothbrush was invented in China. I hear many are still manufactured there today! The first toothbrush used coarse boar hairs and a bone handle. Yuck!

What's His story? Can you imagine life without a toothbrush? If you look back throughout history, particular inventions pop out as being more monumental and impactful than others. The wheel, for instance, changed everything. But I would argue that the invention of the toothbrush literally brought us closer together. Before its invention, the personal space perimeter was probably double what it is now, and perhaps in line with what they call social-distancing. I want you to think about tooth brushing for a minute. Five out of five dentists would recommend you make daily brushing a habit. It helps you maintain good dental hygiene and simply makes you feel fresher, doesn't it? Reading the Bible should be precisely the same. It should also be as routine as brushing your teeth and should leave you feeling just as refreshed. Besides, it is not nearly as dull to read your Bible as it is to brush teeth, but as Joshua 1:8-9 implores, we should never stop reading and obeying. It even says not to let this book of the law depart from our mouth! Besides, five out of five pastors recommend reading the Bible every day. Here is an idea – read your Bible passage or devotional on your phone as you brush your teeth! That is an example of Godly multi-tasking.

JUNE 27

Happy Birthday

Luke 2:8-20

On June 27, 1859, American composer Mildred J. Hill was born in Louisville, Kentucky. Hill composed the song "Good Morning to All," which was later used as the melody for the song "Happy Birthday to You." Now I've got your attention!

What's His story? Not only is "Happy Birthday" the song you should sing twice as you wash your hands, according to health professionals, but it is also a song that elicits happiness and joy. Sure, some people do not like celebrating birthdays because it means you are getting older, but didn't we learn the lesson a few days ago that we should be thankful instead of ungrateful? I believe the song is full of cheerfulness and energy and had the shepherds known about it in Luke 2:15, I think they would have gone into barbershop quartet mode to sing to the sweet seven-and-a-half pound baby Jesus! The message of Luke 2:10 as the angel speaks to the shepherds is not to fear, but a message of good news of great joy that will be for all the people. The keyword there is all. This is the most remarkable event in history and the most celebrated birthday of all time! Instead of sparklers, streamers, and cake, Jesus celebrated with a star, some animals, and the warm love from Mary and Joseph. Today are you singing "Happy Birthday" with joyful energy, or are you lamenting the gift of another trip around the sun? Think about the most glorious birthday of all, and I guarantee it will be put into perspective.

JUNE 28

Van Gogh Steps into the Ring

Psalm 115:6

On June 28, 1997, one of the strangest events in a professional boxing ring occurred. While Mike Tyson and Evander Holyfield were locked in a heavyweight title battle, Tyson bit Holyfield's ear. It led to Tyson's disqualification in the third round, and sent Holyfield to the doctor for some "reconstructive surgery" to repair his ear! Yuck!

What's His story? Undoubtedly, it is not the message of loving your neighbor as yourself. Instead, since Tyson turned our attention to our ears, let's focus on that. Why would Tyson bite Holyfield's ear? Who knows. In Psalm 115:6, the importance of ears is highlighted, and in a way that brings attention to our own lives. It says, "they have ears, but cannot hear, noses, but they cannot smell," and unquestionably, there might be circumstances where this might actually be true. However, in the context of this Psalm, the Psalmist is pointing out that many people worship idols of material things, and miss the ethereal, spiritual things that would fully nourish us. Have you ever listened, but not heard? In today's society, we have a tendency to think about our next statement without hearing what the other person is saying. How often do we do this with God? Perchance we need a "Tyson bite" to awaken our ears to the Lord? Hopefully, it wouldn't take that, but the purpose is to spend more time listening for God than focusing on material objects that offer no nourishment. With God's help, you can stay in the fight and cleanly gain what is yours to win.

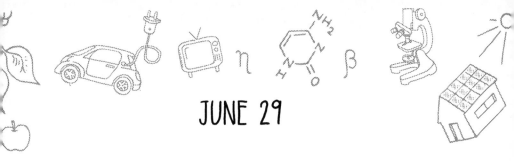

JUNE 29

Canary Yellow

Genesis 37:3

On June 29, 1951, the late, great sportscaster Craig Sager was born. Craig was famous for the outlandishly wild and colorful suit jackets he wore as he covered the National Basketball Association. We are talking canary yellow, bright purple, turquoise, and pinstripes of all colors. Sager always had the unique ability to match wild shirts, ties, and jackets.

What's His story? We can look at Genesis: 37:3, for the story of Joseph and his coat of many colors. Joseph received this coat from his father Israel because he was much loved, and a favorite son. The gift of the coat created a fit of divisive jealousy among his other sons. While the story of Joseph and his coat is ultimately about forgiveness, it is also a story about how God made each one of us special with unique talents. We just have to figure out how we can use those talents to glorify God. Craig Sager found his talent in sports reporting, and he did it with a vitality and style that conveyed professionalism cloaked in brilliance…of colors! He was one of the best in the business. He also celebrated life and the vast array of God's creation through his wardrobe and his demeanor in general. The smiles he created and the joy imparted through his jackets as he celebrated his God-given talent was amazing. How can you be the light today and dress in bright colors to remind others of God's glory?

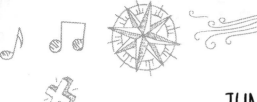

JUNE 30

Swedish Meatballs

Revelation 3:20

On June 30, 2016, in Almhult, Sweden, the IKEA Museum opened to the public. If you have not been to an IKEA with its characteristic blue and bright yellow-colored stores, suffice to say that it is a unique experience, with or without meatballs. It is a large store that sells furniture, household items, and even Swedish meatballs in their cafeteria as a nod to the homeland.

What's His story? Many of you might be thinking there is nothing biblical about building IKEA furniture, and I might agree with you, especially when trying to decipher the instructions! However, IKEA's motto, "To create a better everyday life for the many people," is very biblical. IKEA's mission is not just to sell furniture; it is about building a better life. For us, as Christians in our community or our churches, we have the same opportunity. We are giving life! Yes, at the heart of our own company, which could be a party of one, is the idea that we are leading people to a relationship with Jesus. And that relationship is the only way to eternal life. Although the instructions for how to get there can seem as confusing as IKEA furniture directions, Revelation 3:20 tells us how easy it is when Jesus says, "Here I am! I stand at the door and knock. If anyone hears my voice and opens the door, I will come in and eat with him, and he with me." We do not even have to assemble the door – it is premade, thank goodness! Our heart just needs to open it to him. Once you do, you could even have Swedish meatballs to eat, I suppose. Are you stuck in the wilderness of directions, or are you building a better life by merely opening the door?

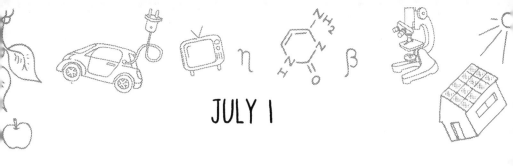

JULY 1

Stamped by Christ

Acts 26:15-18

On July 1, 1847, the first general issue postage stamps went on sale in New York City. One stamp, priced at five cents, depicted Benjamin Franklin. The other was priced at ten cents and pictured George Washington. We now have many designs to choose from, including the heart-warming Love stamp my mom would always ask for at the post office. In fact, the clerks would always have them ready for her.

What's His story? Stamps can be used to send bills, documents, and other items, but I believe the best use for a stamp is a letter, preferably hand-written! It is a lost art these days, but the impact of real ink just seems to make such a difference, right? Speaking of letters and the Bible, there is one guy who probably used more stamps than my mom, who is Paul. Paul really did not get into letter writing until that transformative journey to Damascus when Saul became Paul. After that, he was a Gospel-spreading, letter-writing champ. While Paul did not have to use the stamps we have today, the contents of his letters found in the New Testament were unquestionably stamped with the Holy Spirit. Paul's letters were instructive, informative, motivating, and heartfelt. They were written to encourage new believers facing persecution, to explain Christianity, and to provide everyday life applications. We could also write similar letters today to budding Christians, friends, family, and strangers alike. A postal service stamp is a small price to pay for the opportunity to spread the kingdom of God, stamping others through the Holy Spirit's power! Who is one person you know who could use a short note of encouragement today? Stamp it with the Gospel and send it!

JULY 2

Long Lines & Crazy Outfits

Colossians 3:12-14

On July 2, 1962, a businessman named Sam Walton opened the first Walmart in Rogers, Arkansas. You have probably heard of this chain and perhaps have even visited one. If you have not, I would really like to hear from you, because that is a pretty amazing accomplishment. The store was created because Walton believed that low prices and excellent customer service would bring customers back again and again.

What's His story? The popularity of Walmart, especially around the holiday shopping season, means long lines at the registers. This is not a complaint, but merely an observation. Many of you could attest to this as truth. What happens when we wait in line? Depending on our plans for the day, or mood, we tend to get frustrated and impatient. Impatience can ruin everyone's day, even at Walmart. Rather than focus on the negative, which is standing in line, we could remind ourselves who we are, to whom we belong, and of course, where we are. We are children of God, in whom Christ dwells, and we move about a kingdom in which the Creator cares for our every need. Instead of forcing ourselves to be patient, we change by indirection, allowing the transformative power of the Holy Spirit to invert our typical view of situations that would generally cause frustration or impatience. After we have changed the narrative, we then learn from Colossians 3:12-14 how to put it into action. I invite you to try this on your next shopping trip, no matter if it's Walmart, the bank, or anywhere else you have to wait. Are you allowing yourself to be changed from within, reflecting Christ outwardly?

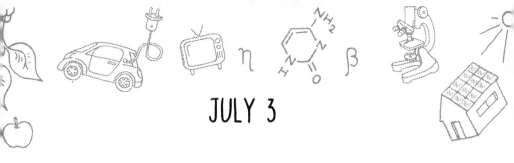

JULY 3

Flux Capacitor

Matthew 6:34

On July 3, 1985, the movie *Back to the Future*, starring Michael J. Fox, was released. This is the movie where Fox's character Marty McFly hops in a DeLorean, hits 88mph, and is suddenly transported back in history. It is an automotive time machine! Marty has to be careful about his interaction in the past because of how it might impact the future. He is also transported forward in time to October 2015 to address his future. It was interesting to watch the movie in 2015 to see if it accurately depicted the future.

What's His story? As someone growing up in the 1980s, this was one of my favorite movies. We probably ran around saying "flux capacitor" just because it sounded cool. Let's think for a minute about the premise of this great flick. How many times have you wanted to either go backward or forward in time? Much of it probably has to do with our innate nature to want to control our lives and the events found within it. When we are unable to control those things, or our grip is slipping, fear creeps into our thoughts. We have probably thought out what the future should look like, either based on preconceived notions or past experiences, but trusting God means that whatever His plan for the future is going to be what we accept. We are invited to live in the present, casting all fears upon our Lord. In Matthew 6:34, Jesus says, "Therefore do not worry about tomorrow, for tomorrow will worry about itself. Each day has enough trouble of its own." It sounds like we don't need that flux capacitor after all. We only need Jesus!

JULY 4

Did You Say Fireworks?

Acts 19:20

On July 4, 1776, in England, King George III wrote in his diary, "Nothing important happened today."

What's His story? To be fair, back in 1776, King George did not have the telephone, newspapers, the Internet, or even Twitter, so he wasn't aware of what was happening in the colonies. Suffice to say he soon would, and it would be an awakening, fireworks included. As *Ferris Bueller* (another 1980's movie reference) says, "life moves pretty fast, and if you don't stop and look around once in a while, you'll miss it." News can also travel fast. In Acts, we see the birth of the church and the growth of Christianity. In it, we see the crowds gather and transform right before our eyes, creating a movement and awakening even more incredible than this one King George would learn about later, which birthed the United States. Acts 19:20 says, "In this way the word of the Lord spread widely and grew in power." The people were hungry for the word of God. Jew and Gentile alike, wanted to hear more of it. They were ready and did not want to miss the awakening that would lead them to a life of blessings that outweighed difficulties. While King George was behind on his news, you have an opportunity today to stay current with your spiritual life and share the good news of the Gospel with someone. It is an opportunity to keep that person from missing out on a life so wonderful it simply has to be shared. Will you do it today?

JULY 5

THE Christian Mission

James 2:15-17

On July 5, 1865, in the East End of London, England, an organization called The Christian Mission, was created. It later became known as The Salvation Army. I knew there was something better to come out of this area of London that that soap opera East Enders! We see the ringing bells and red kettles at Christmas, but The Salvation Army does so much throughout the entire year.

What's His story? The Salvation Army was created to meet the physical and spiritual needs of those who were poor or needy and lack shelter. When you stop to think about how this outstanding organization still operates under the same mission today and how many lives they have indisputably touched, the verse from James 2:15-17 comes into focus. True faith in Christ will always result in good deeds. The Salvation Army provides words of encouragement, but they also offer clothing, food, and other items to those in need. This is the mission we sometimes miss because we are so busy concentrating on our own needs and not directing our abundance to others who may be in need. When we redirect towards those in need, we are abiding by our faith in Jesus, demonstrating that we are truly the hands and feet of the body of Christ. It is always possible to do a better job of caring for others' needs, as The Salvation Army has done. What are some ways in which you take just one small step to join the Christian mission of this army of salvation, which calls for us to love and care for one another?

JULY 6

Heavenly Inoculation

Jeremiah 30:17

On July 6, 1885, chemist, turned microbiologist, Louis Pasteur successfully tested his rabies vaccine on a young boy, Joseph Meister, who had been bitten by a rabid dog. A vaccine works by training the body's immune system, or natural defenses, to recognize and combat pathogens, which could be either viruses or bacteria. The immune system can safely learn to recognize them as hostile invaders and remember them for the future. It sounds kind of like a grudge, right?

What's His story? Pasteur used the vaccine on the nine-year-old boy to hopefully prevent rabies from inflicting its harm. It ultimately worked and led to a host of other scientific advancements. The exciting part here is how the body learns to recognize the pathogens. As you probably know, these germs are not visible to the eye. If they were, we would probably be in even more fear of them, because some look very angry under a microscope. In many ways, God's word performs the same function as a vaccine. While a vaccine inoculates or produces immunity against a disease, God's word protects against the danger and sin, inflicting damage to our spirit and soul. When we repent and turn towards God, as Jeremiah 30:17 says, He will restore our health and heal our wounds. Sometimes this is more than a physical affliction, but it is never too powerful for God to overcome. God offers us a shot of restoration, along with a vaccination against future pain. However, it is up to us to take that first step towards the Father, the doctor who offers to heal our mind, body, and soul. What is stopping you from stepping into His office? There we can receive our inoculation against the things that lead to death and destruction. Nobody likes needles. This is so much better!

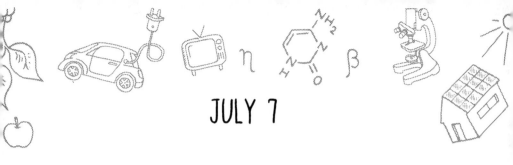

JULY 7

Sliced Bread

John 6:48-51

On July 7, 1928, the Chillicothe Baking Company of Chillicothe, Missouri, sold the first loaf of sliced bread. Whoa! They purchased the slicing machine from inventor Otto Rohwedder. He was responsible for creating the machine that not only sliced the bread but also wrapped it. That is what's known as a double-whammy.

What's His story? You now know the exact date and place to pinpoint "the best thing since sliced bread." However, in John 6, we see several examples of what Jesus can do with bread, sliced or not! It could be referred to as the Heavenly Bakery chapter. It starts with Him feeding the masses with the two fish and five barley loaves that were obviously not sliced. Then, after an intermission in which Jesus walks on water, He affirms that He is the bread of life, and we will never go hungry. The bread of life is greater than bread that is just temporal because it is the only kind offering eternal sustenance and eternal life. Then, in His own version of "best thing since sliced bread" He affirms that He is the true bread that came down from Heaven, not just the manna during Moses' time. He also explains Holy Communion, and once again affirms that He is the bread that came down from Heaven. Through communion, we gain eternal life through His body represented by bread and his blood represented by wine. As you unwrap your sliced bread, think of the convenience that Mr. Rohwedder created, but consider the bread of life that Jesus offers today. Jesus is definitely the best thing since sliced bread! That includes a seven-grain whole-wheat toast that needs a full pat of butter for flavor.

JULY 8

Joseph's Dreamliner

Matthew 1:20

On July 8, 2007, the Boeing Company unveiled its latest airplane, called the 787 Dreamliner. The first flight was on December 15, 2009. This plane was designed to be more fuel-efficient, but it also placed a premium on cabin comfort in terms of seating and pressurization altitude, to name just a few. I can attest to the comfort, even on a sixteen-hour flight!

What's His story? I am an aviation geek, so this naturally interested me. The name Dreamliner was actually the result of an online naming contest. Global Cruiser came in second. Personally, I like Dreamliner. In the Bible, dreams tend to go one of two directions, either revealing God's plan/wisdom or to reveal what might happen if God's way is abandoned. In Matthew 1:20, one of the greatest messages from God was in Joseph's dream in which an angel of the Lord reassured him to take Mary as his wife and name their son Jesus. Being the frequent-flyer dreamer that he was, Joseph again hopped aboard God's Dreamliner in Matthew 2:13 when he was warned to take Jesus to Egypt until King Herod was gone. Can you imagine awakening from a dream like that and the clarity it must have provided to change the course of history in line with God's plan? It is incredible. Do you ever wake up from a dream and wonder if God is sending you a message? We should tune our cockpit radio to the Holy Spirit as one of the first items on our pre-flight checklist, no matter where we are flying.

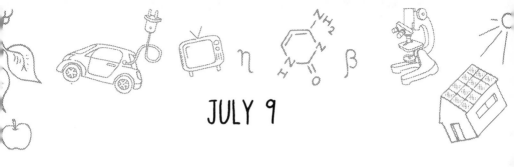

JULY 9

Heart Surgery

Galatians 3:28

On July 9, 1893, Dr. Daniel Hale Williams performed the first open-heart surgery in Chicago, Illinois. His patient was a young man who had been stabbed in a brawl. The surgeon, Dr. Williams, had studied medicine because he did not want to end up as a shoemaker's apprentice. The historic surgery took place at Chicago's first interracial hospital, Provident Hospital, which Williams had helped found during his career.

What's His story? When hearts are hardened, so that skin color is all that is seen, invasive open-heart surgery is required. God has the power to transform our hearts of stone and make them pliable again, allowing the cleansing blood of the Holy Spirit to flow freely, opening our eyes to the knowledge that we are of one race. God has called us to live in community with one another, caring for our brothers and sisters as Jesus taught us. Dr. Williams operated without the usual accouterments of a world-class surgical facility, but it did not impede his mission, which was two-fold. He wanted to heal others both physically and emotionally. With each stitch and suture, Williams was repairing jealousy, hatred, and fears that often keep us from living in the holy harmony as God wants. Williams gave us a stellar example of Christian love to follow. God provides us with the power to integrate servant leadership into our daily lives. Consider how a man who knew he wasn't destined to be an apprentice stepped into the dream that God had over him, changing, molding, and repairing hearts along the way. As Galatians 3:28 attests, we are all one in Christ Jesus. We are children of the one Father. What are the ways in which you are asserting the commonality of our holy lineage today?

JULY 10

The Real Thing

Proverbs 14:30

On July 10, 1985, the Atlanta-based Coca-Cola Company announced they are bringing back the ninety-nine-year old formula for their famous soft-drink beverage. Consumer backlash over the flavor of the "New Coke," resulted in this change being referred to as "One of The Most Memorable Marketing Blunders Ever." I cannot even imagine being in that conference room when the realization hit. It was Coca-Cola's attempt to regain market share against diet sodas and water.

What's His story? April 23, 1985, was the day the formula change was announced. Here we are, not even three months later, changing back to the original. Apparently, the number of calls to the consumer hotline skyrocketed, and folks started hoarding bottles of the old formula in their basements. Protest groups such as The Preservation of the Real Thing and Old Cola Drinkers of America were formed. Sometimes we try to fill our lives, and our cups, with things that were not meant to fulfill or sustain us. The only true fulfillment and contentment we can find are in Christ. Biblical contentment means that Christ's power, purpose, and provision is all we will ever need. It teaches us to overcome anything, including the change in the formula of your favorite soft drink, because we choose to trust in God's promises for our lives, and not in what the world promises. Proverbs 14:30 explains it well: "A heart at peace gives life to the body, but envy rots the bones." In other words, when we are content with the peace that comes from a life in Christ, we come alive for His kingdom and want to make it a better place. Envy causes just the opposite, and it can be so consuming that no joy is found in any single thing. It is a terrible way to live. Soft-drink manufacturers have no control over the joy and sufficiency Christ provides. Are you content, or are you seeking the latest ginger, vanilla, orange, or elderberry Coke? Rest in His formula, which is the real Real Thing!

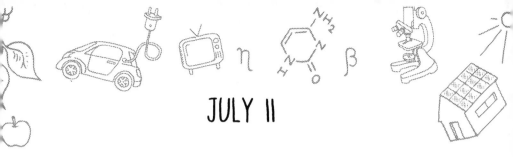

JULY 11

What's the Plan?

Luke 14:28

On July 11, 1979, the first space station the United States put into orbit, SkyLab, came crashing back to Earth at the end of its use in space. SkyLab was not as well known as the International Space Station, but it was a crucial pioneering moment for NASA. Except for the planning part, that is.

What's His story? Did I leave you in suspense? While SkyLab was a success while it was in orbit, the re-entry and crash were not as smooth. As it was coming to end-of-life in orbit, NASA had to figure out how the re-entry and the subsequent break-up in Earth's atmosphere would affect where SkyLab would land. Due to a mathematical error on NASA's part, some populated areas of Australia were showered with bits and pieces of SkyLab. Believe it or not, being a Christian is a lot like the whole Skylab experience. While we may have a great plan to become a Christian and might be fruitful at various points in our lives, many times, our plan to sustain our spiritual disciplines are less than "interstellar." As Luke 14:28 points out, there is a high cost to being a disciple of Christ, and it's not easy. Being a Christian does not guarantee a carefree life. In fact, in many ways, it can mean just the opposite. As this verse points out, we must account for the cost so that we are not easily tempted to turn and run because we did not initially plan on challenges or hardships. It is essential to plan accordingly. Jesus asks us to carry our cross so that we might be His disciples. Will you vacate the Christian faith if it gets too difficult? What is the reward when juxtaposed to the cost of commitment to Christ? It should be easy to see. This could be the opportunity to say and show that you are smarter than a rocket scientist!

JULY 12

Peals of Invitation

Revelation 19:6

On July 12, 1982, in front of a United States Congressional subcommittee, representatives for the United States Postal Service delivered a 300-page plan for how to continue mail delivery after a nuclear war. As you might imagine, this plan was ridiculed and declared futile. Did we not learn anything from yesterday's lesson about planning?

What's His story? Though it is not an official creed or motto, we have all heard the phrase associated with the United States Postal Service, "neither snow, nor rain, nor heat, nor gloom of night stays these couriers from the swift completion of their appointed rounds." We should add nuclear fallout to the list! While the 300-page plan and the unofficial motto are admirable and usually adhered to, there is really only one thing we can genuinely trust: God. Revelation 19:6 brings some good imagery as it says, "Then I heard what sounded like a great multitude, like the roar of rushing waters and like loud peals of thunder, shouting: Hallelujah! For our Lord God Almighty reigns." I want you to stop and imagine those rushing waters and peals of thunder. The use of the word peal gives it great power and emphasis! This entire passage of scripture reinforces our belief that our Lord reigns, and He is the sovereign one. I'm sorry, Postal Service. You do a great job delivering letters of love, but when it comes to where we will put our trust after something like a nuclear war, it's going to be in God, not in a piece of mail offering me a deal on new windows! After confirming the power of God, this passage in Revelation also explains what we receive in return. It is the wedding supper of the Lamb, and we are all invited. The post office didn't even send that invite. God did. Again, God is the only one whose promise we can trust! Are you leaning on your own ideas and understandings, or are you open to trusting God's plan and His power?

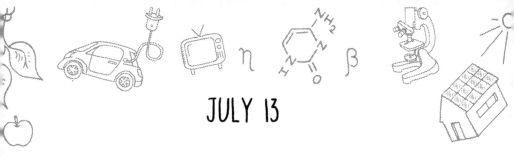

JULY 13

Carrying Burdens

Galatians 6:2

On July 13, 1985, Live Aid was held in London, England. This was a worldwide concert, with simulcast concerts in other locations around the globe to raise money for the relief of millions of Africans who had been affected by famine. It was an amazing sixteen-hour show that raised more than $125 million in relief efforts.

What's His story? We can go to Galatians 6:2 to understand what it means to be compassionate and caring for those in need. We are not independent; instead, we are dependent on one another. We should approach the needs of others, regardless of who they are, or where they live, by just understanding the necessity and fulfilling it. God calls us to do it. Whether you see it firsthand in Africa through the beautiful work of ministries which help abroad, or here in our own backyard community, the need is tremendous. We can reach out as they did in 1985 and care for our brothers and sisters in need and love on them with food, supplies, and prayer. We may not come up with a chart-topper like "Do They Know It's Christmastime?" or "We Are the World," but we don't have to in order to make a difference. All we have to do is take one step in faithful action. Let us glorify God by caring for those in need. What are some ways in which you can carry the burdens of someone else to fulfill the law of Christ?

JULY 14

Not So Plain Vanilla

Acts 4:13

On July 14, 1906, Tom Carvel was born in Athens, Greece. Tom is a special guy to many of us who love ice cream. He invented the soft-serve ice cream machine and established the Carvel brand, which includes ice cream cakes in the shape of various animals. Apparently, Fudgie the Whale was a trendy one.

What's His story? What's your favorite flavor of ice cream? We all have one, and new flavors are being introduced daily, it seems. Mine is vanilla. You are probably thinking, "how boring." Perhaps it is. However, sometimes when things seem to be plain or boring, they turn out completely different! Look at Acts 4:13. Peter and John were appearing before the Sanhedrin, the same Jewish Council that condemned Jesus because they had healed a crippled man. Throughout Acts, the many miracles the disciples performed are documented, including this one. For some reason, this one did not sit well with the Sanhedrin, so they were trying to determine how to punish them. Does that sound familiar? When Peter and John got up to speak, they were filled with the Holy Spirit and spoke powerfully and articulately. The Sanhedrin immediately saw courage and boldness, realizing they were more than just unschooled, ordinary men. They also took note and remembered these men had been with Jesus! There it is. Ordinary, plain vanilla fishermen who spent time with Jesus, absorbed the relational time spent with Him, had been transformed. They were prepared and open to healing in His holy name, but also to defend their faith. Vanilla is not so plain after all! They did not need to be full of knowledge to be empowered or recognized by scholars. Spending time with Jesus can make the ordinary extraordinary for the glory of His kingdom. Are you spending time with Him today? In celebration of Tom Carvel's birthday and this passage of scripture, feel free to curl up with your Bible and a big bowl of vanilla ice cream!

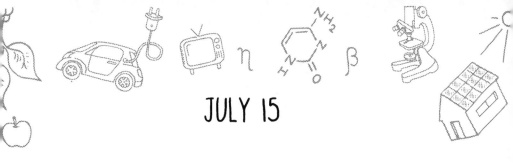

JULY 15

Where's Perry?

Exodus 20:11

On July 15, 1922, the first duck-billed platypus was displayed at a zoo in, you guessed it, New York City. It was at the Bronx Zoo, to be exact. Have you ever seen a platypus in a picture or in person? Perry, the platypus from the cartoon Phineas and Ferb, doesn't count. It is a combination of a duck, otter, and beaver. The males are even venomous with stingers in the heels of their rear feet. I could go on and on about how unique this animal is.

What's His story? In understanding Christianity, you can sometimes get into questions like, "How do you know that God exists?" I would argue that perhaps the simple answer to this question is "because, the duck-billed platypus exists." This animal has baffled zoologists and scientists because it does not fit into standard animal classifications. Is it a reptile, mammal, or bird? In fact, the first scientists who examined it thought it was actually a hoax! Exodus 20:11 tells us, "For in six days the Lord made the heavens, and the earth, the sea, and all that is in them, but he rested on the seventh day." Our creative God designed all living creatures on the face of Earth. Some of His creations, like the platypus, are more interesting than others. However, all have His fingerprints on them, including us! Have you ever thought about the platypus as a reason for believing in our Creator's creativity or His creation? The ability of God to create is so far beyond our comprehension. I'm okay with that because it results in a greater appreciation for what is around us. I'm just thankful the duck-billed platypus is not available at pet stores or rescue shelters as a domesticated pet!

JULY 16

Parking Meters of Life

Mark 16:15-18

On July 16, 1935, the world's first parking meters were installed in Oklahoma City, Oklahoma. Known as Park-O-Meter No. 1, it was the idea of Carl Magee. I wonder if he is also known as the father of the parking ticket?

What's His story? Retail stores loved the parking meter because it encouraged rapid turnover. Magee saw it as a potential solution for crowded urban areas. Either way, the meter maid job was born. Did you ever consider that we also need a parking meter for our lives? Without a parking meter in our life, we might feel content to stay parked in one spot and not move. We would end up being that proverbial moss-covered, jalopy with flat tires. By staying put, are we extending the kingdom of God in a way that glorifies Him? The answer is probably not, because we have taken the route of complacency. There is a difference between being complacent and being content. Reading this, you are probably imagining that time you were running back to your car trying to beat the parking officer who has a ticket in hand. What if that was the catalyst you needed to keep moving? The disciples probably felt like parking it after Jesus' death. When Jesus gave them the great commission in Mark 16:15-18, they realized their meter had expired. They had to keep moving, having been given the strength and wisdom to seek out opportunities to spread His message. You cannot always do that in a parking place, so maybe Mr. Magee has helped us, after all, to see that we really should keep moving. Pack your spare change and get moving! What is one way today that you could go to a new parking place, spreading the message of Christ along the way?

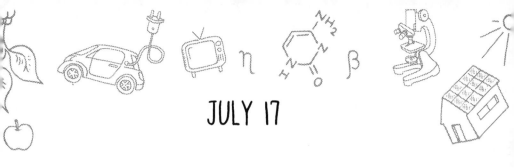

JULY 17

Wrong Way, Buddy!

Jonah 1:3

On July 17, 1938, American aviator Douglas Corrigan took off from Long Island, New York, supposedly bound for California, but he ended up in Ireland! It earned him the nickname "Wrong Way Corrigan."

What's His story? Truth be told, Corrigan had planned the flight across the Atlantic all along, but because his plane was a true heap of a flying machine, his flight plan was denied. Corrigan took off facing west but immediately took a turn back east toward the Emerald Isle. How many turns like this do we see in the Bible? Plenty, but one in particular sticks out to me. It is the story of Jonah. God wanted Jonah to go to Nineveh to preach against the wickedness there and encourage them to repent. However, Jonah had other plans. He thought it would be better to head to Tarshish. That was a big mistake. One big whale enters the scene, and three days later, out exits Jonah from the whale. There was also plenty of praying and negotiating with God while in the belly of the whale. "Right Way Jonah" enters Nineveh and delivers the message God intended. How often do we turn away from what God has called us to do? Why? Many times it is simply too difficult to hear God's voice among the many that we hear, but that is when we must pray diligently to God and seek clarity to listen to His voice. Then, like Jonah, we can vow to make good on the gift of salvation that comes from the Lord and spread His kingdom joyfully. Jonah fulfilled his mission, albeit begrudgingly. Even within Jonah's displeasure over the forgiveness bestowed upon the Ninevites, God reminded Jonah of the enduring mercy poured out on him. When we make a wrong turn and are rescued, the opportunity is there to give thanks to God. We are then reminded of His mercy. To prevent wrong turns, we should always use our GPS – God Positioning System.

JULY 18

The Weinermobile Christian

Philippians 2:15

On July 18, 1936, the very first Oscar Meyer Weinermobile rolled off the assembly line in Chicago, Illinois. It was the creation of Oscar's nephew Carl and was designed to look like a colossal sheet metal hotdog built on a car chassis. Maybe you have seen one driving around your hometown. At any given time, six Weinermobiles are driving around the United States. Occasionally you'll see a news story about one getting stuck in snow or getting a speeding ticket!

What's His story? The Weinermobile is a very unique vehicle. In a world full of cars and trucks, most of which are white for some reason, the Weinermobile sticks out like a sore thumb. I suppose that was the intent from an advertising perspective for Oscar Meyer. We, too, should be like the Weinermobile. Okay, chalk this up to things you thought you would never read, but it is true. When we are filled with the Holy Spirit and are truly abiding in Christ, there is something new and different about us that simply stands out in a crowd. Paul's letter to the church in Philippi gives us instructions on how to do this. In Philippians 2:15, he says, "so that you may become blameless and pure, children of God without fault in a crooked and depraved generation, in which you shine like stars in the universe." In a world full of hot dog choices, and white cars, you are called to stand out like a shining light for Christ. Allow the inner transformation to reveal your outer light. Are you shining brightly or snuffing out your Godly glow? The world needs hot dogs, but more importantly, it needs your light!

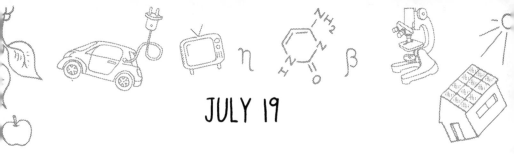

JULY 19

Even Red Clay?

John 9:6

On July 19, 1863, American geologist and one of the founders of modern soil science, Curtis Fletch Marbut, was born in Verona, Missouri. He worked for the United States Bureau of Soils for over 25 years.

What's His story? Soil. It sounds boring, doesn't it? However, as you recently read, with Jesus, even the boring and seemingly ordinary can become extraordinary. Aside from our creation from the dust of the earth, in John 9:6, there is another use, which is healing. There is power in that dirt! In this verse, Jesus rubs together His own spittle with soil to create a healing balm that He applies to a blind man. He then tells him to go wash in the Pool of Siloam, and he can see again! Jesus could have cured him with a word as He did others, but He does not in this instance. Why? He uses it as an opportunity to show two essential things. First, He used what was available and near to Him. There was no water nearby, so He used His own spit. Do we do the same, or put things off until the right arrangement, or what we think are the right tools, finds us? Secondly, His use of His own saliva shows again that there is healing power in everything that is a part of Christ. From spittle-mud to a tassel, to His voice, His healing power redeems us. I live in the South, so references to clay and dirt in the Bible resonate with me, but it could be any soil combined with the touch and power of the Healer, even red Georgia clay!

JULY 20

Touched by God

Psalm 139:13-16

On July 20, 1968, Eunice Kennedy Shriver founded the Special Olympics. The primary mission of the Special Olympics is to provide year-round sports training opportunities for the 200 million children and adults with intellectual disabilities. Today it is the world's largest sports organization for children and adults with disabilities.

What's His story? The first International Special Olympics Summer Games were held in Chicago, Illinois at Soldier Field. How wonderful would it have been to be present on that day! Let's go to Psalm 139:13-16, which says, " I praise you, for I am fearfully and wonderfully made. Wonderful are your works; my soul knows it very well." You have probably seen or watched the Special Olympics and observed the broad smiles and looks of determination on these athletes' faces. Seeing them using their talent and sheer determination is part of it, but recognizing the pure joy of participation is to see God's presence. Each athlete is wonderfully touched and made by God. Through the laughter and smiles, even during the competition, we know each soul rejoices in Him. We truly are one body in Christ. How can you support these wonderful athletes through prayer, participation, or volunteerism? The reward is a heart full of joy and abundance made possible by these amazing and talented image-bearers.

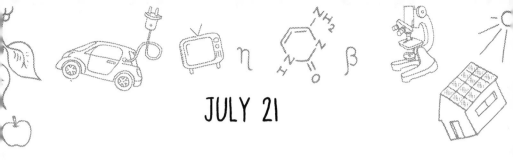

JULY 21

Kicking Dirt

2 Samuel 16:13

On July 21, 1975, midway through the season, the Texas Rangers baseball team fired their manager, Billy Williams. If you are not familiar with Williams, he later managed the Yankees and was famous for arguing with the umpires. His manner of arguing was more akin to an animated act of showmanship and frustration to the point of his signature move, which was to kick dirt on the shoes of the umpire.

What's His story? A few days ago, we talked about dirt and the power it had when combined with Jesus' saliva, but we are not going to even insinuate that Billy's dirt tirades are anything close. Instead, we are going to go to 2 Samuel 16 in which King David and his men have fled Jerusalem after Absalom tried to usurp the throne. In the town of Bahurim, David encounters a critic named Shimei. Not only does he verbally berate David, but he also throws stones and kicks dirt on him. Sounds like a biblical Billy Williams, huh? David's surprisingly patient reaction is just like that of the umpires that came up against Billy Williams. David was calm and patient and even talked down retaliation by his men. You see, David understood Shimei's anger because Shimei is from Saul's clan, whom David has replaced as king. David knew he had no part in Saul's death, so he absorbed the abuse. Maintaining composure in the face of relentless and unwarranted criticism is not easy, but we rest in the assurance that God knows what we are enduring. He will make it right in His time. I am willing to guess that some of those umpires who threw Billy out might even be his friends. How are you reacting to criticism, or dirt, being thrown on you today?

JULY 22

Heavenly Offspring

Acts 17:28

On July 22, 1822, Gregor "Johann" Mendel was born in Austria. Mendel was a botanist whose work was the foundation of the science of genetics. He primarily worked with garden peas to discover what we now refer to as the laws of heredity.

What's His story? Genetics is an overlap between science and religion. Its study allows us to acknowledge the Creator and creation, and form an appreciation and understanding of our role in His kingdom. Heredity is defined as the passing of physical or mental characteristics to an offspring. It is also the inheritance of a title, office, or right. Acts 18:28 articulates it well by saying, "For in him we live and move and have our being. As some of your own poets have said, "We are his offspring."'" Paul's message was to a society that knew of God but did not have a relationship with Him to honestly know Him. There is a distinct difference. Paul dutifully explains the sovereignty of God to them by explaining that while God is in His creation, He is not limited or trapped by His creation. He affirms the closeness of God to His work while remaining the Creator. We are His offspring, children of God created by Him for His creation. Through thousands of pea plants, Mendel discovered how different traits were passed from one plant to another, eventually learning how to predict the offspring characteristics. If we truly live in Christ and move and have our being, we should be unmistakable as His offspring, right? We can then pass those Christian traits on to our offspring and ensure that the next generation knows their rightful place in His kingdom. Are you claiming your inheritance in Christ?

JULY 23

One True Direction

Isaiah 30:21

On July 23, 2010, the pop music boy band One Direction was formed in England. The group was put together during a British singing competition called *The X Factor*. They finished third there, but went on to win many awards and released many chart-topping hits, including "Best Song Ever," "What Makes You Beautiful," and "Story of My Life."

What's His story? Even though I'll admit some of their songs may be catchy tunes, we will focus on the band's name. How often do we feel lost and without the true "one direction" that comes from knowing God's dream over our life? Sometimes we struggle with purpose, direction, or the pathway we are on, not knowing what the next step might be. We feel lost, or like we are in the wilderness. In Isaiah, the Israelites must have felt this way. The book is one part lost, and one part found. In between, we find the turning, or shift in direction toward the Lord that leads to redemption! Isaiah 30:21 is an excellent example passage as it says, "Whether you turn to the right or to the left, your ears will hear a voice behind you saying, "This is the way, walk in it."" One direction rarely means a straight line, but as long as you are walking in the way that is in obedience and trust towards God, it will be the right direction. It is an affirmation that no matter how lost we might feel, God is with us. When we hear His voice of correction, we can then follow it in the direction of our Savior. Are you busy trying to make your own pathway, or are you seeking the one true direction?

JULY 24

Kitchen Debates

Luke 10:41

On July 24, 1959, the fascinating "Kitchen Debate" took place between Richard Nixon, Vice President of the United States, and Soviet leader Nikita Krushchev. It is referred to as the Kitchen Debate because it was a series of impromptu heated exchanges, similar to a debate, that took place in a kitchen mock-up at the American National Exhibition in Moscow, Russia. The kitchen was meant to show the ingenuity of America and the conveniences of a modern kitchen.

What's His story? While the exchange got very testy and terse, it exemplified the Cold War, and the war of words ongoing between the two countries at the time. The exchange was fascinating because it revealed that each man was focused on the wrong thing and was talking past the other. An example of this in the Bible took place in a kitchen and is found in Luke 10:38-42. This is where Jesus is visiting Mary and Martha for dinner. While Mary was intently listening to Jesus' teaching, Martha was busy in the kitchen. Martha was distracted by the work and complained about Mary not helping. In her preparation, she was neglecting her host, and missing the bigger picture and the point of Jesus' visit. It was just like Krushchev and Nixon, who were so busy arguing that they missed the big picture - peace. Jesus set the order straight for Martha's priorities, and He can also do that for us. He did not scold Martha for working, but He reminded her that Mary had chosen better because His teachings would not be taken from her. Are you focused on the right things today, or are you busy debating the conveniences of the microwave with no guests invited for dinner?

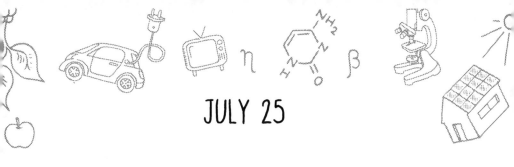

JULY 25

Unexpected Anger

John 2:16

On July 25, 1965, American folk musician Bob Dylan shocked his fans at the Newport Folk Festival in Newport, Rhode Island, by playing electric guitar. It sounds innocuous, but fans of Dylan were not used to hearing this since it represented a shift from folk to rock. He was subsequently booed off the stage. He did not return to the Newport Folk Festival until 2002, playing a headline performance in a wig and a fake beard!

What's His story? Fans at the 1965 festival came expecting to hear folk music, not rock and roll. Dylan threw them something unexpected, and they did not react kindly. It would be like bringing a frozen pizza to a church potluck, and not even DiGiorno's. There are plenty of verses to choose from when it comes to the unexpected in the Bible, but John 2:15-20 is a great example. In the first part, Jesus overturns the tables in the temple of the moneychangers. It is not the patient, slow to anger Jesus we have seen or that comes to mind. First, His righteous indignation fulfills the prophecy from the Old Testament in Isaiah and Jeremiah in keeping His father's house clean. Later, He says, "Destroy this temple, and I will raise it again in three days." Can you imagine the disbelief at that last statement? It was totally unexpected, and there might have even been some boo-birds in the crowd. In our same zeal, we sometimes also miss the reason for righteous anger. We are too busy focusing on our situation that we cannot see how fixing an injustice might lead us back to Him. Are we too busy focusing on ourselves that we look past the needs of others or the power in the unexpected? Think about how something so unexpected could prepare our hearts and minds for His message and His glory. Now go out there today and be ready for the unforeseen!

JULY 26

Aloha Way of Living

Genesis 2:7

On July 26, 1946, Aloha Airlines began service from Honolulu, Hawaii. They operated between the Hawaiian Islands in the Pacific Ocean and beyond until 2008.

What's His story? The name of the airline comes from the dual Hawaiian greeting, which means hello, but it also means goodbye. You might hear it as you step off a plane into the paradise of Hawaii, but the root meaning of the word is the sharing of breath. The Hawaiian people are literally asking you to share breath with them, and the Aloha Way of life involves sharing this attitude in life with one another. As we know from Genesis 2:7, God formed man from Earth's dust and breathed life into his nostrils. Living creatures were thus created. We see other scripture that calls us to love one another and love God, but we sometimes find ourselves holding our breath until we turn blue, and not sharing it or spreading life. Why not adopt the Aloha Way of loving, which is to love by sharing life at the coming and the going? No wonder Hawaii is such a paradise! How will you share life today?

JULY 27

Here's Your Sign

Mark 9:19

On July 27, 1957, comedian Bill Engvall was born in Galveston, Texas. Bill's famous line was "Here's Your Sign." He was an active participant in the Blue Collar Comedy group with Jeff Foxworthy. Their subtle humor had its roots in the comedic value of straightforward, but sometimes off-kilter country sayings.

What's His story? Sure, Bill's trademark line is full of sarcasm, but did you ever look at Mark 9:19 and wonder why Jesus said, "You unbelieving generation, how long shall I stay with you? How long shall I put up with you?" Indeed, He was not insinuating the same thing as Bill Engvall and using sarcasm. But, it does reveal some of the humanity of Jesus. Was He genuinely frustrated, or was He in pain because of their disbelief? Perhaps it was both, but He knew He could not give them what He desired to provide them with because of their lack of faith. We show frustration in a variety of ways, but considering the urgency that Christ faced, it puts this passage into a better perspective. Not to mention the fact that through each miracle, Jesus could state in a different context, "Here's Your Sign! Now trust and follow Me!" He could have used the biggest billboard available based on the power and magnitude of the miracles He performed! How many signs do we miss each and every day?

JULY 28

Sealed for Freshness

Psalm 92:14

On July 28, 1907, a man by the name of Earl Silas Tupper was born in Berlin, New Hampshire. You might know him better because of his last name. Earl invented Tupperware. The story behind Tupperware and how it got off the ground when Tupper joined forces with an extroverted saleswoman named Brownie Wise is a tale of opposites attracts, and other bewildering twists and turns. The legend of Tupperware still lives on today.

What's His story? Tupperware was used to keep foods from spoiling. Tupper's background at the DuPont Company helped him uncover a way to create a plastic container that was airtight and liquid-proof. While many of the Tupperware patents expired in the 1980s, the concept remains. We have all used a Tupperware-like container to store food or leftovers to keep them fresh and prevent spoiling. The righteousness we find in God's word can be the Tupperware we need to stay fresh and green. Psalm 92:14 says precisely that, "They will still bear fruit in old age, they will stay fresh and green." There are no age limits to who can spread the Gospel. Just as the young and energetic can enthusiastically honor God, so can the elderly and everyone in between the two. To praise God and keep His commandments is akin to putting a Tupperware lid over the endless container of the good news: God's word. Have you ever considered your next Bible study to be a Tupperware party? Now you can, using the lesson from Psalm 92:14! And who had one of those bright orange bowls with the lid that had bunches of ridges? Was it just me?

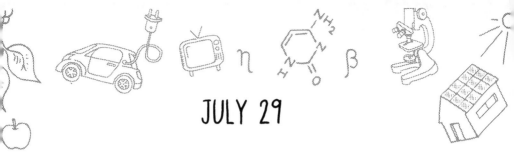

JULY 29

Starry Fingerprints

Psalm 8:3

On July 29, 1958, the National Aeronautics & Space Administration (NASA) was formally created through the legislature in the United States Congress. No doubt, it was created in response to the Soviet Union's launch of Sputnik in the year prior, 1957. One of the greatest accomplishments of NASA was the moon landing on July 20, 1969.

What's His story? NASA's mission continues today, and space exploration has always occupied modern society, but mentions of stars and the beautiful Heavens above are also found throughout the Bible. Psalm 8:3 describes our fascination with the Heavens above as we look for God's fingerprints among creation. It reads, "When I consider your heavens, the work of your fingers, the moon and the stars, which you have set in place," and it gives us such a great perspective. Have you ever found your way to a dark area on a clear, moonless night? The expansive blanket of stars reveals the majesty of God, while sometimes making us feel tiny! But then, when we are reminded of the personal love our Lord has for us, a new perspective is suddenly formed. We realize that if the God who stretched out this expanse of sparkling beauty wants a personal relationship with me, who will deny that? You may not be a starry night nerd like me, but the next time you find yourself on a clear, dark night, look up to the heavenly fingerprints shining through the darkness. Oh, how they sparkle and come alive! While NASA may have been partly about the space-race, admiring space and the heavenly dominion of our Lord can be done in your own backyard. Are you too busy to look up to see the artwork of His canvas? Look up and gain some perspective on just how vast and expansive His kingdom is!

JULY 30

In God We Trust

Psalm 46:10

On July 30, 1956, the 84th Congress of the United States passed a law making the phrase, "In God We Trust," the national motto. It is found on monetary elements and other areas throughout the government. Our state, Georgia, allows drivers to put this phrase on license plates instead of the county name.

What's His story? The backstory behind the introduction of the motto is relatively lengthy but very interesting. Suffice to say that the director of the federal mint in Philadelphia, Pennsylvania wrote, "No nation can be strong except in the strength of God, or safe except in his defense. The trust of our people in God should be declared on our national coins." Trusting in God transcends our personal lives, as well as the political realm. It does not mean elevating government as a replacement for the one true Savior. Trust, as it is explained in Psalm 46:10, is about clearing distractions to focus on the victory of the one true victor. It implores us to recognize and exalt God with the honor and glory due to Him. This particular verse is a great one to try out Lectio Divina, a Latin term meaning "divine reading." It involves reading a passage of the Bible repeatedly, very slowing, and taking time to ponder each word, listening for how the words might impact our hearts. As you break it down, the honor due to our Lord becomes vividly apparent. To be a part of a monetary element bares the exuberant thankfulness we have for what we hold in our hands and our hearts. Look at the money in your pocket. Do you see the motto?

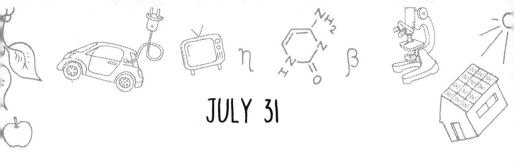

JULY 31

The Armor of God

Ephesians 6:16

On July 31, 1923, American chemist Stephanie Kwolek was born in New Kensington, Pennsylvania. Kwolek is credited with inventing Kevlar! Kevlar is an incredibly strong material used in hundreds of applications, but it is probably best known for its use in the bulletproof vest. By the way, like Earl Tupper, who we learned about a few days ago, Kwolek also worked at the DuPont Company. Perhaps they should have teamed up to create an indestructible Tupperware container. Wait, I think it already is…..

What's His story? Let's focus in on the famous use of Kevlar for bulletproof vests. Police officers and soldiers wear Kevlar to protect themselves. There is no better description of what Kevlar looks like in the Bible than Ephesians 6:10-17. There The Armor of God is defined. From the belt of truth, to the helmet of salvation, to the sword of the Spirit, it is all there through God's word. Just as Kevlar protects, the word of God protects us in our daily battle as Christians against the powers of this dark and sometimes frightening world. The danger is real, but when we don the armor of God, we are protected by something even stronger than Kevlar, which is stronger than steel! God's power has no match. Are you wearing your armor today?

AUGUST 1

The Twist

Galatians 2:20

On August 1, 1960, American singer Chubby Checker released his version of the song "The Twist" and debuted it five days later on Dick Clark's American Bandstand. Some of you can probably do the dance by the same name as if it were second nature. I cannot. It is as simple as that.

What's His story? This song and the accompanying dance has always been popular and is probably one of the most recognizable dances out there today. The Bible also has some twists. Have you ever thought of how many there are? Think about Moses and the plot twists in Egypt under Pharaoh, or of Daniel in the lion's den. Aside from Jesus' resurrection, which is the most incredible plot twist of all time, The twist that turned Saul into Paul is a favorite. It highlights how God is the author of our story. Saul was on his crusade of Christian persecution and had his encounter with Jesus in which he was blinded. The ways of his past disappeared in a flash of brilliant light. He was transformed into a Gospel champion who went by the name of Paul from that point onward. Paul's visionary mission is highlighted in Galatians 2:20. He observes that because of his transformation, he no longer lives for himself, but for Christ. We are the same! We may not feel worthy, or qualified, or as skilled as Paul, but because of grace, we can experience our own plot twist and begin to live for Him. When God calls us, that usually means we are ready, even if we do not think we are. Thankfully, accepting His call does not always require dancing, although you may find yourself twirling for Jesus out of joy! Are you ready to dance with Jesus?

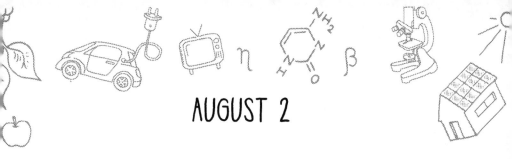

AUGUST 2

The Census

Luke 2:1

On August 2, 1790, the first census took place in the United States. The census is a population count that is used to determine political representation in the United States Congress. It is more than perceived junk mail!

What's His story? The census in the United States takes place every ten years. You may have responded to a few or left it up to the responsible adult in your household. In the Bible, there was a critical census that actually helped to fulfill prophecy. The census that Caesar Augustus called for meant that Joseph and Mary would need to travel to Bethlehem. It was there that the Savior was born. We find the story in Luke 2:1-7, and it is a great example of Joseph's continued obedience to God. This would have been a seventy-mile journey for the two of them, and Mary was almost ready to give birth. It may not have been an enjoyable trip for obvious and not-so-obvious reasons, and perhaps doubt entered their minds as they journeyed across the dusty countryside. Still, God continued to watch over the couple as they completed their task in holy obedience. While the census sounds like a trivial thing, think for a moment about the importance of this census as it helped to prepare the way for the Messiah in God's perfect timing. Are you missing God's role in the seeming monotony of everyday tasks?

AUGUST 3

Talking Donkeys

Numbers 22: 21-34

On August 3, 1952, film star Francis the Talking Mule appeared on the television game show *What's My Line?* This show was a panel show in which a celebrity panel asks questions of the guests to guess their occupation. In this particular episode, the panel was blindfolded for apparent reasons.

What's His story? You may not believe me, but talking mules or donkeys are a rarity. However, in Numbers 22, we find a great story of Balaam the sorcerer and his donkey and how God used him to deliver a message. Balaam was angry at his donkey for disobeying directions. The donkey was doing so because an angel of the Lord was blocking his path, but Balaam could not see the angel. Finally, the donkey speaks to Balaam, and at this point, the Lord opens Balaam's eyes to see. Yes, the donkey spoke! If God can use a sorcerer as a messenger and a donkey to speak, then certainly he can use you and me! God knows how to make His voice heard. Often we wonder if it is the voice of God that we hear. Make no mistake. If a donkey talks, it might just be. Lastly, think about the lowly standing of a donkey. It puts it into perspective to know that God can use the meekest and humblest of creatures to deliver an important message. Could you take a different stance, allowing God to use you as a vessel full of humble desire to listen for His will? Sometimes it is okay to be an all-purpose animal like a donkey. After all, they are hard workers and get things done. Balaam initially resisted God, but God spoke using the donkey as a vessel. Are we like Balaam, or are we like the earnest donkey?

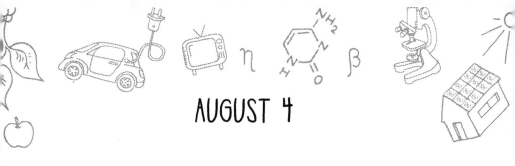

AUGUST 4

What a Wonderful World

Hebrews 13:1

On August 4, 1901, American trumpeter and singer Louis Armstrong was born in New Orleans, Louisiana. The Great Satchmo, as he would later be known, left a lasting legacy of musical talent that still influences today's jazz musicians. Some of his famous songs include "Hello Dolly!" and "Blueberry Hill."

What's His story? One of Satchmo's most-beloved tunes is "What a Wonderful World," which was featured in the 1986 Robin Williams movie *Good Morning Vietnam*. In it, we find the lyrics, "I see friends shaking hands saying how do you do, they're really saying I love you." What a great message that is! You can express love through a smile at church, or in the store, or at a restaurant with a stranger. Perhaps it is through a handshake, except in flu or coronavirus season when a friendly wave is acceptable. Whatever you choose, showing love is an extension of the Holy Spirit's community that lives within us. Hebrews 13:1 should assuage any doubt you may have over whether or not to smile and extend a hand. It says, "Keep on loving each other as brothers. Do not forget to entertain strangers, for by so doing some people have entertained angels without knowing it." Wow. Have you ever thought about that stranger's hand being the hand of an angel? Perhaps you have felt the immediate connection from a warm smile, too. As Satchmo writes, we are really saying I love you! Are you extending your hand in contagious hospitality in the company of Jesus? It really can become the wonderful world of which Satchmo sang if we all do.

AUGUST 5

Traffic Lights of Life

Psalm 27:14

On August 5, 1914, the first electric traffic light was installed in Cleveland, Ohio, at the corner of Euclid Avenue and East 105th Street.

What's His story? Traffic signals are what you might consider to be passive factors in our lives. We have learned to make them a natural part of our commute and do not really give a second thought to what they do in terms of traffic flow and safety. Let's be honest, the only time we really think about them is when we are running late, or running the pink light, which is a technical term for the yellow light that was rapidly turning red! Listening to the Holy Spirit can be a lot like a traffic signal. If we had it our way, all lights would be green, and we would go on our own schedule at our own speed, but there is an inherent danger in controlling our own course. When we are listening for the Advocate, knowing when the answer is no (red light), wisdom tells us that it is for a reason. When the answer is maybe or be cautious (yellow light), it is also for a reason. Green is great, and there is nothing better than getting the proverbial green light, but when we learn to listen for God's voice as we obey the traffic signals, the road of life becomes something joyful and beautiful! Are you gunning it through every yellow light or even the red lights? How is God trying to tell you to pump the brakes a bit? As Psalm 27:14 assures us, "Wait for the Lord; be strong and take heart and wait for the Lord." Sometimes it is okay to sit at a red light. You might have a chance to look to your right or left and share a smile with a fellow driver or Christian journeyer.

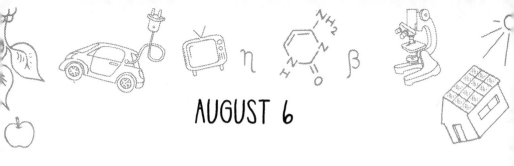

AUGUST 6

Queen of the Waves

2 Corinthians 11:23-29

On August 6, 1926, Gertrude Ederle began her quest to become the first woman to swim the English Channel. This is the narrow body of water between England and France. It is only twenty-one miles wide at its narrowest between Dover, England, and Calais, France.

What's His story? Ederle accomplished the task and even beat some of the prior times by men who had completed the distance swim. She became known as the Queen of the Waves! Before she could finish this historic swim, she had to overcome exhaustion, jellyfish stings, a strong current, and other obstacles. I have trouble swimming just twenty-five meters in a pool, so her accomplishment is incredible! In 2 Corinthians 11:23-29, we find Paul reestablishing his authority with the church in Corinth by walking through all of the trials and tribulations he had overcome and yet was still praising God. Paul was pointing out his differentiation between true Christians and the false teachers of the day. This still exists, and while we do not boast of our sufferings to place ourselves above someone else, giving thanks in all situations is a hallmark of life as a Christian devoted to the authority of God. Living a life of sacrifice may not always be comfortable, and it will include many uphill climbs, but the reward will always be worth it. Are you boasting of your suffering, or are you reflecting on the perseverance it took to overcome it? I'm sure as The Queen of the Waves exited the water, she looked back across the Channel towards France with thankfulness. Let us do the same as we look back across our lives, not focusing on the suffering, but rather the sacrifice for the reward. Remember, if we only had sunshine, life might actually become a desert!

AUGUST 7

The Revolving Door

Revelation 3:7-8

On August 7, 1888, Theophilus Van Kannel of Philadelphia, Pennsylvania, received the United States patent number 387,571 for the revolving door. To many, including myself, this invention is considered to be a thrill ride.

What's His story? The revolving door can be a substitute for a standard door for many reasons, but mostly for energy efficiency. But, I still consider it to be a great ride, and you cannot change my mind! The finest example of the joy that can be found in a revolving door is in the movie *Elf*. To see Buddy the Elf gleefully circling in the door is to know the joy that can be found in Christ Jesus. Unfortunately, in many ways, our spiritual lives and our relationship with God can be a sort of a revolving door. A revolving door keeps going around and around in a circle while a standard door swings one way or another. In reality, a revolving door is one that cannot be shut. In Revelation 3:7-8, we learn that the one who is holy and pure has opened the door. Jesus has opened the door to salvation, and has given you the key, no pun intended. We can stop our own version of a revolving door in which we are hot and cold towards God and instead choose the door that is unlocked by David's key. Are you stuck in the revolving door of a worldly life?

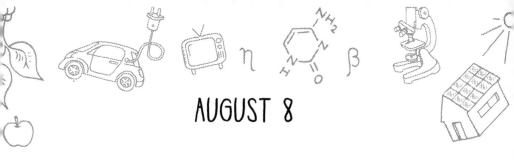

AUGUST 8

Where the Streets Have No Name

Colossians 2:9-10

On August 8, 1961, rock musician David Howell Evans was born in Barking, England, a suburb of London. Evans is better known by his stage name The Edge. He is the lead guitarist and back-up vocalist of the Irish band U2. Since its inception, he has been a member of the band and helped to produce many of their albums.

What's His story? While books have been written about the Christian influences on the band and their lyrics, one song from the 1987 *Joshua Tree* album, "Where the Streets Have No Name" gives vivid imagery of what we might imagine Heaven to be like, even here on Earth. The Edge wrote this song, and the band always put exhaustive thought into its lyrics, drawing upon human experience and translating it into musical feeling. The song is really about Ireland and how if you know the street someone lives on, then you know their social status, religion, etc. The title and some of the lyrics suggest a place where the streets have no name. It refers to a place where we are not labeled by where we live, the neighborhood status, or anything comparable. When we accept the true identity we have in Christ, it can break down walls. The lyrics suggest a way to break away in love from the labels humanity places on us and to only accept the faithful label available through Christ. Colossians 2:9 bolsters our identity in Christ as it declares the fullness of God in Christ's human body. Through Christ, we have everything we need for salvation, and therefore it does not matter which street we call home, so long as we call Christ our neighbor and landlord! Are you living in a world where the streets genuinely have no name?

AUGUST 9

Pure Gold That Is God's

Zechariah 13:9

On August 9, 1876, gold was discovered in the Black Hills of the Dakota Territory. South and North Dakota were not yet established. This land is home to the Badlands and Mount Rushmore today.

What's His story? Gold has been discovered worldwide, in places like Australia, South Africa, and Indonesia, and the United States. Gold prospecting lore is rich and deep. Gold is found throughout the Bible as well, from Genesis to Revelation. Why do you think that is? It could be because of its shine and multiple uses from decorative to utilitarian. Or its prominence evolved from the monetary value inherent in gold. I believe it is more profound and more symbolic. Zechariah 13:9 talks about the refining and testing of precious metals like gold as it says, "This third I will bring into the fire; I will refine them like silver and test them like gold." You see, gold is a material that will not tarnish or rust, thus its value and use in jewelry. But, I want you to look deeper. Precious gold and silver must go through a refinement process to rid it of impurities, or in our case, sin and unbelief. The "third" referred to in the passage is the small contingent of the Israelites that never turned away from God. They trusted in Him as they went through their own refinement, and we see the value God places on this as He refers to them as His people, having gone through the purification and testing process. The importance of being a part of God's people and its pure, untarnished nature is solid gold. Are you allowing God to remove the impurities, knowing that He sees you as valuable as the most elegant gold?

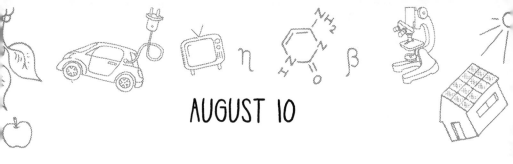

AUGUST 10

The Cornerstone

Isaiah 28:16-17

On August 10, 1675, the cornerstone foundation stone for the Royal Observatory in Greenwich, England, was laid. The Observatory played a significant role in early astronomy and navigation since this is where the prime meridian is located, giving it the name of Greenwich Mean Time.

What's His story? In Isaiah 28:16-17, we see one of many Old Testament references to The Messiah as the "the Cornerstone." In many ways, the cornerstone of the Royal Observatory and the reference to Christ as the cornerstone of the church are similar. Just as Christ guides our lifelong navigation, the prime meridian served as a starting point for early explorers sailing into unknown waters full of fear and anticipation. As we see in the scripture, when we rely on that precious cornerstone (Christ), we will never be stricken with panic. How appropriate that it in Isaiah 28:17, it says, "I will make justice the measuring line and righteousness the plumb line." Cornerstones and lines of demarcation are a great way to remind us to measure twice, cut once, build it on a sure foundation, and rely on Him. Are you relying on the cornerstone as the explorers did? And are you building something great as you lay that cornerstone of the foundation? Navigate, plan, and build with Jesus as the foundational starting point. You will never go wrong!

AUGUST II

The Roller Rink of Life

Romans 15:2

On August 11, 1866, the first roller skating rink opened in Newport, Connecticut. It was actually a dining room in the resort hotel Atlantic House, which had been converted to the roller rink and opened to the public. Talk about "if you build it, they will come."

What's His story? I am not sure if they had these back in 1866, and most of you probably do not need them now, but when you are first learning how to skate, you might use a contraption that looks like a walker with roller wheels. The purpose is the hold you upright while gaining the feel of navigating the roller rink on skates. Sometimes they have catchy names like Mr. Helper or Skater-Aid, but the purpose is the same – to keep you from falling onto the hard floor of concrete or hardwoods. If you are like me, and too prideful to use it, but not skilled enough to skate backward to ABBA, you stiffly slip about the rink, clinging to the wall at times. How often do we live our Christian lives in the same way? The Advocate is there for us, better than any PVC contraption built, and the Holy Spirit can help to keep us upright. In addition, Romans 15:1-3 calls us to build up our neighbors. We are to be that supporting structure that helps to keep them upright. How many times have you seen folks navigating the roller rink, but clutched to each other in fear? Together, and with the Holy Spirit, we are equipped with the courage and strength to live an upright Christian life. Perhaps you are skilled enough to skate in between and around the obstacles of the roller rink of life. Just do not skate blindfolded!

AUGUST 12

Sewing Love

Colossians 2:2

On August 12, 1851, Merritt Singer patented the first sewing machine. While he did not invent it, he patented it and the technique, which used thread to join pieces of fabric together. Although there are other brands of sewing machines out there today, Singer might be the brand you typically associate with sewing.

What's His story? I am sure Betsy Ross would have appreciated knowing Singer during her lifetime, but alas! Sewing is such a necessary part of our lives today. We tend to take it for granted until a rip appears, or a button falls off our shirt. While we usually think of sewing as joining pieces of fabric together, the phrase "the fabric of our lives" comes to mind when we look at Colossians 2:2-12. Paul's letter of encouragement reveals what it means. When he says united in love, he is really asserting the fabric of unity is woven with threads of love. Each action in love is a different colored strand, which, when woven together, reveals the full riches of complete understanding! When sewn together, these threads join different fabrics so that we are all one piece in Christ. Together in love and by His love, we gain the most abundant treasures of wisdom and knowledge that are embedded in this most glorious fabric. Are you sewing with love? What is one way today that you could thread a new needle with a thread of love? And who is that other piece of fabric in the fabric of your life?

AUGUST 13

Faith Like Bambi

Psalm 18:33

On August 13, 1942, Disney's animated feature *Bambi* opened at Radio City Music Hall in New York City. In this movie, after he is orphaned, a young deer named Bambi joins his new friends Thumper the rabbit, and Flower the skunk in exploring his forest home. Together they learn that there is beauty, joy, and sadness in life as he journeys into adulthood. It is a childhood classic.

What's His story? Sometimes movies really can teach us life lessons. Skunks really do not smell like flowers, so there is that. In Psalm 18:33, we find a perfect correlation to a life reliant on God. It says, "He makes my feet like the feet of a deer; he enables me to stand on the heights." Deer are graceful animals, when they are not in the roadways, of course, and like the Bambi story, a great illustration of the Christian life. God does not promise we will not have obstacles, challenges, sadness, or disappointment. A life void of these would not yield growth, leading to maturity. Instead, embedded within His promise is the truth that He will never leave us as we navigate the forests of this life on Earth. Through it all, He is teaching us, molding us, and equipping us to handle the present obstacle and those to come. In turn, and over time, we learn to rely on Him. Bambi learns to do the same through deep friendships. Our deep friendship is with the Father. Are you a young spotted fawn lost in a forest, or are you standing on the heights? No matter, God is present in both!

AUGUST 14

Light in the Darkness

John 1:5

On August 14, 2003, the Great 2003 Northeast Blackout occurred. It was a power outage affecting 50 million people in the Northeastern United States and Canada and lasted up to two days for many. Some seemingly harmless tree branches rubbing against a power line in Ohio caused it, but it set off a cascade of events that triggered this massive loss of electricity.

What's His story? Do we often take electricity for granted? You flip a switch and expect the lights to illuminate. Oh, the travesty if we cannot charge our "smart" devices! Lack of electricity is especially evident at night. Have you ever stepped outside during a blackout to experience the eerie stillness? But what about when it comes to spirituality? Do we sometimes suffer a spiritual power outage where nothing works, no food can be prepared, and no traffic lights of God are lit? In John 1:4-5, we learn right out of the gate that the Son of God was the light of men! The light shines in the darkness, but the darkness has not understood it. In this passage, we get a taste of the light that God was bringing into the world by becoming human, and just how powerful it was. His true light can penetrate the darkness and light the path before us. We always wonder if we are on the right track. If we follow the one that is lit, there will be no mistaking. The joy from His light can also recharge our spiritual life so that our inner spirit and outer glow penetrates the darkness. As reflectors of Christ's light, we can spread the Heaven-sent light so that no one stumbles in the dark. It is more than just having electricity to heat up a Hot Pocket. It is the light of life! How are you allowing Christ's light to end your own spiritual blackout? Can God's word be the power generator that kicks the lights back on for you?

AUGUST 15

A Flamin' Hot Purpose

Proverbs 20:5

On August 15, 2017, the pop-up restaurant The Spotted Cheetah opened for a short three-day run. In this restaurant, everything on the menu was made using Cheetos, including dessert. Yes, they used that orange, stick to your hands' snack. Television chef Anne Burrell was at the helm of this rather adventurous endeavor.

What's His story? One of the dishes included not just Cheetos, but the Flamin' Hot Cheetos, the spiced-up version. The story behind how this particular varietal of Cheetos came about reveals an individual who listened for God's dream over his life. A janitor at one of the Cheetos manufacturing plants noticed there was no spicy version and decided he would be the guy to mention this to the senior leadership. Long-story-short, access to corporate management was not easy! Nevertheless, Richard Montanez knew his purpose and place in God's workforce and walked in confidence towards his goal, buoyed by guidance that surpassed corporate limitations. He is now a senior executive for Cheetos parent company. How often do we miss the plan spread out before us by God's dream over our life? Is it because we fall victim to the lie that our lives are too insignificant to make an impact? Had Montanez done that, we would not have Flamin' Hot Cheetos today, and subsequently no Spotted Cheetah restaurant. Instead, as Proverbs 20:5 says, "The purposes of a man's heart are deep waters, but a man of understanding draws them out." Sure, it is not always easy to figure out, but understanding is formed out of a deep relationship with God. By actively reading His word, praying earnestly, and loving as He loved us, clarity begins to arrive. It may not come in the form of a career move from janitor to senior executive, but it could. Developing a life plan on the foundation of this passage in Proverbs and Ephesians 2:10 will certainly glorify God. Do you know your purpose? What would it take to find out your life's dream?

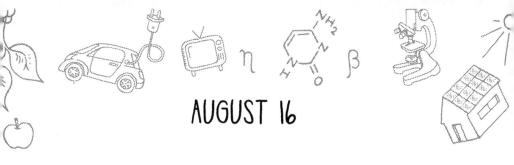

AUGUST 16

Finding Grace at Graceland

Luke 6:37

On August 16, 1977, American singer Elvis Presley died at his home, Graceland, in Memphis, Tennessee. He was only 42 years old.

What's His story? Elvis performed many of the Gospel favorites like "Amazing Grace," "How Great Thou Art," and "Peace in the Valley," among others. Elvis had a deep faith, and his Bible showed that, although some would argue that his music did not always reflect it. One annotated note in his Bible sheds light on his perspective of life. It read, "To judge a man by his weakest link or deed is like judging the power of the ocean by one wave." This note emphasizes our own need for God's forgiveness to wash over us like a wave. We are quick to judge others, withholding a cleansing and healing mercy for them. Luke 6:37 says, "Judge not, and you will not be judged; condemn not, and you will not be condemned, forgive, and you will be forgiven." Just as we love, because He first loved us, Elvis' Bible note reminds us of the words found in Luke that lead us to love one another unconditionally. Are you judging someone else by one action, or are you looking deeper in loving forgiveness? It is freeing to do so, and divine by nature. Not so divine for your diet are those grilled peanut butter, banana, and bacon sandwiches Elvis loved. Although Graceland is not named as you might think, grace can still be found in his home. Can it be found in your home?

AUGUST 17

Hit Me One More Time

Ezekiel 36:28

On August 17, 1957, Philadelphia Phillies baseball player Richie Ashburn fouled off a pitch that struck Alice Roth in the stands. The ball rocketed off the Hall of Famer's bat, hitting Roth squarely, breaking her nose. When play resumed, Ashburn fouled off another pitch. As "luck" would have it, this one also hit Roth as she was being stretchered out of the stands to be treated!!

What's His story? Ashburn and Roth mended fences later. Wishing for the best, her kids asked to go to an Eagles game where they could get hit by a football in hopes of getting a few autographs. What is the chance of someone getting hit by a foul ball in the same at bat twice? Repetition is also extensively used in the Bible, usually for positive impacts, although sometimes it truly is to liturgically hit us over the head! For example, the phrase "fear not" appears almost a hundred times in many versions. It is often used to emphasize a point, theme, or person. Or, as in the Gospels, repetition is there to offer greater credibility. One phrase found in Ezekiel 36:28 spells out God's covenant promise to His people, "you will be my people and I will be your God." It establishes a foundational relationship with God. We are His people, and He is our God. There is no mistaking that, and because it is found in multiple places (Genesis 17:7, Numbers 15:41, Jeremiah 7:23), its importance lands like a hard-hit foul ball hitting us squarely in the face! Hopefully, the result is not a broken nose, but rather a mended spirit, and a heart of flesh molded by our heavenly Father. Can you imagine getting hit twice? Now, can you imagine a life without a relationship with God? No question which one would be worse.

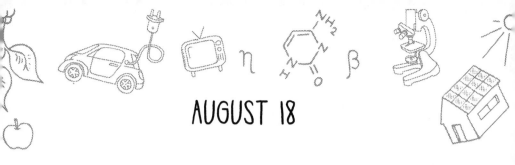

AUGUST 18

The Weather Channel

Psalm 135:7

On August 18, 1926, the first weather map was telecast using radio facsimile. The radio facsimile was an early version of the fax machine. This weather map was introduced for naval purposes and the need for weather assessments before missions. This came in handy for the D-Day invasion in WWII.

What's His story? I am a self-avowed weather nerd, and could probably watch The Weather Channel nonstop. Have you ever just paused to watch the clouds, their movements, and the shapes they make? You will find that there are more than just dolphins, dinosaurs, and hippo shapes in the clouds! In Psalm 135, which is a hymn of praise that contrasts the power and greatness of God with the feebleness of idolatry, we find some great descriptions of His sovereignty, including the weather! Psalm 135:7 says, "He makes clouds rise from the ends of the earth; he sends lightning with the rain and brings out the wind from his storehouses." Many times, we can see God's power and majesty in the weather, but beauty and promise also exist. The rainbows after the storm or the freshness in the air after a cleansing rain are just a couple of examples. Take it a step further and think about how the cycle of weather enables His kingdom to thrive. When we think of praising the Lord for the weather and how it elevates Him so much higher than any idols, it minimizes the sassy disappointment we have in our modern weather forecasts! After all, every day should be a ten on a weather meter since God created it, right? Today, go outside and for just a few minutes, observe the weather and see if you, too, can find God.

AUGUST 19

The Pull of Gravity

John 20:29

On August 19, 1934, the first Soap Box Derby was held in Dayton, Ohio. It moved to Akron, Ohio, the next year and has been an annual event since then. A soapbox derby is a downhill race between cars that are powered by gravity. They have no engine. The event evolved from a day in Dayton in 1933 when journalist Myron Scott was photographing a few boys rolling downhill in a crate strapped to some baby-stroller wheels.

What's His story? The Soap Box Derby is definitely environmentally friendly. There is no exhaust being emitted, and no noise pollution produced other than the wildly enthusiastic fans who always line the one-thousand feet of the straight downhill track. The cars are powered by something we cannot see, but we know exists – gravity. It sounds similar to our faith and our belief in God and the Holy Spirit. We find ourselves like Thomas in John 20:27-31 doubting because we cannot touch or feel it tangibly. As Jesus says in John 20:29, "Because you have seen me, you have believed; blessed are those who have not seen and yet have believed." Clearly, it takes more exertion and effort to believe and have trusting faith in something we cannot see. The downhill trek each soapbox car takes is also a lot like the Christian journey. It is long, and sometimes arduous with risk, and again, it is powered by something you cannot see, but you know it exists! Verse 31 hammers it home to the finish line with this, "by believing, you may have life in his name." Who doesn't want that?! Are you being guided home to the finish line, or are you still stuck at the start line? If you allow it, the power of the Holy Spirit can get you rolling!

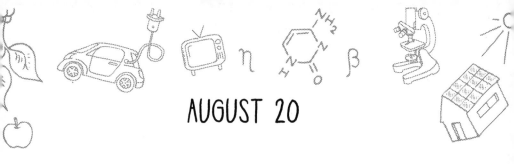

AUGUST 20

Tuning Into God

Hebrews 3:7

On August 20, 1920, the first commercial radio station in the United States began to broadcast in Detroit, Michigan. The AM radio all-news station had the call letters WWJ. It might have been easier to write today's devotional if it were WWJD. You know…what would Jesus do? Alas.

What's His story? In today's modern society, tuning a radio is sometimes as simple as calling out to our "smart" device. Even just a few years ago, you would need to turn a dial to tune the radio into a broadcasting station like WWJ in Detroit. How we tune into the Holy Spirit is very similar. When you are not on the right radio frequency, you end up hearing nothing but static, or a garbled message or music. The same applies to our daily lives as we attempt to tune into the Holy Spirit to listen for discernment. For some people, you like talk radio, and for others, you prefer country or pop. No matter your genre, if you are not tuned properly, you are just going to hear static. In Hebrews 3:7-8, it says, "So, as the Holy Spirit says: Today if you hear his voice, do not harden your hearts." Notice it is not "the Holy Spirit said," instead it is, "the Holy Spirit says"! If we do not tune in, and if we do not listen to the continual broadcasting night and day, day and night, our hearts are hardened. We tune out God and miss the beautiful redeeming message He is playing just for us. It is our own soundtrack, almost like a well-planned mix-tape from the '80s or '90s! Are you tuning in, or listening to the static? Who can help turn the dial for you?

AUGUST 21

What's Old Is New Again

Isaiah 53:7-9

On August 21, 1904, American jazz legend William James "Count" Basie was born Red Bank, New Jersey. Count Basie was an impactful bandleader and piano player during the Big Band era of jazz music that included the likes of Duke Ellington and Glenn Miller.

What's His story? Although always a jazz musician, Count Basie was said to have had different eras that his fans referred to as Old Testament band (1935-1950) and New Testament band (1952-1984). The Old Testament band was broad, impactful, and up-tempo, while the New Testament band was minimalist and more laid-back. Not necessarily the way the Bible unfolds, right?! I would not refer to Deuteronomy or Leviticus as up-tempo, but some might argue with me. Conversely, Paul's letters in the New Testament are far from laid-back! We have identified the common thread of the jazz genre between Basie's New and Old Testament. The fulfillment of Old Testament prophecy through Jesus in the New Testament is extensive. Isaiah contains many, many references, including Isaiah 53:7-9, which is one of the most magnificent descriptions of Jesus in the Old Testament. Some fans of Count Basie might argue that you have to listen to both eras to understand his musical talents and greatness. I would say that both the Old and New Testaments of the Bible are likewise necessary to even begin to understand the complete power, glory, and greatness of God. Even then, it is often too much for our minds to comprehend! When you read the Bible, are you recognizing the common thread of Jesus between the Old and New Testaments?

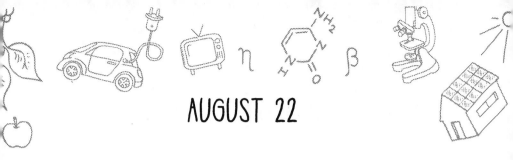

AUGUST 22

The Cup of Salvation

Psalm 116:13

On August 22, 1851, *Yacht America* won the initial Royal Yacht Squadron Cup. This nautical event later became known as the America's Cup. No, America does not win it every time, but it was named as such, because at the first race near the Isle of Wright, an American schooner called *America*, won it!

What's His story? This is one of the most prestigious sailing competitions in the entire world. Even if you are not into sailing, it can be fun to watch. If the leaning of a boat makes you queasy, then perhaps you get a hall pass not to watch. The prize for winning is a giant silver cup. A lovely award, but not as grand as the one in Psalm 116:13. It says, "I will lift up the cup of salvation and call on the name of the Lord." To take the cup is to worship God and accept the cup of saving grace that He offers us. The opportunity for us to drink from it and be refreshed is what is available for us at the table with our Savior. You might hear this when we take the sacraments during communion, because it is our way of receiving this blessing by faith and with thanksgiving. Just as in Psalm 23, our cup does overflow with the fullness of His blessing. Today, are you taking the cup of salvation in your obedient and grateful hands, or are you sending it out to sea with the sailboats? What is stopping you from coming back to the table to receive the blessing?

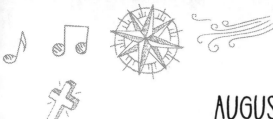

AUGUST 23

In Open Rebellion

Psalm 107:10-16

On August 23, 1775, King George III of England declared the colonists to be in open rebellion. He issued a Proclamation of Rebellion in response to the Battles of Lexington and Concord and the Battle of Bunker Hill. Little did he know what was coming.

What's His story? The American colonists did not need a monarch thousands of miles away and across the Atlantic Ocean to declare them in rebellion. They knew it, and they knew exactly why they were rebelling, or at least most of them did. Keep in mind, there was no social media, no nightly news, etc. to stoke the fires of rebellion! What about us? Do we feel like we are in rebellion towards God? Psalm 107:10-16 describes what our cycle is like. First, we are in darkness, facing the deepest gloom that holds us prisoner. Then, we rebel against the words of God and despise the counsel of the Most High. We cry out to Him, and He hears us and saves us from distress. The second half of this passage is the redemption we receive from His unfailing love. Yes, there was no love between King George III and the colonists, but our Heavenly King offers an everlasting love that squelches any rebellion within our hearts. Would you consider yourself to be in rebellion today? If so, what would it take to seek the counsel of the Most High, knowing He can solve the root cause of your disobedience?

AUGUST 24

Clunkers for Christ

1 Thessalonians 3:13

On August 24, 2009, the month-long "Cash for Clunkers" program ended. This was a United States government incentive program designed to get some of those ancient, wood-paneled, gas-guzzlers off the road in exchange for more fuel-efficient cars. A clunker is technically defined as a bucket of bolts. But, many of us use it to describe an old, run-down jalopy (second use of this word in the book!) The government ended up spending $2.9 billion on 690,000 cars that were traded in for cash.

What's His story? Do you sometimes feel like you are a clunker for Christ? Maybe you are worn to the nub from stress and believe you have no more to give. Perhaps you think you are just an inefficient Christian that only consumes and does not offer? 1 Thessalonians 3:13 says that you do have something to provide, "May he strengthen your hearts so that you will be blameless and holy in the presence of our God and Father when our Lord Jesus comes with all his holy ones." While this is a reference to the second coming of Christ, we know that God can strengthen us so that we do not need a clunker buy-back program to improve our heart and prepare it for Him by creating a good work in us. Because He strengthens us, we can work tirelessly, no pun intended, for God. We will never be a clunker if we are doing it for Him. You can be a gas-guzzling Ford Explorer yet run like a Toyota Corolla because He strengthens you. It does not matter your situation. If the fuel of the Almighty powers you, anything is possible, and it will be accomplished through Him. No one is a clunker in the realm of Christ. Do you feel like you are ready to be traded for a newer model? Why not ingest the cleansing power of the living word?

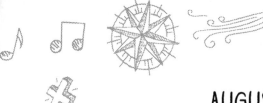
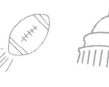

AUGUST 25

Biblical Rolodex

2 Timothy 3:16

On August 25, 1910, Arnold Neustadter was born in Brooklyn, New York. He invented the Rolodex. Oh dear, this is probably another outdated invention I need to describe for younger readers. The Rolodex was a desktop rotating card file containing names, addresses, phone numbers, etc. for essential people or those of meaning in your life and available for quick reference. Today, many of you know this as contacts on your phone.

What's His story? Do you have a Rolodex for your Bible? What would that look like? I wonder if it would contain favorite books, or more appropriately, favorite scripture? The power of God's word is found in having familiarity with it. Staying intimate and close to scripture is staying close to Him. Scripture memorization is for more than just Sunday school or vacation bible school. Having scripture at hand, or a Biblical Rolodex, is one of the best ways to apply scripture to everyday life. As 2 Timothy 3:16 says, "All scripture is God-breathed and is useful for teaching, rebuking, correcting and training in righteousness so that the man of God may be thoroughly equipped for every good work." That is a perfect reason for creating your own Biblical Rolodex. Just like a regular Rolodex (or contacts file) keeps your vital people at hand, it could allow you to engage in any number of those useful attributes for the sake of the kingdom! What verse might be the first card in your Biblical Rolodex? Mine would be 1 John 4:19. Pick yours and let me know sometime via social media! #BiblicalRolodex

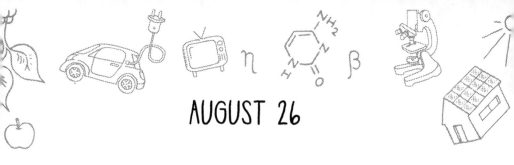

AUGUST 26

Mother Teresa

Deuteronomy 15:11

On August 26, 1910, Agnes Bojaxhiu was born in Macedonia. She later became known as Mother Teresa, and most recently was canonized by the Pope to become Saint Teresa of Calcutta. She was recognized with many awards and accolades for her work with the poor and needy in India. She once won a Nobel Peace Prize.

What's His story? Mother Teresa is a shining example of what being Christlike is. As Jesus did, Mother Teresa ran to the people in need, not away from them. She learned this at an early age from her own mother, who would routinely invite strangers and the destitute for dinner at their house. Mother Teresa listened to what she felt was a calling from Jesus to help those in need. Someone in need did not just mean the poor. It included the neglected, the sick, the marginalized. Deuteronomy 15:11 describes how she lived her life. She understood there would be poor people everywhere, yet she wanted to do something about it and obeyed the command found in this verse to be openhanded. What is it like to be openhanded like this? She believed it was not about how much you do, but how much love you put into what you do that counts. Love is where caring begins. It is an action taken to address the needs of someone in your own Calcutta. All we have to do is open our ears and eyes to hear and see the cries that beckon us to love. Mother Teresa's example of love as an action is something we should be reminded of every day. Have you found your Calcutta? Is it nearby or in a faraway land? Take the first step, because as the verse says, there are people in need everywhere.

AUGUST 27

No Fences

James 4:7-10

On August 27, 1990, American country music artist Garth Brooks released the album *No Fences*. It launched Brooks' career into another orbit. It sold over 10 million copies and was one of the most popular albums of the 1990s across all music genres. I have no idea how it beat the likes of Michael Bolton, Kenny G, and Weird Al Yankovic, but it did. Just kidding.

What's His story? With tracks like "Friends in Low Places" and "Unanswered Prayers," we could use either of those, but instead, we will focus on the album title, *No Fences*. When it comes to a relationship with God, do you ever feel like you are either straddling a fence or busily building a charming white picket fence protecting your comfortable life? Why do we do that? When we straddle a fence, we are not giving our full selves to God, holding back, or holding onto the things and ideas of the world. Furthermore, when we build a fence, we are penning ourselves inside spiritually because we think we can protect and control what we know. In James 4:7-10, you get five tools with which you can break down those fences and live a life that allows you to get closer to God. Use the tools found in scripture, but do not allow rust and dirt to collect. Use them in your community and in your family to break down fences wherever you see them. Who knows, you might even learn to love country music. But seriously, what are the fences you are either straddling or building? Garth and God say, "No More!"

AUGUST 28

I Have a Dream

Psalm 119:130

On August 28, 1963, Civil Rights Leader and minister Dr. Martin Luther King, Jr. delivered his "I Have a Dream" speech at the Lincoln Memorial on The Mall in Washington, D.C. It is an iconic seventeen-minute speech that is incredibly moving and memorable. King certainly did have a dream of a world devoid of racism and full of civil rights for all individuals.

What's His story? King's speech was one of the critical moments of the civil rights movement. It was a plea to live as a symphony of brotherhood based on character, not skin color. King's speech is more of a sermon because it was a call to action! It delivered then and still does today. Apparently, part of the back-story of his speech was that he improvised some of it – especially the "I have a dream" part! That speaks to the passion within his heart and the plea for action that came through his words. It was an awakening, a prompting, and a deliverance of hopeful expectation rooted in his faith in God, and what should also be ours. If you listen to the entire speech, or read the transcript, you will feel it. As Psalm 119:130 says, "The unfolding of your words gives light; it gives understanding to the simple." King knew that the urgency of his message was grounded in the understanding we are all created in our maker's image. To advance unification according to this, was to glorify God. The unfolding of God's words lights the world around and allows those seeking it to understand. King's sermon was a reminder that we are all equal in the Lord's eyes, and an invitation to join in that brotherhood of love. I invite you to find some time today to listen to the dream that King shared.

AUGUST 29

Melted Lump of Sheetmetal

2 Corinthians 3:18

On August 29, 2013, the building known as The Walkie Talkie Building in London, England, melted a Jaguar sports car. You may need to reread that sentence. The building, located at 20 Fenchurch in the City of London, is unusually shaped with curves and really does look like a thirty-seven-story tall walkie-talkie. How did it melt a car, you ask? Read on, please!

What's His story? The building's shape meant that the sun was reflected on a slightly different angle than a typical skyscraper. It is also very potent, because of the vast expanses of glass the building's architects incorporated into the design. When the Jaguar's owner parked on the street below, it was like that old "use the sun and a magnifying glass during the summer to set a piece of paper aflame" trick. The side of the car got so hot from the reflection that it melted. Shouldn't the way we reflect the Spirit and love of Christ be just as fiery? We cannot blame it on a cloudy day, because the Lord is always shining! I guess the crucial part of how we show that Christ lives within is our ability to reflect His light. What that means and how to do so is found in 2 Corinthians 3:18. As we reflect God's glory, the Holy Spirit helps drive inner change, and the outward transformation becomes so apparent that others feel the heat of our passion for Christ. Indeed we do not want to melt anyone, but we can undoubtedly shine the light brightly enough that others know transformation is taking place! How are you reflecting God's glory today?

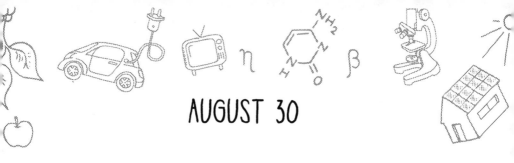

AUGUST 30

Hotline to God

Psalm 4:3

On August 30, 1963, a hotline communication link was established between Moscow, Russia, and Washington, D.C., in the United States. This link, similar to the one you might find in a baseball stadium between the dugout and the bullpen, allowed leaders of each country to pick up the phone and immediately talk to sort out any misunderstandings. No quarters were involved, and no busy signals.

What's His story? The communications link implementation came during the Cold War, which was mainly a war of words in which the two countries were either talking past each other or not talking at all. This link was designed to improve communications after the Cuban Missile Crisis. To varying levels of success, it did help. These days you have a whole group of contacts you consider being on a hotline link, but what about God? Do you know that we are born with a hotline link to God? There are no installation charges, no missed appointments, and it is pretty easy to use. It comes through the Holy Spirit and allows us to improve our own relationship with God. This communication is two-way. We speak to God through prayer and then listen to His words. According to Psalm 4:3, "the Lord will hear when I call to him." God is always on the other end. Have you picked up the hotline to talk to Him recently? Why or why not?

AUGUST 31

Producing Fruit

John 15:8

On August 31, 1960, the Agricultural Hall of Fame was established in Bonner Springs, Kansas. It honors individuals who have made outstanding national or international contributions to the establishment, development, advancement, or improvement of agriculture. Inductees include George Washington Carver (agricultural scientist), Eli Whitney (cotton gin), and even Squanto (Pilgrim helper).

What's His story? Have you ever heard the Paul Harvey "So God Made a Farmer" speech from 1978? Farming itself is fueled by science, but rooted in faith. Technology drives many of the farmers' lives today to help complete the incredibly long list of tasks he or she has each day. John 15:1-8, where Jesus teaches about the vine and the branches, explains why farming is rooted in faith. Jesus is the vine, and we are the branches. We are in a life-sustaining relationship with Him. To produce fruit, spiritual, or otherwise, we are reliant upon Him. Apart from Him, we can do nothing. We must abide in Him, and to abide in Him means to allow Christ to live in your heart. Through this living prayer, we are rooted in faith, and only then do we begin to produce the spiritual fruit of which Jesus spoke of here, and Paul in Galatians 5:22. Farming is a remarkable profession full of trust, hard work, and faith. It sounds a lot like being a Christian, which is why Jesus uses farming in many parables. Are you relying on Jesus to produce fruit, or are you trying to do it yourself? You do not need a rooster to wake up to this knowledge. Abide in Him!

SEPTEMBER 1

The Buddy System

Luke 10:1

On September 1, 1980, Terry Fox ended his Marathon of Hope. Terry was a Canadian who had a goal to draw attention to cancer research since he had personally been affected by it. He came up with a vision to run a marathon across Canada from East to West. On this day, Fox had to call it quits in Ontario, after 143 days and 3,339 miles, due to health issues. He called it the Marathon of Hope because he believed in miracles, and it captured the qualities of compassion, commitment, and perseverance he saw in others.

What's His story? Terry Fox started his Marathon of Hope in Newfoundland with just a handful of observers. His close friend drove the travel van and cooked meals. Terry's frustration with parts of his journey led the two of them to argue so much that Terry's brother eventually had to step in as a buffer and became a part of the buddy system. Sometimes similar to us, huh? We may not always listen to God, find ourselves arguing with Him, or not on speaking terms with Him. Yet, He still offers us a buffer and buddy system for our own journey through Christ Jesus! In fact, in Luke 10:1, Jesus appoints seventy-two messengers and sends them out two by two. Why do you think He does this? It could be to support one another, or to provide a more credible witness. Either way, the mission was to raise awareness of Jesus' power and to spread the Gospel. Find your buddy, and do it today! Now here is the kicker. Terry ran with a prosthetic leg and a crazy hop so the springs in his leg could reset after each step. Cancer took his leg, but it could not take his hope, courage, or dedication to loving and helping others. How is your buddy system helping others?

SEPTEMBER 2

Smoky Mountains Full of Glory

Exodus 40:34

On September 2, 1940, United States President Franklin Roosevelt dedicated the Great Smoky Mountains National Park. It is an area of land found in the southern Appalachian Mountain range covering 800 square miles of beautiful mountains in Tennessee and North Carolina. This was the first national park I ever visited as a child, and I still remember walking up Clingman's Dome in thick, thick fog.

What's His story? My personal account gives some insight. They are called the Smoky Mountains because of the thick layer of fog or blue mist that regularly settles over the hills and valleys of these grand mountains appearing like a perpetually cloaking smoke. The Old Testament has many examples of God appearing in a cloud, and for a good reason. The cloud symbolizes His presence. As in Exodus 40:34, "Then the cloud covered the Tent of Meeting, and the glory of the Lord filled the tabernacle." The tabernacle was where God was present on Earth, and He filled it with His glory. Can you place yourself in a thick fog, surrounded by a cool mist that held the glory of God? When you watch a fog roll in, all of the sudden things have changed, and perspective is new. It is in this type of mist or fog that we must do as Moses did by relying on God, sensing and seeing His presence, and responding in reverence. The next time you see thick fog or mist, especially in the cool of the evening in the mountains, think of God's glory surrounding you.

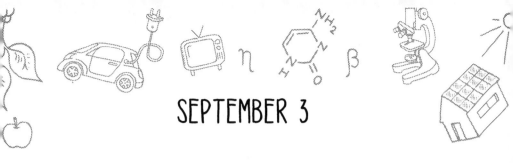

SEPTEMBER 3

Great Works in the Wilderness

Isaiah 43:18-19

On September 3, 1964, United States President Lyndon Johnson signed the 1964 Wilderness Act into law. This piece of legislature ordered the protection and designation of 9.1 million acres as wilderness. It sought to add additional land to secure its enjoyment for present and future generations. Johnson and Congress were astutely aware of population expansion's impact on the natural beauty, and rightfully acted to protect it.

What's His story? We reflected on other days about the beauty of God's creation found in the natural grandeur of the wilderness, but in Isaiah 43:19, God reassures the exiled Israelites that there is something greater to come. Starting in the prior verse, it says, "Forget the former things; do not dwell on the past. See, I am doing a new thing! Now it springs up; do you not perceive it? I am making a way in the desert and streams in the wasteland." Can you imagine what it must look like? God is practically yanking our sleeve at that scenic outlook imploring us to look up from our map and see the glory He has created in the wilderness! He accounts for our sense of ingratitude when He rhetorically asks if we do not perceive it. He knows that we tend to look past the exquisiteness all around us in selfish thoughtlessness, blinding us to how He is moving in our lives. The Wilderness Act protected land for future generations. How can your relationship with God today and acknowledgment of what He has created in the proverbial wilderness be your gift and guide to the next generation?

SEPTEMBER 4

The Rest of the Story

John 16:33

On September 4, 1918, American radio host Paul Harvey was born in Tulsa, Oklahoma. I believe that Paul was probably telling stories right out of the womb. If you have never heard Harvey and his absurd ability to weave fantastic stories, I encourage you to find some. His velvety voice and seamless transitions will leave you in awe.

What's His story? Harvey was famous for his "Rest of the Story" segments on his show. He was undoubtedly a storyteller and would share tales on a wide variety of topics, holding onto one key piece of information or detail until the very end. He would then deliver it, along with the punch line of, "and now you know the rest of the story!" Emphasis was on the word rest because that allowed Harvey to deliver the plot twist with a gripping effect. Often, in our lives, we feel lost or confused until we learn the rest of the story. In the Gospel of John, we find Jesus sharing the Last Supper with the disciples. He was giving instructions and wisdom on how to pray, how the world would react, and on the Holy Spirit. While Jesus was the ultimate in story-telling through parables, always delivering the punch line at the end of the story, John 16:33 is different. Jesus was speaking directly and not using parables; therefore, the disciples finally understand. This is especially true as Jesus says, "In this world you will have trouble. But take heart! I have overcome the world." Little did the disciples know that they would get the rest of the story in just a few days. But, that is not even the end of it. We know that the rest of the story is when Jesus is resurrected! Are you ready for the rest of the story when Jesus comes again in His triumphant return?

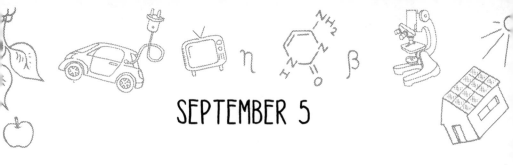

SEPTEMBER 5

The Amazing Race

2 Timothy 4:6-8

On September 5, 2001, the reality television show *The Amazing Race* premiered on CBS. On this show, eleven pairs of contestants traveled across the globe, performing a myriad of culturally-aligned tasks based on clues provided along the way. The team that deciphered the clues, completed the tasks, and finished fastest went on to the next stage. The wounded antelope, as I like to call it, or the last-place team was sent home each week.

What's His story? In the first episode of each season, the host Phil ends his opening dialogue with, "The world is waiting for you. Good luck. Travel safe. Go!" Along the way, they use every form of transportation known in the country in which they are located. The prize at the end of the marathon race is a million bucks, but I am not sure if that makes eating chicken feet during a challenge-stage worth it! Have you ever thought about the Christian journey as a race? It can sometimes feel the same, loaded with obstacles and roadblocks, but ever since we said yes to Jesus' calling, we have been in an Amazing Race that delivers a grand prize worth more than money. As Paul attests in 2 Timothy 4:6-8, if we fight the good fight, keep the faith, and finish the race, we are awarded the crown of righteousness. With this knowledge, it makes our race seem more rewarding and less hectic all at the same time. If you have ever seen The Amazing Race, you will agree. You do not see them walking to a bus, subway, taxi, or plane. They are always running! But, if we keep the faith, the blessed assurance in Jesus allows us to savor the journey and reap a much greater reward! Where are you on your Amazing Race? Are you just starting out, or are you well on your way? God is always willing to be your partner, no matter where you are.

SEPTEMBER 6

Being Big on the Pig

1 John 2:1-2

On September 6, 1916, Clarence Saunders opened the first Piggly Wiggly grocery store at 79 Jefferson Street in Memphis, Tennessee. It was the first store to be known as "self-service" in which customers were able to roam aisles and pick what they wanted. What a novel concept, huh? With grocery-buying and delivery services today, everything really does come full circle.

What's His story? The next time you are in the cereal aisle spending minute after minute trying to decide which flavor of Cheerios to buy, you now know Mr. Saunders is to blame! By the way, he picked the Piggly Wiggly name because he liked the way it sounded, and it rhymed. He is my kind of guy. There is a poem called "Heaven's Grocery Store." Reading its verses, you can imagine yourself traveling up and down the aisles, picking out everything a human being would need like patience, love, boxes of wisdom and faith, courage, and some loving grace. As the poem continues, the writer notices that Salvation was advertised as free! When you get to the cash register and ask how much you owe, you are told it has already been paid! Of course, it has. We get everything we need to live, thrive, and survive for free because Jesus has already paid the cost. 1 John 2:1-2 reminds us that Jesus is the atoning sacrifice for our sins. Sin in our lives is like the fifty-pound bag of dog food that barely fits under the shopping cart. Even though it is cumbersome, and you want to forget it is there, you cannot. The burden is just too heavy. Thank goodness we have Jesus. All the marvelous things we have picked up in Heaven's Grocery Store are paid for, not only our tab but also the world's! Go ahead and shop with Jesus at Heaven's Grocery Store!

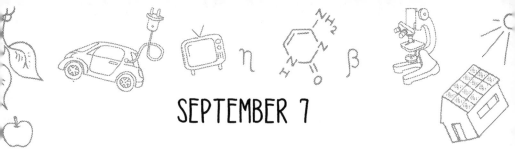

SEPTEMBER 7

Caring for Tigers

Proverbs 27:23

On September 7, 1936, the last remaining Tasmanian tiger, named Benjamin, died in captivity at Hobart Zoo in Tasmania, Australia. The Tasmanian tiger, or thylacine, was a meat-eating marsupial, which is like saying it is a large opossum that likes leftover steak.

What's His story? The thylacine's population had already dwindled due to overhunting and invasive species like the dingo. I guess dingoes eat more than we knew. Unfortunately, Benjamin at the Hobart Zoo died of neglect and not a dingo. Proverbs 27:23 reminds us that we should not take possessions for granted. We know they are not ours. They are God's creatures, and we are just their stewards. As caretakers of the animals (Genesis 2:19), we must not neglect them. Neglecting what God has given us, whether it is possessions or animals, is not pleasing to Him. It is all an opportunity to glorify Him through love and care that we can share. Recently there was a rumor that the thylacine had come out of extinction in Tasmania. I have no way of knowing if this is true, but I do know it would probably receive exceptional care and comfort. Do you have a pet, livestock, or a furry/scaly friend? You know the connection you share with them and the attention they deserve, but do you see this as a chance to give praise to God? Show them the love that God shows us. Who are you caring for today, and does it reveal your love for God?

SEPTEMBER 8

Aid That Knows No Bounds

Hebrews 13:16

On September 8, 2005, two Russian aircraft landed at a disaster aid station at an Arkansas Air Force Base in response to Hurricane Katrina. This was the first time in history that a Russian plane had completed this type of aid mission on North American soil.

What's His story? This is an incredible humanitarian example in a time of extreme need. Consider the post-World War II history of relations between the United States and Russia. The Russians put all disagreements aside and acted out of compassion for others, as Christ would want us to do. Putting the kingdom ahead of self-interest and acting on behalf of others in a time of great need is divine. The lesson we can all learn from a rather dull factoid is that when we put aside our differences to be compassionate and caring, it represents a move towards Christ. It can motivate others to extend a helping hand. Acts of compassion can transcend and overcome years of discord and distrust, but also self-righteousness, bringing us back into a relationship with God. That is precisely what He wants. As Hebrews 13:16 says, "And do not forget to do good and to share with others, for with such sacrifices, God is pleased." Acts of kindness and love should be our focus. Today, how can you show someone else that they are loved?

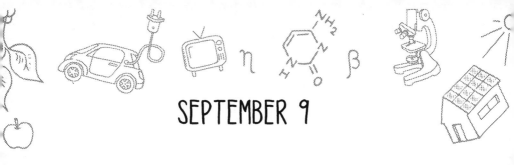

SEPTEMBER 9

Father Figures

1 John 3:1

On September 9, 1938, the movie *Boys Town* opened, starring Spencer Tracy as Father Edward Flanagan. It was a biographical film drama based on Flanagan, who was an advocate for delinquent and disadvantaged boys and founded a boys' home outside of Omaha, Nebraska. His story is one of seeking justice, which is well represented in the movie.

What's His story? Father Flanagan believed there was good in everyone, including rebellious, angst-filled young men. He believed in the redeemed power of Christ, as well as the hunt for justice where injustice seemed to prevail. Father Flanagan lived up to his title because he knew these young men needed a fatherly figure to help regain order in their lives. We may not think we are as rebellious as these young men (although I once participated in a food fight…. in college…), we know that we also need our heavenly Father figure to order our lives after Christ's example. 1 John 3:1 assigns our position in the holy family with God, and aligns with Father Flanagan's role in these boys' lives accordingly. It reads, "See what great love the Father has lavished on us that we should be called children of God! And that is what we are! The reason the world does not know us is that it did not know him." The reason the world does not understand our relationship as a child of God is that they do not know him, nor do they know they could become a member of the family right this moment! Do you feel as though you are a member of God's heavenly family? Think of how He lavishes His love on you. Just the word lavish should tell you how deep this love is!

SEPTEMBER 10

Quite a Shortcut

Romans 3:23

On September 10, 2000, thirty-three participants in the Berlin Marathon were disqualified. You might think, well, that seems like a high number, but perhaps there is more to the rest of the story. See what I did there? I pulled a Paul Harvey! The reason they were disqualified? They had taken the subway somewhere between the 15 ½ mile mark and the finish line. Apparently, they forgot about their timing chips. And now you know the rest of the story. Almost.

What's His story? I want to ask these runners why run over half the race only to cheat on the backside?? Then again, how often does this apply to our own life? We run solidly out of the gate at the start, but soon enough, we begin to falter in a variety of ways. It would be easy to point a finger and say, "how dare you," but the reality is that we all fall short. Jesus was the only reference point of perfection we have. Paul's letter to Rome is an excellent source of directional wisdom for the forgiveness of sin through Christ. In Romans 3:23, we find confirmation that we fall short of God's glory, but there is hope in the very next verse! After a slight chuckle, I am sure the race organizers eventually forgave these runners. Just as they fell short and were forgiven, Romans 3:24 reminds us that we are justified by His grace through redemption found only in Christ. Our sorrow over failure in sin can take that subway to cross the finish line of redemption! Do you acknowledge the sin in your life? That's step one. Now take the next step to turn away from whatever it might be, and turn back to God in repentance for forgiveness.

SEPTEMBER 11

A Day of Remembrance and Healing

Psalm 147:3

On September 11, 2001, the United States was hit by a historic and devastating terrorist attack. New York City, Washington, D.C., and Shanksville, Pennsylvania, were locations of the attacks that left almost 3,000 people killed, 6,000 injured, and thousands more traumatized or affected in the cleanup and aftermath.

What's His story? It was a shocking day, and generations will remember where they were when the events unfolded. It has since become a day of remembrance for those precious lives lost. Every year since it took place, it is an opportunity to heal hearts and assuage anguish. The words of Psalm 147:3 appropriately read, "He heals the brokenhearted and binds up their wounds." The context of this Psalm is the Israelites returning to Jerusalem from exile. The setting of the verse is a triumphant return, and the application on this day is the same. After the September 11th attacks, the United States triumphantly unified as one nation under God to help one another see the healing power in God. Today, I invite you to pray over the lives that were impacted, whether that is your own immediate family or someone you do not even know. When we accept God's healing, we do so jointly with our brothers and sisters to our right and to our left.

SEPTEMBER 12

The Man in Black

Romans 10:17

On September 12, 2003, the legendary singer Johnny Cash died in Nashville, Tennessee. Cash, who sold more than ninety million records worldwide, crossed over several genres of music. Not only did he play and sing country music, but also rock and Gospel. He is probably one of the few musical artists in the Country, Rock, and Gospel Halls of Fame!

What's His story? The Man in Black, as he was known because of his consistent wardrobe color selection, recorded eight solo gospel albums. Funny enough, he even recorded a song about the Apostle Paul called, "The Man in White." In 1990, Cash recorded a reading of the entire New Testament in the King James Version! It is over nineteen hours long! Can you imagine that distinct voice reading the word of God? I would compare it to Norman Vincent Price reading a scary tale, but not nearly as impactful! In Romans 10:17, we learn that faith comes from hearing the message, and the message is heard through the word of Christ. How important it is to listen to the word of God! It does not matter if it is in a church pew, or from The Man in Black. When we hear the word of God, we are transformed. It forces us to look at our own lives and evaluate how we do or do not align with what we hear and read in scripture. Do you need to hear God's word in such a distinctive way that it leaves an impression? If so, does it move you into action?

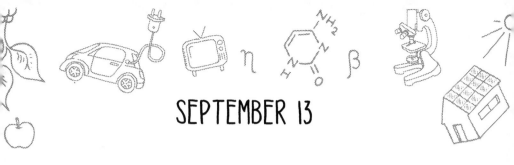

SEPTEMBER 13

The Secret Ingredient

Jeremiah 33:3

On September 13, 1857, Milton Snavely Hershey was born in Derry Township, Pennsylvania. You probably recognize the last name. The Hershey Bar was introduced around 1900, and Hershey's Kisses were around 1907. In 1912, Hershey was slated to travel on the *Titanic*, but canceled his reservations at the last minute! That is one close call.

What's His story? Everyone loves chocolate. Okay, maybe not everyone, but close to everyone! Ironically, on this same day, not only is it International Chocolate Day, but in 1909 the operetta *The Chocolate Soldier* opened in New York City, and in 1916 Roald Dahl, who wrote *Charlie and The Chocolate Factory* was born! Whew, that's a lot of chocolate. What set Hershey apart in the confectionary business was his use of fresh milk. It is what led him back to his childhood state to build a factory for the candy of the future. The milk was his secret ingredient. When you compare your life to a magical chocolate bar, what do you see as your secret ingredient which sets you apart? That's right; it is God. Having God in your life is the secret ingredient you need to really make a difference. Many times He uses that secret ingredient of love in ways we do not fully understand. Our natural instinct is to try to create the recipe on our own, without God. That is akin to trying to make milk chocolate without milk. In the promise of restoration for the Israelites, in Jeremiah 33:3, we find the reason why we need God, "Call to me and I will answer you and tell you great and unsearchable things you do not know." Are you calling out to God for the secret ingredient needed for the recipe in your life? My guess is that it always starts with love.

SEPTEMBER 14

Ring the Bell

Ephesians 6:18

On September 14, 1849, Ivan Pavlov was born in Ryazan, Russia. Dr. Pavlov was a Russian physiologist and introduced the world to something called conditioning or a conditioned response. Today we refer to his studies by his name because of his groundbreaking work in the late 1800s. This is known non-technically as "ring the bell and the dog slobbers!"

What's His story? Not to get too deep in the weeds, but conditioning or a conditioned response refers to a learning process by which a previously neutral stimulus, such as a bell, causes a reaction similar to a potent stimulus, such as food. In Pavlov's studies, a bell replaced food and made the dogs drool. How often as Christians do we come conditioned in almost the same way? Sometimes we make an immediate judgment about someone or something, or our conditioned response is not one of love or prayer. In Ephesians 6:18, the passage is wrapping up the description of the Armor of God. It instructs, "And pray in the Spirit on all occasions with all kinds of prayers and requests." How can we make this a habitual or conditioned response to every situation we encounter daily? It can be just a quick prayer. Whatever it might be, God wants us to be conditioned to react to all bells, whistles, and situations with prayer and love. Is prayer second nature to you? What would it take to become so, and what is your first step to making it your bell?

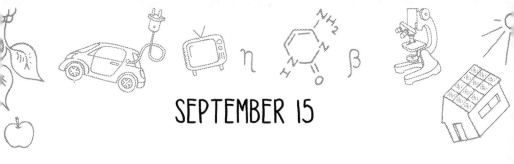

SEPTEMBER 15

Plague Three of Ten

Exodus 8:18-19

On September 15, 1946, The Brooklyn Dodgers beat the Chicago Cubs 2-0 in the second game of a double-header at Ebbetts Field. The game had to be called in the fifth inning due to swarming gnats! You may not know, but you won't be surprised when I inform you that Ebbetts Field was in New York City!

What's His story? It turns out that throughout the history of Major League Baseball, and as of this writing, two other games have been called due to gnats. One game was the White Sox against the Orioles in 1959, and the other game was the Blue Jays against the Brewers in 1990. This should remind us of the ten plagues inflicted on Egypt, as described in the book of Exodus. Gnats are the third of the ten plagues, and the first one in which the magicians or sorcerers under Pharaoh were unable to replicate. The significance is found in Exodus 8:19 when the magicians tried to tell Pharaoh that it must be the finger of God, yet Pharaoh's heart was hardened, and he was unrelenting. How often do we see the signs affecting someone we know? Do we try to counsel and restore gently as we are instructed in Galatians 6:1, yet they will not yield? I believe they are often referred to in the Bible as "stiff-necked!" Even the magicians saw that the gnats inflicted on them were of God. God tries to reach us and bring us back into a relationship with Him. Should it take a field of gnats to get your attention?

SEPTEMBER 16

Play-Doh for God

Jeremiah 18:4-6

On September 16, 1956, the toy known as Play-Doh was introduced. The clay-modeling compound had actually been around since the 1930s, but it was used then as a wallpaper cleaner. To me, it is like Legos in the way imagination drives unique creation. You can make almost anything with Play-Doh, but for me, balls of all shapes and snakes with different colored eyes tends to be the extent of my creativity.

What's His story? For both adults and kids, there is just something about the feel of the clay in your hands. It is one part stress relief and two parts "why does it smell this way?" Putting aside the fragrance, it always taps into our desire to make something out of nothing. It can be a challenge to create a masterpiece out of a lump of colored clay. God looks at us the same way, especially our hearts. At the potter's house in Jeremiah 18:4-6, we hear the Lord say, "Like clay in the hand of the potter, so are you in my hand, O house of Israel." Just like when we get our hands on a lump of Play-Doh, the Lord takes us and molds us in His likeness with a heart that yearns to glorify Him. We long to worship him, and just as Ephesians 2:10 says, we are His masterpiece. When you plop that lump of clay out of the carton, you think, "How can I create anything out of this blob?" There many days that we could ask God the same thing? Only God could make something so beautiful and full of love as you. Are you allowing Him to mold you into that masterpiece created by the Master Potter? God can shape you into a vessel for His love, no matter your defects!

SEPTEMBER 17

The Daffodil

Isaiah 58:8

On September 17, 1909, Scottish horticulturist Peter Barr died. He was known as the Daffodil King for his work studying and popularizing this bright and cheery spring flower. The daffodil is a typically yellow flower that pops up in late winter or early spring. Its happy yellow face is a harbinger that our short, cold, gray days will soon transition into sun and warmth.

What's His story? The daffodil is planted as a bulb in October or November, a few weeks before the first freeze. It gives the bulb a chance to settle into the ground and get established in preparation for a long cold winter. But, here is the neat thing about the daffodil. It requires that cold spell to trigger the flower to start developing. I was a horticulturist in college, but will not bore you with the details of this, but suffice to say that the cold is a necessary part of the process for this happy plant. It is sometimes like our lives in the way we must go through rough seasons or cold snaps to produce spiritual fruit or flowers. In Isaiah 58:8, the transformation of a daffodil bulb is described, "Then your light will break forth like the dawn, and healing will quickly appear; then righteousness will go before you." Just like the bulb, to break forth and flourish, we must store up God's word as energy, hiding it away in our hearts. As we use our Biblical Rolodex to locate it, we draw strength to heal and burst forth with joy and happiness that rivals the happy face of the daffodil. Do you see how the cold snaps in your life are preparing you? Are you storing up God's word for something big?

SEPTEMBER 18

Racing Horses

Jeremiah 12:5

On September 18, 1830, near Baltimore, Maryland, in a race between a locomotive and a horse, the horse won! It was not just a horse; it was a horse pulling a stagecoach! Today's trains are faster, but can you imagine what it must have been like to see the horse outrunning a train? It was probably much to the chagrin of one embarrassed engineer.

What's His story? No one would have ever thought a horse would outrun a train, but the message is more profound in Jeremiah 12:5, in which God is answering Jeremiah's complaint that the wicked always seem to prosper. Hear God's response as He uses the horse analogy for us to turn the perspective upside down, "If you have raced with men on foot and they have worn you out, how can you compete with horses?" We have all asked that question, haven't we? This is appropriate considering the event marking a horse outrunning a train. If we are worn out competing with people who are just like us, how can we expect to step into the big leagues of suffering and injustice? In the scripture, God is reminding Jeremiah that if he cannot handle the injustice he has already seen, then how can he handle what is to come. When you stop to think about it, if we got what we truly deserved for the sin in our own lives, we might contemplate rethinking our complaint! Are you busy trying to outrun God's wisdom today? How is God preparing you and your heart for what is to come? Sometimes it is not easy to see, but God helps give us vision by changing our perspective.

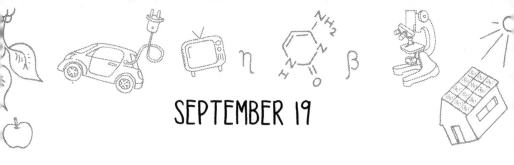

SEPTEMBER 19

Barred from The Happiest Place on Earth

Genesis 3:24

On September 19, 1959, Soviet leader Nikita Krushchev was barred from visiting Disneyland while he was on an extended tour of the United States. Yes, this is the same Krushchev we last saw in the testy Kitchen Debate with Richard Nixon. He had a very quick temper, so to deny him entry into Disneyland led to a bit of a childish spat. This was, of course, during the Cold War!

What's His story? Out of an abundance of caution, Krushchev was barred from visiting Disneyland with his wife because security could not guarantee his safety with all of the crowds. While Krushchev did not do anything wrong, when you look at this and see someone barred from "The Happiest Place on Earth," it harkens us back to Adam and Eve getting bounced out of Garden of Eden for eating the apple. I have heard that there is a church mural in the nursery or kid's section of a church somewhere in this country with very vivid imagery on its wall. Supposedly it refers to Genesis 3:24, and is a cherubim with the flaming sword flashing back and forth guarding the way back into the Garden of Eden. Yikes! When found on a wall in a nursery, it is not a very reassuring image to the youngsters, but this scene shows how serious disobedience to God is. And for us, as we read it in scripture, it should serve as a reminder to everyone that because Adam and Eve disobeyed God, they had to leave paradise. When we are in a deep relationship with God, through prayer and worship, we live in a place that is happier than the "Happiest Place on Earth." Our desire is to be back with him in paradise for all eternity. What lessons can we learn from someone getting barred from Disneyland that reminds us of why we had to leave the Garden? Because of Jesus, the pathway is lit, and He can lead us back.

SEPTEMBER 20

Time to Make the Donuts

Proverbs 13:4

On September 20, 2002, William Rosenberg died at age 86 in Mashpee, Massachusetts. Rosenberg was the founder of one of my favorite places, Dunkin Donuts! It started in Quincy, Massachusetts, as a place called the Open Kettle. Rosenberg wrote a memoir before his death, and it was titled "Time to Make the Donuts," and he explained how attitude was everything. He further described the difference between Positive Mental Attitude (PMA) and Negative Mental Attitude (NMA). This should be obvious, but Rosenberg gave us some valuable insights.

What's His story? The title of Rosenberg's book, and his PMA approach, are both crucial to our role as followers of Christ charged with spreading the good news of the Gospel. Time to Make the Donuts could be our mantra as well, just try not to think about the Daniel diet in the book of Daniel. The positive attitude emphasizes the impetus of not sitting around, expecting someone else to do it for us. God has equipped us with tools, talents, and abilities. Proverbs 13:4 spells out what we need to do with them when it says, "The sluggard craves and gets nothing, but the desires of the diligent are fully satisfied." Many times, we are the sluggards, wanting Heaven and happiness, but not willing to put in the effort and work that is required. However, we can become rich in spiritual inheritance, through studying God's word, prayer, and even Rosenberg's PMA. NMA will never help you make that transition, because you will be too busy focusing on the negative aspects of everything. Is it time for you to make the donuts? Will that require a change of career, a spiritual discipline, or something else that enables you to meet the *Missio Dei* that makes kingdom impact?

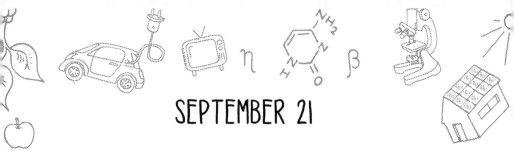

SEPTEMBER 21

Two Great Minds

Proverbs 27:17

On September 21, 1937, the book *The Hobbit* by J.R.R. Tolkien was published. It is a classic tale and often required reading in a high school literature class. Tolkien was an incredibly talented author, and the inspiration for this book came as he was grading student essay exams one morning.

What's His story? You may not know this, but Tolkien shared a close friendship with fellow author C.S. Lewis. That is incredible, right?? Through their friendship, Tolkien brought Lewis back to the Christian faith. It was Lewis that encouraged Tolkien to write his fantasy novels, which by the way, carried some overt Christian themes. Tolkien and Lewis challenged each other, pranked one another, and veritably enjoyed each other's company, while both focused on God's will for the world. They lived out Proverbs 27:17, which says, "As iron sharpens iron, so one man sharpens another." One can only imagine the conversations these two had as they walked the grounds of the University of Oxford in England. We can also learn from this friendship that had incredible emotional depth. We have an opportunity to build each other up, sharpening one another in preparation for the ensuing battle that will inevitably take place. While we may not have the same level of intellectually stimulating conversations as these two, we can create a meeting of the minds that spreads the kingdom in a new and meaningful way. Who are you sharpening today?

SEPTEMBER 22

Wicker Baskets of Faith

Exodus 2:3

On September 22, 2003, David Hempleman-Adams became the first person to cross the Atlantic Ocean in an open wicker basket balloon. The journey was from New Brunswick, Canada, to Blackpool, England. To call him an adventurer is an understatement.

What's His story? Let's go to the book of Exodus 1 and 2:1-10, where we find the story of Moses as a baby left in a wicker basket among the reeds and bulrushes of the Nile River in Egypt. Moses' mother, Jochebed, put him in a basket and placed it in the river to protect him from Pharaoh, who had decreed that Hebrew boys be drowned at birth. His crying alerted one of Pharaoh's daughters, and she decided to adopt him as her child and, through God's grace, used Jochebed as his nurse. You could say this was just the beginning of the adventure for Moses. To call him an adventurer would also be an understatement! Do you see the underlying theme between the two stories? Both Hempleman-Adams and Jochebed believed and had faith, but they also trusted and put their faith into action! Both are great examples of pure trust placed into a simple wicker basket. Will you take that first step to put your faith into action? What is your adventure, and how will you trust God along the way?

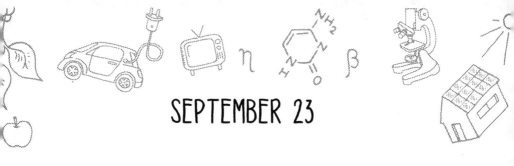

SEPTEMBER 23

Trusting a Bucking Bronco

Psalm 28:7

On September 23, 1897, the first Frontier Days Rodeo took place in Cheyenne, Wyoming. If you have never been to Cheyenne during Frontier Days, I highly recommend it! This is one of the most popular rodeo events in the United States, if not the world. There is something about Wyoming and a rodeo.

What's His story? While there are mixed opinions about rodeos and the interaction between man and animal, one thing remains certain. There is a distinct connection between horse and man, especially at the rodeo. As a prey animal, the horse inherently lacks trust until a bond is established between its owner, trainer, or rider. It is incredible to observe the transformation. Even better is the change from unbridled mustang to obedient horses through human horsemanship. This is what is required to perform the barrel racing or roping competitions you might see at rodeos. This requires trust in both ways. A horse must trust rider, and a rider must trust a horse. It is also how we must trust Jesus. Psalm 28:7 reminds us of the wonder and joy that awaits our hearts when we believe. It says, "The Lord is my strength and my shield; my heart trusts in him, and I am helped. My heart leaps for joy and I will give thanks to him in song." My heart leaps like a bucking bronco when I trust in God. Why do we find this so difficult to do? What can horses teach us about God? There is more than you might think. Today, what is stopping you from hopping back on the horse to trust God and feel your heart leap for joy?

SEPTEMBER 24

Dodging Dodgers

1 Samuel 19

On September 24, 1957, the last baseball game was played at Ebbets Field in Brooklyn, New York, where the Brooklyn Dodgers beat the Pittsburgh Pirates. The Dodgers then moved to Los Angeles, California, and became the Los Angeles Dodgers.

What's His story? Usually, team mascot names are self-explanatory. There are many birds like Cardinals, Orioles, and Jays (all mean birds, by the way...), but the Dodgers were initially called the Brooklyn Trolley Dodgers. We can all agree that the team mascot name was better than the minor league Montgomery Biscuits or Rocket City Trash Pandas! They were the Trolley Dodgers because that was what New Yorkers had to do as they got used to the transition from the slower horse-drawn carriages. Trolleys were much faster and required Frogger-like skills to navigate the busy streets, ducking and dodging. The story of David ducking and avoiding Saul in the desert is similar. We find this story in 1 Samuel 19, and it is an incredible tale of ducking and dodging, near misses, and Spirit intervention. At its culmination, we have David in prime position to eliminate his threat, but he abides by the honor due to a king, even one who would rather have him dead due to his jealousy. This story in the Bible is an intriguing one, and we can probably relate. How often do you feel like your troubles are pursuing you? Do you feel like you are just one step ahead like David was? Do you realize, like David did, that the reason you are a step ahead is that God goes before us? It might seem like a stretch to tie a baseball team name like the Dodgers to this story, but think for a minute about how we try to dodge things for what we believe to be our own safety. What if we truly trusted? Then, how much dodging would we need to do?

SEPTEMBER 25

Come On Get Happy

Acts 16:25

On September 25, 1970, the television show *The Partridge Family* debuted on ABC. This was a show about a fictional family in which the widow and her five children form a musical band. They get signed to a record deal, and the show follows how their lives change.

What's His story? It was a fantastic show. Even though I live amid a musical family, I cannot sing or dance, but I love the theme song for *The Partridge Family* show. It is titled "C'mon, Get Happy." You will hear it once, and it will get stuck in your head all day. The lyrics start out, "Hello world, here's a song we're singing, C'mon get happy." You are probably humming along right now as you read the verse. Psalm is an outstanding source of singing scripture, but let's look at Acts 16:25. Paul and Silas are in prison, but are they downtrodden? No! They are awake at midnight, praying and singing hymns. The crucial part of the verse is this, "and the other prisoners were listening to them." Music is contagious, and when we are singing praise to God in the midst of pain and suffering, other people take notice. They want the happiness and joy that only comes from knowing and praising our Lord. We actually sing our way to freedom, and others join us for the ride. In other words, we sing the same song as the Partridge Family. Come on and get happy, because we are singing in joy. Who hears you singing today? Is it possible to sing with a smile? Absolutely, I believe it is.

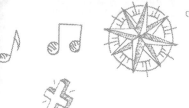

SEPTEMBER 26

The Showdown

1 Kings 18:38

On September 26, 1957, the musical *West Side Story* opened on Broadway. This play was inspired by William Shakespeare's play *Romeo and Juliet* and became a modernized version set in the Upper West Side neighborhood in New York City during the 1950s.

What's His story? The *West Side Story* plot involves two rival gangs, the Sharks and the Jets. There are plenty of showdown scenes between the two, which reminds me of another rather big showdown in the Bible. In 1 Kings 18:16, it starts with Obadiah picking a fight with Elijah. How could Elijah turn it down when he begins like this, "Is that you, you troubler of Israel?" Wow. We then progress through chapter 18 further until Elijah challenges the prophets of Baal to reveal the real power of God. This is where Elijah builds the altar of wood inside the twelve stones and then has them pour water over it again and again. After Elijah prays and calls out of God, the fire of the Lord consumed everything, doing what the prophets of Baal could not do, even though they ranted and raved all afternoon. God answered Elijah's prayer, and although His answer to our prayer may not be as dramatic, it demonstrates the faith we can have in a God who will provide everything we need to continue on the path. Like the Sharks and Jets, Elijah and the prophets of Baal were locked in a showdown, but the one true God revealed Himself to the one who had faith. Wouldn't it have been great to witness this showdown in 1 Kings? Are you bringing God to your confrontations? Why not?

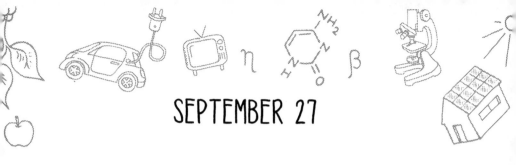

SEPTEMBER 27

Burning Flame Within

2 Timothy 1:6

On September 27, 1892, the company called Diamond Match patented the matchbook. The matchbook is a small foldable item that has paper matches on the inside, which could be torn away one by one and struck against a strip of rough paper on the side to light the match. It is easier to just use a "clicker" lighter than to explain a matchbook. Either way, the point is to create fire.

What's His story? In 2 Timothy 1:6, it says, "For this reason, I remind you to fan into flame the gift of God, which is in you." As spiritually young individuals, we have a spark within us that is of the Holy Spirit. As with a campfire, you start with a spark and feed the small flame with oxygen, turning it into a burning hot fire that provides warmth and utility. We are the same. There are so many ways we can fan our own flame within such as prayer, songs of praise, acts of servitude, or calling on the Lord. Or are we fanning the flame of others? Words of encouragement and prayer are ways in which we support others. Our human spirit has been ignited with the Holy Spirit to burn hotly for God. You want to burn so hotly that the marshmallows are toasted as you walk by them in the candy aisle of the store. What are you doing today to fan the flame of the Spirit within so that it burns intensely for God's kingdom?

SEPTEMBER 28

Love Apples

Luke 12:23

On September 28, 1820, a man named Robert Johnson ate an entire bushel of tomatoes just to prove that they were safe to eat. This took place on the steps of the Salem County Courthouse in New Jersey. Back then, the prevailing thought was that the "love apples" were pretty to look at, but had to be poisonous. Johnson was an agriculturist and was willing to risk it all to show how tomatoes could improve the local economy.

What's His story? When we think about what must have been going through the spectator's minds and their looks of horror, we can go to Jesus' warning about worry in Luke 12:23 when He says, "Life is more than food, and the body more than clothes." He gives some of the best instruction on worry in the Bible when Jesus says, "Who of you by worrying can add a single hour to his life?" No, you cannot make the Daylights Saving Time argument. Think for a moment about Johnson and his belly-ache-inducing bushel of tomatoes. He knew there was more to life than food, and he knew that he could prove that worry over a love apple was misplaced. He saw the bigger picture. Johnson overcame the anxiety paralysis of the time to meet the more significant needs. Jesus did the same in this verse, and He continues to do so today. All we need to do is call on Him. He reassures us that we are worth more than ravens. Ravens, by the way, are brilliant birds! Jesus also reminds us that worry will lead nowhere. A bushel of tomatoes helped Johnson demonstrate what you can do when you suppress fear. You do not need to do this by eating a bushel of strange vegetables, do you? Or will the words of Jesus be all the assurance you need?

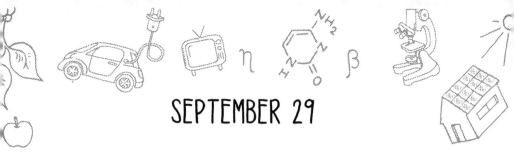

SEPTEMBER 29

The Chief Cornerstone

Ephesians 2:19-22

On September 29, 1907, the cornerstone was placed for the National Cathedral in Washington, DC. President Teddy Roosevelt gave a ceremonial speech, but the cathedral was not completed until 1990. The stone itself came from a field near Bethlehem (Pennsylvania, not Israel!) and was set into a larger piece of American granite. The inscription on the stone read, "The Word was made flesh, and dwelt among us." (John 1:14).

What's His story? Besides the inscribed scripture, think about the cornerstone and consider the building not being completed until eighty-three years after the cornerstone was placed. Look at Ephesians 2:19-22. In it, you will find the reference to Jesus as the chief cornerstone. "And in him, the whole building is joined together and rises to become a holy temple in the Lord." We know that Jesus must be the cornerstone of our own lives for real transformation to take place. We also know that by His instruction, we join together, support each other, love one another, and create the body of Christ, the church! He is our foundation, and with Him as our cornerstone, we can build a beautiful and magnificent temple that glorifies God! As for the length of time it took to complete the building of the National Cathedral? Think of the human journey. Our fear and hesitation can sometimes prevent us from realizing that we must have a cornerstone of Christ. Our transformation from vision to first step, then to completion as a child of God who genuinely trusts God, can sometimes take a long, long time. Place the cornerstone of Jesus in your life, create that holy temple in the Lord, and invite people to experience the wonder of Christ in your life!

SEPTEMBER 30

MacGyver Lives

1 Peter 2:10-11

On September 30, 1985, the television series *MacGyver* debuted on ABC. Do you remember this show? This was a television series that had virtually the same plot each week. It revolved around the main character, named MacGyver, getting himself or others into a sticky, harrowing situation, and it always involved some type of explosive device. Cue the paper clip, banana peel, and chewing gum, and all of a sudden, MacGyver has created a contraption that could fly a man into space and freed everyone from harm mere seconds from disaster.

What's His story? Now, do you remember the show? I have known friends who could create something out of nothing like MacGyver did on the show. Naturally, they earned the nickname, "MacGyver." Some readily accepted. The point is that the character on the show could always create something out of nothing, or an ordinary article, which represented no perceived value. 1 Peter 2:10-11 is an outstanding example of how God "MacGyvers" us into something of extraordinary value! "Once you were not a people, but now you are the people of God, once you had not received mercy, but now you have received mercy." The work God is creating in you is a tremendously more significant transformation. It is a transformation for the good of His kingdom. This selection of scripture assigns our value to God, not our accomplishments. The mercy we receive from God is worth more than our value and possessions. Are you busy trying to MacGyver your life, or are you willing to accept the value your Lord assigns to you? We are a part of the royal priesthood of God!

OCTOBER 1

The True Magnificent

Daniel 5:8

On October 1, 1962, the late-night talk show *The Tonight Show* with Johnny Carson premiered. I remember watching this show as a kid, and although there are new late-night talk hosts who are clever and entertaining, Carson was one of the best. His antics, facial expressions, and sidekick Ed McMahon made it so enjoyable.

What's His story? Carson had multiple characters he played from time to time. One of them was a character called Carnac the Magnificent. Carnac was a "mystic from the East" who knew the answers to the questions that were in envelopes that he would hold to his forehead. Carnac would provide the answer like, "Rose Bowl" and then open the envelope to reveal the question, which in this case was, "What do you say when it's Rose's turn at the bowling alley." Often we are like Carnac, and we think we know the answers before even hearing the question. Or, you have heard that phrase "the writing is on the wall." In the Bible, Daniel 5 tells the story of Daniel interpreting the writing. Unlike Carnac, Daniel is equipped and enabled by the Most High to reveal what is right and what is just. Sure, we would love to have someone give us the answers before we hear the question or interpret the writing on the wall, but in truth, if we have a relationship with the Holy Spirit, we have it all. It is the listening part of finding the answer that snags us in a web of confusion, fear, and control. When we finally come back to the place where faith and a belief in the sovereignty of our Lord reigns, the answers practically write themselves on the wall. Are you jumping ahead like Carnac without considering the one true Magnificent's answers?

OCTOBER 2

The Reason for the Season, According to Linus

Luke 2: 8-14

On October 2, 1950, the *Peanuts* cartoon by Charles Schulz debuted in the comic section of newspapers around the country. This is the cartoon with woe-is-me Charlie Brown, Linus, Lucy, Snoopy, and the whole cast of characters, including Woodstock, the little yellow bird that flies upside down. It is a favorite cartoon of many, simply because of the genuine and heartfelt nature, Schulz presented in the strips…and Snoopy!

What's His story? If you pay close attention to some of the themes in the *Peanuts* cartoons, you will find a good bit of Christian theology sprinkled throughout them. One deliberate example was in a made-for-television special based on the comic strip called *A Charlie Brown Christmas*. In it, Charlie Brown finds himself unsurprisingly depressed during the most wonderful time of the year. Lucy suggests he direct the Christmas pageant, and that materializes as poorly as you would expect. But when Linus explains the true meaning of Christmas to him, he finally gets it. You have probably already seen Christmas decorations up in your local store or neighborhood. While they are pretty and put everyone in a good mood, it is still not the true meaning of Christmas. Instead, Linus pulls it straight from the Bible! Charlie Brown asks if anyone knows the true meaning of Christmas. Linus quickly indicates that he does. He then asks for the stagehands to cue the lighting as he recites Luke 2:8-14. Linus tells the story of the angels visiting the shepherds and announcing the most glorious news in the history of the world. If Schulz can deliver this message through kids in a cartoon strip, we can discover the true meaning of the season for ourselves, right? As the Christmas season approaches, how will you prepare your heart to accept the gift, the true gift of the season?

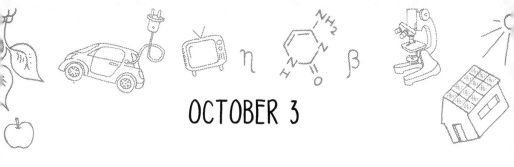

OCTOBER 3

Thanksgiving and Praise

1 Timothy 4:4

On October 3, 1863, amid the Civil War in the United States, President Abraham Lincoln proclaimed the last Thursday of November officially as Football Thursday…I mean Thanksgiving. In 1789, George Washington had declared a day of giving thanks. Yet, Lincoln put it on the books to consolidate all of the various Thanksgiving celebrations in different regions of the country.

What's His story? Lincoln's proclamation did not just call it a day of thanksgiving. It was officially called "a day of Thanksgiving and Praise." Throughout the proclamation itself, which I would encourage you to find and read, Lincoln acknowledges the blessings and gifts poured out on the country. Again, keep in mind this is during the very contentious Civil War! In fact, Lincoln asks for people to fervently implore the Almighty to heal the land as only He can. For Lincoln to focus on giving thanks in all things at all times reminds us of 1 Thessalonians 5:18. This theme is also especially apparent in 1 Timothy 4:4, where the acknowledgment can be found that "everything God created is good, and nothing is to be rejected if it is received with thanksgiving, because it is consecrated by the word of God and prayer." There it is – thanksgiving and praise! Even during one of the most lamentable times in our nation's history, we are reminded at least once a year to pause in remembrance of all the good that God created and to praise Him for it. Why can't it be every day? You do not have to have turkey and all the sides every day, but you do need to greet each day in thanksgiving and praise. That is a proclamation found everywhere in the Bible!

OCTOBER 4

A Stormy Masterpiece

Mark 4:35-41

On October 4, 1669, the talented Dutch artist Rembrandt Harmenszoon van Rijn died in Amsterdam, Netherlands. I believe he shortened his name to just Rembrandt because it would have taken up a large portion of the canvas to sign his entire name. Rembrandt was famous for his use of light in his pieces to portray emotion and action. A painting called *The Night Watch* is one of his most famous, but he produced many works during the Dutch Golden Age.

What's His story? Rembrandt realized he had been given a gift by God and put it to use. There are several of his paintings to choose from, but I believe one of his paintings, in particular, resonates biblically. *The Storm on the Sea of Galilee*, which he painted in 1633, is an incredible piece. Although you did not come here for an art lesson, I urge you to find a copy of this online to admire it. The original was stolen in 1990 and has not been recovered. An empty frame hangs in the museum awaiting its return. In the painting, your eye will be drawn to an area full of light and action, a section of shadows, and then finally to an area of peace where Jesus is sitting in the boat. His face is the preeminent calm in the storm. The painting captures the story from the Gospel of Mark 4:35-41. While the scripture covers seven verses, Rembrandt was deft enough to capture its emotion on just one canvas. Scripture tells us that problems will always be a part of our lives, but Jesus is the one who can calm the wind and the waves. With Him in our heart, we can pray, trust, and turn into the oncoming wind knowing that only He can right our ship. Are you trapped in a storm? Have you called on Jesus to calm the waves as only He can do?

OCTOBER 5

Unlimited Spirit

John 3:34

On October 5, 1947, United States President Harry S. Truman delivered the first presidential address televised from the White House. Truman gave the address asking Americans to sacrifice for the good of the Europeans, who were reeling from the effects of World War II. He asked people to avoid eating meat on Tuesdays and eggs and poultry on Thursdays. He also urged Americans to eat one less slice of bread daily. He was an early low-carb diet advocate. These limits were implied so that the supply around the world would stabilize, and order would be restored.

What's His story? In John 3:34, it says, "For the one whom God has sent speaks the words of God, for God gives the Spirit without limit." God's Spirit was upon Jesus without limit, which for us was what we needed then, and today. In the Old Testament, people were given the Spirit for a limited time, but not Jesus! Jesus has the Spirit of God without limit. This permanent presence and the fact that Jesus came from Heaven is proof that He is, in fact, God incarnate. So while Truman was asking Americans to sacrifice for the greater good, which is what we should do, we should also not forget that our supply comes from the one who has the Spirit without limit! Are you operating today from a position of scarcity or abundance? Which do you think Jesus would prefer for you?

OCTOBER 6

Hobby Lobby

1 Corinthians 12:4

On October 6, 1937, the radio show *Hobby Lobby*, not the craft store, started with Dave Elman as its host. The show was based on people who wrote to Dave "lobbying" for their hobby to be picked. If Dave selected them, they would join his show, and he would help describe their hobby and talent to the radio listeners. One lady trained kangaroos to box, but my favorite was a gentleman who put hot coals in his mouth and cooked bacon on his face.

What's His story? In 1 Corinthians 12:4, it notes there are different kinds of gifts, but the same Spirit distributes all of them. Later, in 1 Corinthians 12:12-27, just as a body, though one, has many parts, but all its many parts form one body, so it goes with Christ. Yes, each person on the *Hobby Lobby* radio show had all kinds of different gifts and talents, but the same Spirit distributes them. Christ unites us, even with the bacon guy, through our formation in Him. Our uniqueness is one of the beauties of His creation, and it undoubtedly contributed to the popularity of this radio show! Just as there are different kinds of work and service, in all of them we find God. As our physical body is made up of many different and interesting parts, so is the body of Christ! *Hobby Lobby* was a great illustration of just how diverse this body is. Do you know which part you are?

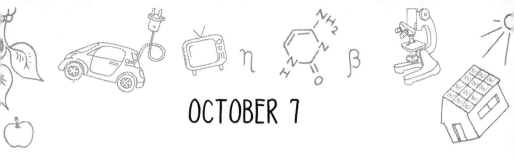

OCTOBER 7

The Perfect Team Win

1 John 4:4

On October 7, 1916, the Georgia Tech Yellow Jacket football team coached by John Heisman (yes, that John Heisman!) defeated Cumberland College 222-0! The statistics for the game are astounding, especially the fact that Georgia Tech scored at least forty-two points each quarter. Cumberland had a patchwork team because they had ended their football program, but Heisman would not let them out of their obligation to play.

What's His story? This comparison could quickly go down the road to David and Goliath, but that would be too obvious. Instead, let's dig deeper into the power of the triune God! If you were to put a team together with the only three positions, who would you pick? The Father, Son, and Holy Spirit are all you need against any trouble, any doubt, any demon, or any fear. The score would still be a shut-out! 1 John 4:4 tells us, "The one who is in you is greater than the one who is in the world." When we truly know this and let it soak into our soul, the realization that the power to overcome comes through us because of God. His power allows us to overcome the things of this world that inhibit our ability to step into the path that He has lit before us. It is daunting sometimes, like facing a team against whom you have no chance. We have to show up for the game each and every day. The good news is that we do not need a coach the caliber of Heisman to win, because we have the Father, Son, and the Holy Spirit on our team. Do you sometimes feel like Cumberland College? Hop over to the other side and enjoy the game.

OCTOBER 8

Perfection

Matthew 5:48

On October 8, 1956, sticking with the sports theme, pitcher Don Larsen of the Yankees threw a perfect game against the Brooklyn Dodgers in Game Five of the 1956 World Series at Yankee Stadium. As of this writing, it remains the only perfect game in World Series history.

What's His story? A perfect game is sometimes confused with a no-hitter. A pitcher can pitch a no-hitter, which means no player from the opposing team got a hit, however, they could have reached a base via a walk, error, or a hit by pitch. A perfect game means the pitcher faced twenty-seven batters during the 9 innings, and no one reached first base. It is the ultimate in a clean scoring sheet with no hits, no walks, no errors, no nothing except perfection. That is the baseball world. In our society, Jesus remains our perfection. He is without sin, without blemish, and a perfect sacrifice for our sins. Jesus is no comparison to a perfect game because He is much more than we can comprehend. In Matthew 5:48, Jesus actually calls us to, "Be perfect, therefore, as your heavenly Father is perfect." That sounds like an unachievable task because, after all, only Jesus was perfect. However, there are ways in which we can move towards His desired perfection for us. It is only through character, spiritual maturity, and love that we can think of approaching this lofty, yet necessary, watermark. Christ calls us to excel, outperform what the world expects, and always move towards that one day where we will rest in perfection with Christ. Larsen accomplished perfection under the incredible pressure of the World Series. How can you strive to live in Christian perfection? It is not easy, and we will continue to mistakes along the way, but the scripture tells us to try! What is stopping you today?

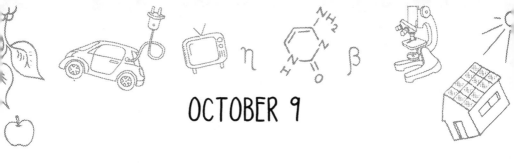

OCTOBER 9

The Unclean

Mark 1:40-45

On October 9, 1953, Lebanese American actor Tony Shaloub was born in Green Bay, Wisconsin. Shaloub has been in many movies like *Cars* and *Men in Black*. He has also acted in television sitcoms such as *Wings*, but his most famous role may be that in the show *Monk*, which ran from 2002 to 2009.

What's His story? Shaloub's character on Monk was Adrian Monk. Sounds benign and unrelated, but Adrian Monk had an obsessive-compulsive disorder, which made him afraid of 312 things. Yes, very specific. He was primarily fearful of germs and dirt. As a firm believer in hand sanitizer and no-touch greetings, he already knew what to do in a pandemic. We know this is far from who Jesus was. How many times do we act like Adrian Monk when we see someone in need? Whether it is on a street corner somewhere, or in our own neighborhood, do we sometimes act like we will be afflicted if we stop to help? Jesus sets the example for us. Instead of running from the lepers, He met them where they were and offered healing and wholeness. The unclean were His mission field. The Gospel of Mark 1:40-45 marks a turning point. When the man with leprosy approaches Jesus and asks to be made clean, Jesus responds willingly, and the man proceeds to spread the news. As a result, Jesus could no longer enter a town openly, but the people still came to Him. Jesus knew that the value of a person is inside and not by appearance. By healing this man, many came to know Jesus' power. He always welcomed the outwardly and inwardly unclean, along with the diseased who desired healing. Jesus would never use anti-bacterial wipes or gel the same way as Adrian Monk, because His compassion and power are like nothing the world had seen. Are you a germ-a-phobe? What would have happened if Jesus had been one? We do not have to physically touch to actually touch someone's heart!

OCTOBER 10

Joined Out of Love

Mark 15:38

On October 10, 1913, United States President Woodrow Wilson remotely pushed a button to blow up the Gamboa Dam in Panama at the site that would become the Panama Canal. This allowed waters from the Atlantic and Pacific Oceans to meet for the first time. The Panama Canal would enable ships to bypass navigating all the way around the bottom of South America through the dangerous Drake Passage and Strait of Magellan.

What's His story? I thought the guys in the hard-hats that implode dilapidated old buildings and stadiums had a cool job when they hit the button, but can you imagine pressing a button and joining two massive oceans? That is power! But, it is nothing like the power of tearing the veil in two that we find in Mark 15:38. It says, "The curtain of the temple was torn in two from top to bottom." The separation of humanity from God because of our sins was immediately removed through Jesus' sacrifice on the cross. Jesus opened the way for us to approach God. With the push of a button, Woodrow Wilson linked two massive bodies of water together, and it was good for mankind. What Jesus did on the cross was infinitesimally better! As Hebrews 9:15 points out, "Christ is the mediator of a new covenant." Christ's sacrifice allows us to communicate more directly with God, just as the Panama Canal allowed ships to navigate similarly, avoiding danger and peril. Direct communication with God can do the same thing for us today! Are you allowing Jesus to push the button in your life to detonate the obstacle blocking your relationship with God?

OCTOBER 11

Like a Polaroid Picture

Mark 2:22

On October 11, 2011, The Polaroid Company filed for bankruptcy. To that date, it was one of the largest companies to fail. The downfall stemmed from not keeping up with technological advances. More people were using digital cameras, or their phone cameras, but not film cameras. Though there is still a nostalgic appeal to the Polaroid, it could not keep pace with the newer technology. As the saying goes, "windshields are larger than rearview mirrors!"

What's His story? Unless we are actively in God's word each day, we often find ourselves going the way of The Polaroid Company. While it may not be technology that passes us by, cultural and social influence cannot be ignored. God's word does not change, nor does it need to, which should give reassurance to us that as we abide in His word, we will never be antiquated or outdated. Think about the wineskins Jesus talks about in Mark 2:22 when He says, "And no one pours new wine into old wineskins...No, he pours new wine into new wineskins." Old wineskins cannot expand and stretch to accommodate the process of making new wine. Therefore, what He is pointing out here is that our hearts can be like the old wineskins, becoming rigid and unable to accept the newness in life that Christ offers us. If we keep ourselves fresh and new, and open to what Christ is revealing daily, then we are able to accept new wine, allowing it to mature and improve over time. The old wineskins were the Pharisees, whose rigidity around rules made them unable to accept Jesus. Picture them (pun intended) in a faded Polaroid group picture. You have those who have taken the newness of Christ, staying fresh in the word as it reveals His will. Are you stuck in the past, unable to move forward, or are you moving ahead as a fresh, new creation in Christ?

OCTOBER 12

Scottish Raincoats

Isaiah 54:17

On October 12, 1823, Scottish chemist and inventor Charles Macintosh began selling his raincoat. Macintosh developed the waterproof fabric. The Mackintosh (for some reason, they changed the spelling) raincoat is named for him. Some inventions are neat, and some are wacky. This one is just plain awesome and useful. I am still amazed at how waterproof fabric works, especially if it is slightly breathable.

What's His story? In Macintosh's eyes, the purpose of a raincoat was to keep water out and to protect the wearer from the elements. In Scotland, I am sure he was able to conduct a plentiful field study! What else is meant for protection? It is certainly God's word. You may think there is no way words can provide the same level of tangible protection a raincoat could, but it is true. We get a real sense of this as we look at Isaiah 54:17, "no weapon forged against you will prevail, and you will refute every tongue that accuses you." The Lord's protection is greater than that of any thick Mackintosh raincoat. This scripture gives vivid imagery of arrows just bouncing off like raindrops rolling off a raincoat, falling to the ground. The Lord encamps around us and protects us as we trust in him and obey. Today, are you wearing a permeable coat, or have you put on the protecting gear of our Lord? He has already created the color or pattern to match your wardrobe, so do not worry.

OCTOBER 13

The 33

Daniel 3:25

On October 13, 2010, the last of the thirty-three rescued miners, referred to as "Los 33," emerged out of the collapsed mine in Copiapo, Chile. They had been trapped since August 5th, for a total of sixty-nine days!! They were trapped 2,300 feet below the ground and three miles from the mine entrance. After the initial collapse, it was not immediately known that they were alive, but once it was revealed, the people of Chile, and many from around the world, mounted a monumental effort to save them.

What's His story? This is an exceptional example of maintaining a steadfast and unwavering faith in the face of dire circumstances. It illustrates how we can also make our faith work. Think of all of the families who were praying all across the globe. After receiving so much media attention, some of you may even recall praying for Los 33. The miners spent their days in prayer and even set up a makeshift chapel in their confined space. As they were brought up to the surface, each wore a shirt that said, "Thank You Lord!", along with Psalm 95:4, "In His hands are the depths of the earth; the heights of the mountains are His also." So half a mile below the ground in a dangerous, cramped space with limited air, their focus was prayer. When asked about his experience, one of the miners said that there were actually thirty-four of them, because as he put it, "God never left us down there." It sounds a lot like the parallel stories in the book of Daniel with the inferno and lion's den. Read Daniel 3:25 and Daniel 6:21 if you are playing along at home. We could all learn from Los 33, and today is a good reminder of how to maintain faith in unfathomable situations. Have you ever seen the power of prayer in action?

OCTOBER 14

The 100-Acre Wood Around Us

Hebrews 10:24-25

On October 14, 1926, English author A. A. Milne published the book *Winnie-the-Pooh*. It is a tale about a boy named Christopher Robin and his adventures in the Hundred Acre Wood with his stuffed animals Pooh, Piglet, Eeyore, Kanga, Roo, Owl, and Rabbit who come to life to join him. Before this book, Milne was a very accomplished playwright and poet, but the success of *Winnie-the-Pooh* overshadowed those works!

What's His story? This was one of my childhood favorites. I must admit that I did not watch the movie because the book seemed much more authentic. What about you? I did realize that as a Christian community, we are a lot like the makeup of the characters in this book. Milne probably did not intend this, but Christopher Robin could be viewed as the image-bearer of Christ, bringing a message of hope and love to the Hundred Acre Wood. In contrast, Eeyore, through all of his grumbling, complaining, and woe-is-me, does occasionally find appreciation in small things. Many of us, in joyful enthusiasm that comes from knowing Christ can be so much like Tigger! We all have a Tigger in our lives, right? Do we sometimes turn into Eeyore because of them?! Then there is Piglet, a faithful and trusted friend at our side. Even Rabbit, through his standoffishness, eventually embraces the intrinsic value of those that are different from him, like Kanga and Roo. Just as Hebrews 10:24-25 encourages us, as a community, whether in The Hundred Acre Wood or your own neighborhood, we must build each other up, spurring one another on in love and encouragement! Look around you today. Do you see a community in need of the good news of the Gospel? Of course, you do! Tiggers engage! Eeyores, y'all feel free to sleep in a bit longer.

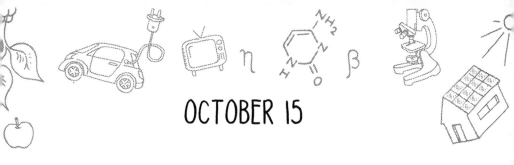

OCTOBER 15

Fishing for Followers

Luke 5:1-11

On October 15, 1881, American Angler, the first fishing magazine in the United States, was published in Philadelphia, Pennsylvania. Of course, this happened on a Saturday. The magazine only cost ten cents!

What's His story? While the early issues did not have many pictures, it was full of useful articles for those who loved fishing. Fishing was, and is, woven into the fabric of this country for men and women, old and young. Some of you out there (I hope I am not the only one) will drive by a lake, pond, or seashore, and your mind immediately goes to what kind of fish would be in there, what lures or flies to use, etc. I believe that was Jesus' thought as He walked along the Sea of Galilee in Luke 5:1-11 and gave Simon some advice regarding proper net placement. When the haul of fish nearly broke the nets, Simon immediately fell to his knees in unworthy confession. You see, Jesus saw the opportunity. It is exactly like any angler looking out across a body of water or a stream. He sees opportunity. Simon, later known as Peter, knew about Jesus' power, and seeing this miracle in his daily life as a fisherman was enough for him to drop everything and follow Jesus. As Jesus said, "Don't be afraid; from now on you will catch men," meaning as a disciple, Peter would be leaving his past behind to help grow Jesus' ministry. The best fishing advice is captured two-fold in the Bible, and it should be enough for us to want to set our own hooks for the Gospel to spread and multiply in others. Today, are you fishing, or is your gear packed away? What kind of tackle or fly should you use? Ask the Holy Spirit for the answer, and you might be surprised at the angling advice you receive!

OCTOBER 16

More Than a Book of Words

John 1:1

On October 16, 1758, Noah Webster was born in West Hartford, Connecticut. Would you recognize Webster if I tell you he was a lexicographer? I had to look it up too...in a dictionary.... now, you are with me! Webster is the dictionary guy. He is best known for his *American Spelling Book* (1783) and *American Dictionary of the English Language* (1828).

What's His story? Webster helped to instill and give American English its own dignity and vitality to distinguish itself from British English. When you consider the timeframes around which his works were published, that makes perfect sense. It is natural to look to the dictionary as an authoritative source for all things spelling and definition-related. We should look to the Bible in the same way. After all, the Bible can be described in four ways: a library collection of 66 books about the story of God, sacred scripture, God speaking to us about salvation through the writers and the words therein, and a guide to faith and life allowing us to apply principles in our daily lives for the sake of His kingdom. That is one long sentence, but all four are vitally important descriptions of the Bible. It forms so many parts of our worship lives, yet there is rampant biblical illiteracy. The only way to change that is to open this transformational book and let the scripture come alive. Yes, it sounds strange, but this is how we can hear God. We can do this by deliberately reading, thinking, praying, and living. Those spiritual disciplines do not happen overnight, but just as the dictionary is an integral building block to language, the Bible should be a cornerstone of our lives. Open it, and be amazed! After all, John 1:1 tells us everything we need to know about why the Word is important.

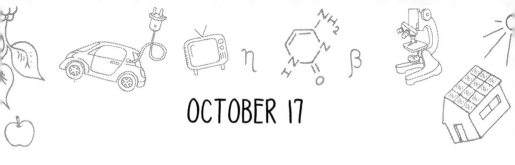

OCTOBER 17

Cracking the Christianity Code

Matthew 22:37-40

On October 17, 1917, during World War I, the American Code Talkers began their essential work. The Code Talkers were members of the Choctaw Indian tribe and were enlisted to develop a communication method and code that could not be deciphered by the opposing forces. It gave the Allies the element of surprise and turned the tide in several battles. The Code Talkers played an even more prominent role in World War II.

What's His story? These Native American heroes put aside differences and injustices to fight for their country and ended up aiding in a way no one expected. The story about how the use of the Code Talkers developed is fascinating. In many ways, Christians and non-Christians sometimes look at Christianity as a complex set of rules and laws, and they begin to look for their own double-super-secret decoder ring. When that does not work, frustration or rebellion sets in, and all momentum ceases. In Matthew 22:34-40, Jesus simplifies it for us. The Pharisee was trying to trick Him by asking, which is the greatest commandment. In other words, Jesus, can you decipher this complex code of rules and laws and tell us which one is most important? Jesus' answer cracks the code for us, "Love the Lord your God with all your heart and with all your soul and all your mind. This is the first and greatest commandment. The second is like it: Love your neighbor as yourself." Everything hangs on these two commandments. Are you making things more complicated than it needs to be?

OCTOBER 18

The Last Frontier

Psalm 36:9

On October 18, 1867, the United States took possession of the territory of Alaska from Russia. Their loss, our gain! It is a rugged land full of natural beauty and wildlife. As far north as Alaska is, it experiences some rather interesting periods of lightness and darkness. You could call Alaska the Psalm state instead of The Last Frontier, which comes from the untamed wilderness throughout the state. You had to reread that to make sure it didn't say palm, right?

What's His story? While the winter days in Alaska are extremely short, the summer days are long, and the sun does not even set. On average, Alaska receives ten to seventeen more minutes of daylight per day than the rest of the United States. That can be your factoid to impress friends. Here is where we see that Alaska really is the Psalm State, full of light, because our text comes from Psalm 36:9, "For with you is the fountain of life; in your light, we see the light." This is not Ponce de Leon's fountain of youth. That is in Florida, where there really are palms. Instead, let's focus on the light. God is the source of all light, and all light proceeds from Him. As in Genesis, God said, "Let there be light; and there was light." In this verse from Psalm, our satisfaction and joy rest in the life and light that comes from God. Everything away from God is dark, and everything near Him is light. It is similar to John 1:9 in which John writes that Jesus is the pure light. No doubt, he had this Psalm in mind as he wrote of the divinity of Jesus. So as we reflect on the abundance of light in Alaska, we begin to turn inwardly and concentrate on that last piece. In God's light, we see the glorious, conquering light. How could we not see it? Today, how is your ability to see God's light around you? Are you in the darkness? Move to the light and experience the satiating happiness.

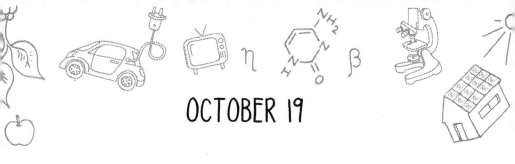

OCTOBER 19

Movie Night

Joshua 24:15

On October 19, 1985, the first Blockbuster Video store opened. I can still recall the sights and smells of our local Blockbuster, the feel of my laminated card for checkout, and the bright blue and yellow company colors everywhere. What about you? The company once had 9,000 outlets, but they are all gone, except one that may still be open in Bend, Oregon. Netflix, Redbox, and other modernity ended the reign of this onetime fixture for family movie night.

What's His story? While Blockbuster went the way of the Polaroid Company we read about recently, the message is different. Blockbuster was a big part of family movie night, and by offering movies of all genres, it provided an opportunity for devotions. Many films have an underlying moral or lesson that could be reinforced. *Caddyshack* and *Animal House* are not on that list. However, movies like *Noah*, *The Passion of Christ*, *The Ten Commandments*, and others come to mind. Even secular films can offer an opportunity to evangelize as a family. Joshua 24:15 and the covenant of renewal offers us guidance as a family. "As for me and my household, we will serve the Lord." It is a solid testament to how we can set our families apart as Christians. Even though we do not have Blockbuster today, the opportunity to reflect on a movie remains, along with a chance to learn and grow from it. How do you use movies to set an example or demonstrate Christ's love for us? Remember, no *Caddyshack,* although the lightning strike scene might make for a solid lesson about talking back to God...

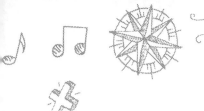

OCTOBER 20

The Opera House

Ephesians 5:19

On October 20, 1973, the Sydney Opera House in Sydney, Australia, opened. This stunning piece of architecture at the tip of Sydney Harbour looks like white shark fins laying on top of one another. Next to the koala, boomerang, didgeridoo, Uluru, kangaroo, and the meat pie, it is one of the most iconic symbols of Australia. Designed by Danish architect, Jorn Utzon, it was completed ten years late and $95M over budget. Oops. At least it got done. I recently had an opportunity to see a concert there with my musically inclined kids, Liz and Joey. The inside of the building concert experience met every expectation and dream I had about it.

What's His story? The first performance in the Opera House on this day back in 1973 was Beethoven's Symphony No. 9. For the vocals, Beethoven used Friedrich Schiller's "Ode to Joy" poem. He composed the symphony while he was virtually deaf, which makes the piece even more impressive. The opening of the Sydney Opera House was a celebration of God's gift of music, and this awe-inspiring piece was appropriate for the structure. We see mention of music throughout the Bible, especially in Psalms, but you will enjoy this passage in Ephesians 5:19, "..speaking to one another with psalms, hymns, and songs from the Spirit." Music really does come from the Spirit and is just one way to glorify Him. That is also found in Beethoven's Symphony No. 9 through this translation from the "Ode to Joy":

Do you bow before Him, you millions?
Do you sense your Creator, o world?
Seek Him above the canopy of stars!
He must dwell beyond the stars.

What is a memorable musical performance you have experienced? Reflecting back, do you remember one that brought pure joy?

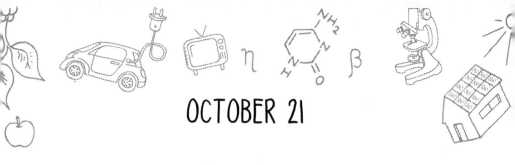

OCTOBER 21

Ultimate Irony

Mark 2:17

On October 21, 1833, Alfred Nobel was born in Stockholm, Sweden. Of course, you recognize the last name, since it is one of the most famous and prestigious awards one can earn. He was a chemist, engineer, inventor, and philanthropist. He was also responsible for hundreds of patents.

What's His story? If you didn't already know this, you would never look at the Nobel Peace Prize the same way. One of Nobel's inventions was none other than dynamite. Yes, you know the stuff made by the cartoon's Acme Company with Wiley Coyote as the most frequent customer. It is the ultimate in irony! Not to be outdone by himself, he also invented the blasting cap. That is called a double-whammy. Mark 2:17 contains similar irony from Jesus. When Jesus is rebuked by the Pharisees for eating with tax collectors and sinners at Matthew's house, He simply says, "It is not the healthy who need a doctor, but the sick. I have not come to call the righteous, but sinners." While Nobel invented such a destructive force, it was also used for good. Remember the Panama Canal construction? Yes, dynamite was used. Jesus teaches us those that need His message of salvation do not always appear as we think they should. Do you sometimes judge a book by its cover without considering the underlying needs? Let the Holy Spirit guide and equip you! How can you show your explosive love for Jesus?

OCTOBER 22

Slow of Tongue

Exodus 4:10

On October 22, 1924, the social group Toastmasters International was founded. Headquartered in Englewood, Colorado, this educational organization's goal is to help promote communication, leadership, and public speaking.

What's His story? Do you like public speaking? Some folks are great at it, but it can be a terribly daunting task for many. I am from the South, so I naturally talk slowly and occasionally fumble my words. In Exodus 4:10, I can totally relate to Moses. He says to God, "O Lord, I have never been eloquent, neither in the past nor since you have spoken to your servant. I am slow of speech and tongue." Ha, did Moses think God did not know? He knew that He had equipped Moses just as He has provided you and me boldness for His kingdom's purposes. We underestimate our ability because we do not first consider He who gives us strength, power, might, and skill! When we stop to discover how God gives us the tools to accomplish so much, everything else falls into place. God gives us the courage to face our fears and overcome perceived weaknesses. Whether it is in front of a group of five or five hundred, it does not matter because He is greater than the battle that takes place in our mind! Moses did just fine. God knew then, and He knows now. Do you become filled with doubt or excitement when opportunities to speak in front of others arise? Renew your mind with the knowledge that God strengthens you and then see what happens.

OCTOBER 23

Close But No Cigar

Revelation 3:16

On October 23, 1915, the first National Horseshoe Throwing Contest was held in Kellerton, Iowa. Horseshoes, for short, is a game in which you toss actual metal horseshoes towards a stake set into the center of a square pit or small area about forty feet away.

What's His story? Scoring in horseshoes is relatively straightforward. You get three points for a ringer, when your shoe is wrapped around the stake. That is obviously the goal with each throw, but you may also accumulate points if your shoe is the one closest to the stake. Thus we get the phrase, "close only counts in horseshoes and hand grenades." Sometimes as Christians, we do not aim for the ringer, but simply try to get close to the stake. Why is that? Just as there is something so satisfying in scoring a ringer and hearing the shoe clang against the stake, hitting the evangelistic stake of the Gospel brings joy and fullness to the heart. Revelation 3:16 reminds us, just getting close by being a lukewarm Christian will not cut it. When we choose the easy way out and leave the rest for someone else, indifference rules the day, and we make no room for Christ in our hearts. We then become hardened to the message of the Gospel with no incentive to spread it. Just aiming to get close is not what God asks of us. He wants us to throw a ringer. He seeks our whole heart, and close simply misses the mark. We can be so much more when we repent and allow His voice to fill our hearts. What is one way you can throw a ringer for Christ today?

OCTOBER 24

Birthday Barrel Roll

John 5:44

On October 24, 1901, on her birthday, a sixty-three-year-old schoolteacher from Auburn, New York named Annie Edson Taylor, took a wild ride. It was not just a joy ride celebrating her sixty-third trip around the sun. No, this was a trip over one of the most powerful waterfalls in the world, Niagara Falls, in a barrel! Have you ever been to see Niagara Falls? The thunderous noise exhibits just how powerful they are. Plenty of people before young Annie attempted the same feat, but only a few made it. Annie was the first to successfully use a barrel.

What's His story? Annie was widowed during the Civil War and was apparently cash-strapped and thought going over Niagara Falls in a wooden barrel would generate some cash and desired attention. After she survived, it did accomplish her goal, but the spotlight quickly dimmed. In John 5:44, we are warned about fame-seeking: "How can you believe if you accept praise from one another, yet make no effort to obtain the praise that comes from the only God?" It is a valid question. Why do we tend to seek the attention of those around us, but neglect God? We should not act out of legalistic approval from God, but rather in jubilant praise for the prospect of building a deeper and more meaningful relationship with Him. When we seek the approval of this world, our values are misaligned, and worthiness voids abound. However, when we seek counsel with God, we can become content with His wisdom and will. No barrel is required thank goodness. The simple question is, whose approval are you seeking today?

P.S. If you are keeping score, today was also the day in 1861 a transcontinental telegraph was sent, putting the Pony Express out of business. That was short.

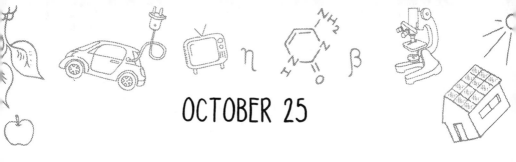

OCTOBER 25

Postcards from Paradise

1 John 4:9

On October 25, 1870, the United States Postal Service first used postcards in the United States. Postcards used to be more popular before digital cameras, phones, texting, and social media. It was a quick way to share a touristy picture from a vacation or trip and quickly describe what was going on for those back home.

What's His story? When you picture a postcard, what comes to mind? Mine is a picture of a tropical island with the words "the weather is here, wish you were beautiful." Wait, that can't be right! Maybe it is the other way around. Either way, it is an expression of thanksgiving and longing. I believe that God sends us postcards in the form of people who are in our lives, events that impact us, and conversations with the Holy Spirit. Prayer time is our opportunity to send a postcard to God, and in return, He might send us one through a beautiful sunrise or sunset, or even a stranger's smile. The truth is, God sent us the most beautiful postcard in the form of Jesus Christ. In 1 John 4:9, we learn of God's message: "This is how God showed his love among us; He sent his one and only Son into the world that we might live through him." This is how God shows us His longing for us to join Him in paradise. God did not have to use the postal service. He used something so much grander than that. By the way, He does not care if you have a really terrible bathing suit, because all He wants is you. He sent something infinitely more valuable than an Earthly postcard. Are you receiving His postcards, or do you have a permanent forwarded mailing address in place? Every day is an opportunity to check the mailbox for God's postcards!

OCTOBER 26

Overflowing the Dam

Romans 15:13

On October 26, 1936, the first electric generator powered up at Hoover Dam on the border of Arizona and Nevada. The 726-foot high dam is a masterful piece of architecture holding back the waters of the Colorado River and Lake Mead. There are now seventeen generators at the dam, producing enough electricity to serve upwards of one million people! While there are no people "lost" in the concrete, the construction workers' mascot dog is definitely buried on site.

What's His story? What is the purpose of a dam? It is usually to hold water back, but through ingenuity, innovation, and creativity, we have figured out a way to generate electricity when water is released and passed through the dam. Sometimes, we allow ourselves to act as a dam, inhibiting the Holy Spirit's power from flowing through us. However, like the release of water to generate electricity, when we allow the living waters to flow through us, we become less like a dam holding something back, and more like a fully-functional, beneficial creation of God. Romans 15:13 summarizes it well, "May the God of hope fill you with all joy and peace as you trust in him, so that you may overflow with hope by the power of the Holy Spirit." This verse is such a great visual for an immense, powerful dam full of potential power poised to be released into the world in His name's sake. What is stopping you or holding you back? Release the living waters of the Holy Spirit and be energized! Whew! Made it through a dam devotional without one misspelling.

OCTOBER 27

Subway Grace

1 Samuel 24:6

On October 27, 1904, the first underground line of the New York Subway system opened. One of the oldest public transit systems, it is also the world's largest with 469 stations in operation. Although some of the 233 miles of track are above ground, most are below the surface of Manhattan and the other boroughs.

What's His story? Have you ever noticed the number of references to caves, caverns, and tombs in the Bible? There are plenty! We can start with Jesus' tomb or Lazarus awakening from the dead, but my favorite might be the irony of Saul's choice of caves when nature called. 1 Samuel 24 is where you will find it. It is worth it to read all of this chapter to understand the power of courage to do the right thing and how it can change those around you. Subways and caves are synonymous because they are dark, dank, and smelly. But in the darkness of that cave in the desert of En Gedi, David became a shining light. To say he is the light of an oncoming subway train would be a bit of a literary and metaphorical stretch. We can all agree that he was Christlike in the mercy he showed his enemy Saul, in that cave, and we can learn from him! What about you, how are you seeking out and creating light and happiness in the deepest, darkest places around you? Are you praying for an opportunity this very day?

OCTOBER 28

Gateway to God's Promise

Joshua 3:17

On October 28, 1965, the St. Louis Arch, or Gateway Arch, was completed in St. Louis, Missouri. The Arch, a 630-foot remarkable feat of architecture, is called The Gateway to the West. If you find yourself driving across the country, its position along the mighty Mississippi River really does make it seem like you are going through a gate to the Western United States.

What's His story? The St. Louis Arch was constructed to commemorate the expansion into the Wild West and St. Louis' role as a gateway or stepping off point for so many seeking a better life out west. In Joshua 3, we find a similar story of a nation seeking its Promised Land, crossing the River Jordan instead of the Mississippi, but all the same trusting God. God kept His promise to the people of Israel and delivered them. He was with them all the way from beginning to end. As the settlers headed west in search of a better life, the Gateway Arch represented their starting point. Some might look at the entrance into the Promised Land as an ending point. I believe that these pivotal moments can be both when we realize that God keeps His promises throughout our journey. Miracles like the Jordan River parting or a monument like the Arch can serve as reminders of His power and presence in our personal mission walk. What does it feel like when you set foot in a new experience? Are you full of trust in God, or is it a tentative action? Look back at some monumental pivotal moments in your life and reflect on God's presence. He was there then, and He is here now.

OCTOBER 29

Underlined Faith

Hebrews 11:3

On October 29, 1945, the Reynolds pen, named after Milton Reynolds and sometimes called the Reynolds Rocket, became the first modern ballpoint pen sold in the United States. It was sold in the Gimbels department store. During its first week, thousands of the $9.75 pen were sold. It was an improved version of a pen the world already knew, but Americans loved it, and demand was high.

What's His story? Have you ever stopped to think of how integral pens are in our lives? There are those of us out there who still like the feel of ink flowing across a page. The pen is a utensil, which enables the fruits of the Spirit. Through it, you can share kindness, joy, peace, love, and many other things. It can also serve as an instrument of remembrance when we use it to underline or make notes in our Bible. Do you do this today? It is a great way to highlight impactful or meaningful scripture. You will be surprised how often something you underline will play a role in your life. Therefore, it becomes a communication tool between God and us. You cannot judge a person's faith by the number of underlines, colors, stars, or doodled notes found among the pages of scripture, but know it is a way to customize a book that should be very personal. Reynolds pen is just one of many tools we can use to galvanize our relationship with God. Hebrews 11:3 states, "By faith we understand that the universe was formed at God's command, so that what is seen was not made out of what was visible." When we underline scripture in our Bible, God's word gets louder and louder and can impact our faith in a way that declares His awesome power. All this can be enhanced through a simple ballpoint pen. Have you written in your Bible this week? Will you start?

OCTOBER 30

Spreading the Truth

Acts 6:7

On October 30, 1938, Orson Welles' radio broadcast of *War of the Worlds* took place. Millions of radio listeners were tricked into believing that martians were attacking Earth. It was a reading of H.G. Wells' book, *War of the Worlds*, and it was broadcast through a series of radio news alerts. I am sure folks were a little upset when the truth was revealed, but relieved it was not actually an invasion.

What's His story? Back before television and the Internet were around, families gathered around a radio to hear about news events or entertainment. Today, some rely on social media to stay informed. Whether that is a good or a bad thing is debatable, but back in 1938, social media platforms that we know today were not even glimmers in someone's eye. The shepherds did not see that Jesus' birth was trending. Instead, a multitude of angels told them! Similarly, after Jesus ascended back to Heaven, the spread of Christianity was firmly on the shoulders of the apostles. Acts contains so many great stories of the Gospel being spread to thousands. Unlike the *War of the Worlds* broadcast, this was not a hoax. Acts 6:7 says it best, "So the word of God spread." We know radio broadcasts are meant to reach scores of people, and Jesus told the apostles that they would also need to reach the flocks, and it would start in Jerusalem. The miracles performed by them as they were filled with the Holy Spirit reassured the people who received it that the message was pure and true. Are you listening for the one true God, or are you tuned in to something far from the truth? What would it take to turn the dial towards God?

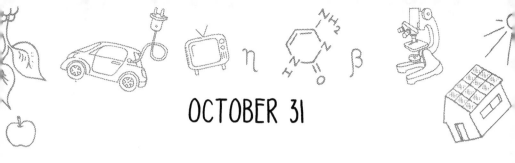

OCTOBER 31

The Price WAS Right

1 Corinthians 6:20

On October 31, 2006, legendary game show host Bob Barker retired from the show *The Price is Right*. You have probably seen it, but the show begins with a group of people who have their name called out of the crowd to be a contestant. Once up front, the contestants have a chance to win prizes by playing a variety of pricing games in which you must guess the correct price of different items. It is an entertaining and exciting game to watch, and Barker was one of the best. I am biased because I grew up as a kid watching him, but he really was good.

What's His story? Watching this show, I always thought I knew better than the people on television about how much something costs. Do you think we do the same thing when it comes to God? We often do not realize the price that was paid for us. The price was right and good and justified. The sacrifice of His only Son gives us grace and salvation. We do not deserve it, but God has called each one of us to "come on down" and accept it. He is not just calling the crazy one with the amusing air-brushed t-shirt. He is calling us all! Lucky for us, the game has already been won. 1 Corinthians 6:20 says it all, "you were bought at a price. Therefore honor God with your body." Yes, the price was right!

NOVEMBER 1

Look Up

Psalm 123:1

On November 1, 1512, the Sistine Chapel ceiling in Vatican City was first exhibited to the public. It is a stunning and remarkable piece of art that is still hard to fully comprehend and appreciate. Famed sculptor and reluctant painter Michelangelo completed the masterpiece, which includes various frescoes that highlight humanity's need for salvation.

What's His story? Pope Julius II decided to do some remodeling that included more than just some new curtains. He obviously felt the ceiling should be painted. More dental offices should consider this. Contrary to popular belief, Michelangelo was not lying down as he painted. Instead, he was standing with his head locked into a looking-up position. It was grueling work, but the beauty he created is exquisite. We could take a lesson from both the location and manner in which the artist painted. When we look up, away from a device, a book, or our shoes, we see the world around us in all of its beauty. We might also see its need. When we look up, we see God, and opportunities to serve Him. Psalm 123:1 says, "I lift up my eyes to you, to you whose throne is in heaven." We look up to the Lord for mercy. When we are on this journey together, one of the greatest gifts we have is the opportunity to look up and see His hand in everything. What do you see when you look up from the distractions?

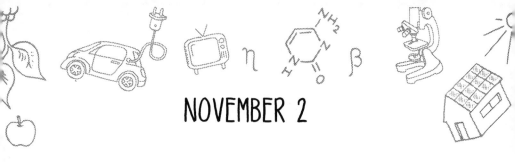

NOVEMBER 2

Noah & The Spruce Goose

Genesis 6:14

On November 2, 1947, American businessman, inventor, engineer, investor, and pilot Howard Hughes flew the Spruce Goose for the first time. It was given this unique name because it was made entirely out of wood due to all metals being used in the war effort at the time. It was six times larger than any airplane of its time, and even though it only made one single, solitary flight, it left an impression.

What's His story? Hughes was a visionary, but he also received ridicule for his massive dream to build and fly the Spruce Goose. By the way, if we are being specific, it was constructed of birch, not spruce. Who is someone else we have seen on the receiving end of ridicule for building something massive, but beneficial? You are correct - Noah! Think of the jeers and sneers Noah must have received. But, he knew that God was equipping him for a mission, and he trusted in faithful obedience to God. If you ever see a picture of the Spruce Goose, it may remind you of Noah's Ark. The Goose was also a seaplane, drawing another relative comparison! Genesis 6:14 tells us about the construction of the Ark, and when you read about the dimensions, you quickly realize just how massive it was. Hughes eventually proved the doubters wrong with a short, one-mile long, seventy-foot high flight, and we all know Noah's story had a happy ending with a rainbow! While you do not need to build a massive wooden plane or ark, what are you creating today with God as your architect?

NOVEMBER 3

The Best Sacrifice Fly of All Time

Hebrews 9:28

On November 3, 1954, Major League Baseball reinstated the use of the sacrifice fly. Earlier, it had been removed from the rules in 1939. The sacrifice fly is a play in baseball where a batter intends for a teammate to score a run after the batter's hit is caught. Usually, the batter hits the ball deep to the outfield for an out while the runner runs from third base to home plate to score, even though the runner has to wait until the fielder catches the ball before he leaves the base.

What's His story? A sacrifice fly on the baseball field is minuscule compared to the sacrifice Jesus made for us and for our sins on the cross. There is NO comparison. It is even a little cheeky to compare the two, but if it helps remind you of His sacrifice for you every time you see this play in baseball, then it was worth it! Why did Christ do it? In faithful obedience Hebrews 9:28 reveals the answer, "so Christ was sacrificed once to take away the sins of many people; and he will appear a second time, not to bear sin, but to bring salvation to those who are waiting for him." Today we are thankful that because of His sacrifice, we have scored on the field of life. It may sound cheesy, but thank goodness it is true! Have you accepted the sacrifice Christ has made for you? Do you know the depths of what it means, or are you uncovering new meaning each and every day?

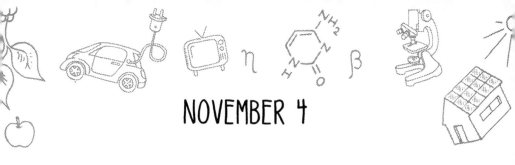

NOVEMBER 4

And That's The Way It Is

Luke 1:1-4

On November 4, 1916, American journalist and newscaster Walter Cronkite was born in St. Joseph, Missouri. Cronkite was a familiar face in homes across America during the 1960s and 1970s as anchorman for the CBS Evening News. He was once noted as the "most trusted man in America" in an opinion poll. Cronkite's sign off as he ended his program was a classic. He simply said, "And that's the way it is."

What's His story? Cronkite was the anchorman for some of the most pivotal moments in modern human history. He was there for JFK's assassination, the lunar landing, MLK's assassination, Watergate, and Vietnam, just to name a few. It was how Cronkite delivered the news and events that earned him the opinion poll title. Cronkite believed the news needed gravity, a tone, and a voice. When we look back at Jesus' ministry and the important news He shared in those three short years, Matthew, Mark, Luke, and John come to mind as the Cronkite of Jesus' time. Their recollection and collection of details related to Jesus are the most important news stories of all time, and they each gave the Son of Man gravity, a tone, and a voice. While each is unique in delivery, details, and perspective, some common threads and dynamics give each one unique power. All four are essential, integral components of the Bible. All four are great places to start reading the Bible, and you can pick which to read first. It can be Matthew's focus on His divine lineage, Mark and John's affirmation of His divinity, or the Walter Cronkitish writer Luke. Luke 1:4 is our guiding principle, but one could argue it was Cronkite's mantra as well as he delivered headlines. Check it out and then read the rest as you prepare your heart for the upcoming season of hope!

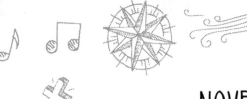

NOVEMBER 5

The Incredible Way to God

John 14:6

On November 5, 2004, the Disney-Pixar movie *The Incredibles* was released. It is a delightful comic movie about a family of superheroes trying to live out a normal life because the government has banned superpowers. In this movie, there is still a good vs. evil theme. Ironically, the sinister character is really just a kid named Buddy.

What's His story? As you will find out in the movie, Buddy turns to the dark side, because of one pivotal encounter with Mr. Incredible, head of the Incredible household. In this encounter, Buddy is trying to be just like the Incredibles and earn notoriety through his superhero actions. When he did not receive the recognition he thought he deserved, he continued down his dark pathway. We have a tendency to act like Buddy, even though we do not have the nifty superhero costume. We believe that our identity rests in recognition of what we do, how much we make, who our friends are, and where we live. Instead, our identity is found in Christ, and none of that matters in our Savior's eyes. In John 14:6, Jesus confirms, "I am the way and the truth and the life. No one comes to the Father except through me." This direction is what Buddy was missing, but he missed the point, just like we sometimes miss the point. We are rewarded with a relationship with God through our actions and words. It defines our identity, and others can clearly see it. Are you trying to gain your identity elsewhere? Why not turn to Jesus and ask him to show you the way back to a relationship with the Father?

NOVEMBER 6

A Better Mousetrap

John 10:9

On November 6, 1894, American inventor W. C. Hooker received the United States Patent #528671 for the mousetrap. First of all, who sits around thinking about how to develop a mousetrap? I wonder if Hooker really used cheese as bait? He named it "Out of Sight," after all. I still have so many questions.

What's His story? British inventor James Atkinson who made the "Little Nipper" eventually improved the mousetrap. There you have it! That is confirmation of the quest to build a better mousetrap. Atkinson's trap has a closing speed of $1/38,000$th of a second. Yikes! Aside from these guys trying to improve each other's mousetrap, what exactly does the trap do? There is a bait designed to draw the unsuspecting rodent in and then POW! While our situation may not be so draconian, we are sometimes in the same position. The things of this world tempt us, and before we know it, the trap has snapped, and we are stuck. John 10:9 sums it up by saying, "I am the gate; whoever enters through me will be saved. He will come in and go out and find pasture." If we abide in Christ, we go from being the mouse trapped in the clever trap of worldly things to a country mouse free to roam in the pasture and enjoy the things that freedom and joy have to offer. Which would you rather be, a city mouse fooled by the trap of worldly things or country mouse at pasture? You may never look at a mousetrap the same way, but think of this, Jesus offers you a pathway out, even quicker than the "Little Nipper." Are you ready to follow the path?

NOVEMBER 7

The Mighty Pacific

Philippians 4:6-7

On November 7, 1805, explorer William Clark of the famed Lewis & Clark exploration team first set his eyes upon the Pacific Ocean from the Oregon coast. The beauty of this area is striking. One second, you are in a lush evergreen forest, and the next, you are in an open hillside pasture overlooking the indigo blue ocean as far as the eye can see. For this party exploring the Louisiana Purchase, it must have been quite a sight.

What's His story? Clark wrote of this day and the sight before his eyes, "Great joy in camp we are in view of the ocean, this great Pacific Ocean we have been so long anxious to see." The famous explorer Ferdinand Magellan named the ocean the Pacific, which means peaceful. When Magellan first saw it while in search of the Spice Islands, the expanse of water was calm and tranquil. Philippians 4:6-7 ties these two perceptions together bound by the word of God through Paul. He writes, "Do not be anxious about anything but in everything, by prayer and petition with thanksgiving present your requests to God. And the peace of God, which transcends all understanding, will guard your hearts and your minds in Christ Jesus." It is ironic that Clark was anxious to see an ocean named because of how peaceful it was. While it sometimes seems implausible not to worry about anything, the next verse tells us why. The peace of God overcomes what we believe to be peace. God's peace is much greater than anything we can imagine. It is dependable peace in the knowledge that God is the leader of our own exploration party, and He grants us the assurance that He is in control. This should allow us to relinquish all worry and anxiety to Him. Are you full of anxiety and at peace about nothing? What would it take to swap around those two?

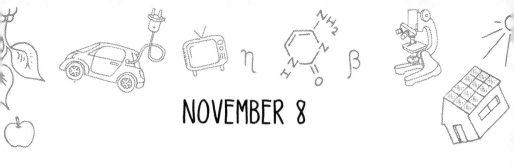

NOVEMBER 8

Precious Treasure

Revelation 21:18-21

On November 8, 1889, the Big Sky Country state of Montana was admitted to the United States as the 41st state. It is a beautiful state with open prairie on the eastern side and the gorgeous Rocky Mountains on the western side.

What's His story? Montana is rich in geological treasure, so much so, it is nicknamed the Treasure State. While gold and silver led to the nickname, Montana has a vast number of other treasures in its fertile soil. Revelation 21:18-21 is also rich in gemstones and describes the walls of the New Jerusalem. Fittingly, in the Treasure State of Montana, you can find nine of the twelve precious stones mentioned in the verse from Revelation! Even more intriguing is that the twelve precious stones mentioned are all anisotropic gems, which means they show colorful patterns under pure light. In contrast, seemingly priceless stones like diamonds and garnet are not mentioned, perhaps because they are isotropic, meaning light simply passes through them. A diamond's fire comes from its cut and not the stone itself. The twelve stones all disperse light in a colorful pattern that illuminates the throne of God in brilliance! I believe there is a deliberate message that we are meant to disperse our light to others. Revelation 4:3 makes reference to the rainbow of light that these stones produce when struck by true and pure light. Back in Montana, precious stones are hidden in the dirt, awaiting the warmth of pure light to disperse the beauty inherently found within them. Are you just like each gemstone mentioned in the passage? Are you also hidden in the dirt? Who or what is the shovel that will pry you out of the darkness to shine?

NOVEMBER 9

The Walls Came Crashing Down

Joshua 6:20

On November 9, 1989, the destruction of the Berlin Wall began. This wall divided Eastern (Communist) and Western Germany and was erected in 1961 as a result of Soviet participation in Germany's post-WWII occupation. The wall itself became a significant source of discussion during the Cold War. It resulted in a couple of memorable speeches by United States presidents Kennedy and Reagan, demanding that the wall be taken down in the name of freedom.

What's His story? We open the Bible to the book of Joshua. In chapter six, we read about the fall of the walled city of Jericho. As Joshua led the nation into the Promised Land, this was one of their first obstacles, and it was a seemingly unconquerable city. However, Joshua was faithful and obeyed God's instructions. Astonishingly, his faith was rewarded. When I read, "Make six laps and then on the seventh lap I want you to play trumpets and scream at the top of your lungs," it did not necessarily sound like a "plan," but it was God's plan. His plan can be much different than our plan. In this scripture, we learn that while the instructions may not make sense, believing God's plan teaches us how to have faith in insurmountable situations by trusting and obeying Him. Imagine seeing the walls of Jericho fall juxtaposed against the Berlin Wall as it fell. God was present in both. We simply have to trust that God is who He says and will do what He says He will do. Do you trust Him to tear down the walls that are holding you in, or holding you back?

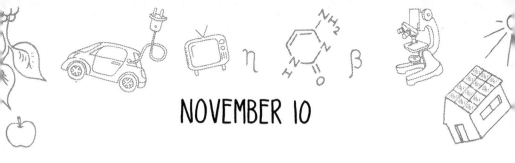

NOVEMBER 10

God Bless America

Psalm 33:12

On November 10, 1938, composer Irving Berlin's song *God Bless America* was first heard on the radio. The First Lady of Radio, Kate Smith, performed it.

What's His story? You have plausibly heard the song often, but have you ever read the lyrics line by line? It is a revealing view of the proper backbone of a nation, which is God. As it says, "Stand beside her and guide her," we know that our reliance is not on our own perceived power, but that which comes from divine guidance. Psalm 33:12 affirms this as it says, "Blessed is the nation whose God is the Lord, the people he chose for his inheritance." Singing this song is a reminder of the blessings God has poured out on all of us. We begin to understand this even more, when we sing "God Bless America," saying, "God Bless America, my home sweet home." We are proud to be Americans with freedoms to worship that other countries do not enjoy, so let us not take that for granted. Now, when you hear them sing the song at a baseball game or other sporting event, you will hopefully be reminded of the grace God pours out on you each day.

NOVEMBER 11

The Ugly Duckling

2 Corinthians 4:16

On November 11, 1843, Danish author Hans Christian Andersen published the fairy tale *The Ugly Duckling*. This delightful and still-appropriate tale is about a "duckling" that is actually a swan. However, he does not know this and tries to fit in with the ducks, only to receive abuse and isolation because he does not look like them. As he matures inwardly, he eventually joins the swans that readily accept him.

What's His story? This tale by Andersen is a story of inner personal transformation leading to a changed outward appearance. The ugly duckling is the result of a swan egg that accidentally rolled into a duck nest. This little "duck" was considered ugly and not worthy by all of the other animals since it did not look like them. Have you ever seen a baby swan, or cygnet as they are called? It is not so pretty. In this story, the ugly duckling, which was really a swan, matured and realized that inner beauty is what matters. Inner transformation results in outward appearance that is unmistakable. 2 Corinthians 4:16 reminds us, "Therefore do not lose heart. Though outwardly, we are wasting away, yet inwardly we are being renewed day by day." Why has Hallmark Corporation not picked up on this one? This should be on every birthday card, especially the milestone years. The point here is that even in the case of the ugly duckling, as our hearts are renewed each day by the power of the Holy Spirit, outward appearances may not tell the whole story. After all, it is actions like love that positively reveal the beauty of God within, not the clothes or feathers we wear. Are you focused inwardly, building your spiritual strength? Or, are you dressing an outer layer that is wasting away? Renew your heart and begin to realize the inward transformation that reveals itself outwardly through actions that are unmistakably the mission of God!

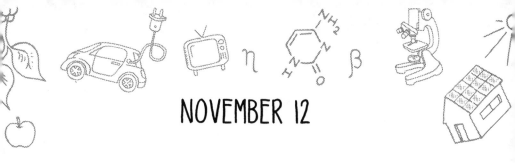

NOVEMBER 12

Human Tunnels

Matthew 21:1-11

On November 12, 2015, Otto the Bulldog earned his place in the *Guinness Book of World Records* as he skateboarded through thirty people's legs. Yes, you read that right! This English Bulldog rode a skateboard down a slight hill through their legs without touching. Apparently, touching is against the rules.

What's His story? What comes to mind when you hear about someone going through a "human tunnel" like this? Maybe you recall the scene with Dracula from the cartoon movie Hotel Transylvania? Now think of the most glorious human tunnel of all time. Yes, Jesus' entrance into Jerusalem that we celebrate each Palm Sunday. Admittedly, it is hard to think about His grand entrance, because of what happens just a few days afterward, but the Son of Man knew what He had to do. All four Gospels tell the story of His entrance into Jerusalem, but I believe Matthew 21:1-11 does the best job of forming the imagery similar to Otto's feat. The crowds gathered and greeted Jesus with praise, saying, "Hosanna to the Son of David! Blessed is he who comes in the name of the Lord! Hosanna in the highest!" The people threw down their cloaks and waved palm branches for Him. Can you imagine the scene? He rode in on a donkey's colt, fulfilling prophecy, but also sustaining His humility. The King of Peace rode through a human tunnel full of hopeful expectation. Sadly, it would turn just a few days later. Today are you greeting Christ with hope and expectation, or are you demanding something else, just as the people of Jerusalem did? They were expecting a military conqueror. Little did they know!

NOVEMBER 13

Tunnels Part II

2 Chronicles 32:30

On November 13, 1927, the Holland Tunnel in New York City first opened for traffic. This tunnel, underneath the Hudson River, allows traffic to flow from New Jersey into downtown Manhattan. The tunnel is 1.6 miles long, has 3.1 million ceiling tiles, and 2.9 million wall tiles. That is a lot of grout, huh?

What's His story? Yes, I realize it is another tunnel, but it is an entirely different type! The purpose of the Holland Tunnel was obvious - to save time when traveling into New York City. Have you ever stopped to think about the engineers who created these plans and then bring them to life? 2 Chronicles 32:30 contains a story of a tunnel and one man's trust in God. This chapter also has the downfall of this man due to the pride he took in his accomplishment. Our focus today is on the inspiration and building. Hezekiah, king of Judah, was preparing for an attack on Jerusalem by the Assyrians when he built his own tunnel. It is known today as the Siloam Tunnel and was built to divert water from the Gihon Spring to the Pool of Siloam. The goal was to continue to provide enough water in case the city was placed under siege. Hezekiah prayed and trusted in God, knowing that he had God on his side. I cannot help but think that the engineers who were building the Holland Tunnel regularly said a few prayers. I also say a quick prayer each time I pass through a tunnel! Today, are you trusting God to build the tunnels you need to handle your situations at hand? It may sound strange to pray for that, but to trust God in the darkest of places is what we are called to do. Hezekiah's creative solution was certainly God-inspired. What does God have in store for you when you do it?

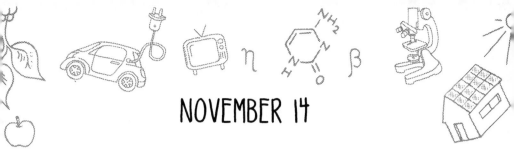

NOVEMBER 14

BOGO Faith

1 Samuel 17 & Genesis 22

On November 14, 1910, Eugene Burton Ely performed the first takeoff in a plane from a ship in Hampton Roads, VA. He took off from a makeshift deck on the *USS Birmingham* in a Curtiss pusher plane. In related news, fifty-nine years later, the Apollo 12 mission launched to become the second crewed mission to the moon's surface. That's right, today is BOGO...two events for the price of one.

What's His story? Think of the walk in faith that Eugene Ely and the crew of the Apollo 12 mission took to accomplish great things. Can you imagine what the feeling would be right before you hit the throttle on that plane, or sitting on the launchpad just before taking off into space? What gives them the confidence to push through the fear? Where can you find such extreme examples of having faith in the Bible? There are many places to find His story, but the two that stand out to me are David against Goliath, and Abraham offering his son Isaac as a sacrifice in obedience to God. While they did not, both men could have tried to run away from the challenge. Not only were they rewarded for their faith, but the example of steadfast faith they set and their belief in God's divine wisdom has impacted generation upon generation – quite literally! Do you believe that they also had that sense of uneasiness? Of course, they did. They replaced fear with faith in God. What is the goodness or greatness you can spread when you supplant fear with God? How can we begin to step out in faith today? What is one way you can start?

NOVEMBER 15

A Tale of Two Cities

Galatians 4:21-31

On November 15, 1859, the final installment of the Charles Dickens book *A Tale of Two Cities* was published. This classic is a gripping story about revolutionary unrest in Paris and relative calm in London, the respective locations of the main characters, and the backdrop for much of the book. The stark contrast is very apparent, and Dickens builds his characters Charles Darnay, Lucie Manette, and Sydney Carton in this context.

What's His story? Clearly, the two cities are very different in the story, thus the title. What about in the Bible? Do we find evidence of a tale of two cities? We do! In Galatians 4:21-31, Paul takes a page out of Jesus' book. He uses his own allegory about Abraham's wives and his two sons to explain how being born into slavery versus being born into freedom differentiates. He uses scripture to support it. Paul mentions the two covenants God made. The first is on Mt. Sinai, speaking to the current Jerusalem, and the other corresponds to the New Jerusalem that is to come in Heaven, which represents freedom! New Jerusalem embodies the freedom that is to come when we trust in Christ to save us. Just as there are two very different cities in Charles Dickens' classic, there are two very different Jerusalem's in the Bible. Which city do you choose, freedom in Christ, or bondage in the hollowness of the things of this world?

NOVEMBER 16

The Hills Are Indeed Alive

Psalm 121:1

On November 16, 1959, the musical *The Sound of Music* premiered on Broadway at the Lunt-Fontanne Theater. This musical is an enchanting musical tale of the real-life von Trapp Family Singers just before World War II. Oscar Hammerstein II wrote the lyrics, and Richard Rodgers composed the score music.

What's His story? There are several biblical messages in this musical. Whether it is the repeated phrase, "when the Lord closes a door, he opens a window," or main character Maria's commitment to God, there are plenty to find. I believe the best message is one that ties directly to Psalm 121:1-2 when it says, "I lift up my eyes to the hills – where does my help come from? My help comes from the Lord, the Maker of Heaven, and Earth." One of the most distinct and memorable Rodgers & Hammerstein lyrics comes from the title song as it says, "The hills are alive, with the sound of music." Further, Maria sings, "I go to the hills when my heart is lonely." In other words, as music heals, we learn that our help comes from the Lord. We can trust in Him who has made the hills, but also the Heavens and Earth. The last verse of Psalm 121 reminds me of the *Sound of Music* movie in which Maria is in the high mountain pasture circling around singing this song. Psalm 121:8 says, "the Lord will watch over your coming and going both now and forevermore." Her coming and going as she twirls about the meadow reminds us of the joy we find in God when we lift our eyes to Him. What is your attitude towards God? Is it a happy twirling as in the *Sound of Music*?

NOVEMBER 17

The Heidi Bowl

1 Corinthians 2:10

On November 17, 1968, the television network NBC left the live broadcast of the Oakland Raiders vs. New York Jets football game to start their broadcast of *Heidi*. The Jets were leading 32-29 with just sixty-five seconds left, so I am guessing the television executives felt safe switching to regularly scheduled programming.

What's His story? There was a dramatic turn of events in those last sixty-five seconds. A couple of plays later, Oakland scored and took the lead. The cherry on top was another Oakland touchdown to secure the win 43-32. The Raiders scored twice in nine seconds. It was a record until recently when the Atlanta Falcons did it in two seconds! As Yogi Berra says, "It ain't over 'til it is over." That is so true. Many times we think the same thing about God's dream for our lives. We think we know how it is going to end. In doing so, we do not take into account the things that God reveals to us daily. How often are new things, friends, talents, or discoveries revealed to you in a way that has God's fingerprints all over them? 1 Corinthians 2:10 says, "but God has revealed it to us by his Spirit." The depths of His nature and His kingdom are available to us, but we must accept God's message and take it into our hearts. We may think we know the full story, or how it ends, just like all those folks watching the "Heidi Bowl" that night in 1968. However, we do not, and that is okay. We only need to trust in the Lord and His plan for our life. He has beautiful things in store for us. He brings us near to reveal His glory! Are you sticking around until the end, or are you leaving because you think you know the ending?

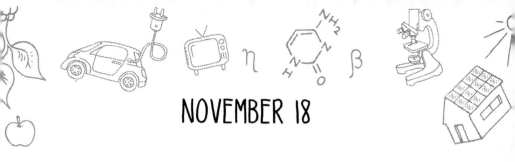

NOVEMBER 18

The Bond of Life

Colossians 1:17

On November 18, 1952, the Borden Company registered the Elmers trademark. Did you know that the bull on the Elmers glue bottle is the spouse of Elsie the Cow, who is the corporate symbol of Borden? Borden is famous for its milk products. I have learned so many new things in writing this book!

What's His story? Let's talk about Elmers for a second. Who can forget Elmers glue? It is that pasty, white, distinctively fragrant adhesive that literally stuck with you through childhood. What is something sticky that holds you together today, also quite literally? I believe it is Jesus Christ. Colossians 1:17 affirms this, "He is before all things, and in him all things hold together." Without Jesus, all things fall apart! You may have heard the Laminin, the Cross, and this scripture sermon, but it is worth looking up if you have not had a chance. It illustrates the point very clearly that the adhesive power of Jesus is the glue that literally holds us together. Jesus most definitely holds us collectively better than the adhesive strength of Elmers glue, no offense Borden Company! Is Jesus the glue holding you together, or are you experimenting with some false adhesive that loses its bonding power over time?

NOVEMBER 19

Eatin' Good in the Neighborhood

Luke 14:15-24

On November 19, 1980, Bill Palmer and his wife T. J. opened T. J. Applebee's Rx for Edibles & Elixirs in Atlanta, Georgia. In 1983, they sold the Applebee's concept to W. R. Grace & Company, and the rest, as they say, is history! Today there are almost 2,000 locations worldwide.

What's His story? One of Applebee's slogans they revived recently is, "Eatin' Good in the Neighborhood." English teachers, you just have to let this one slide. Nevertheless, do you know who always ate good (well) in the neighborhood? Jesus!! That guy was always around a meal, whether helping with the accouterments, providing the meal itself, being served a meal, or dining with sinners, Jesus found His way to the table. Clearly, because He was getting His steps in, caloric intake was not His concern. Instead, His interest was the salvation of others and to make sure all felt welcome at the table with Him. The parable of the great feast in Luke 14:15-24 is His way of reminding us of God's invitation for us to join the Father, Son, and the Holy Spirit at the table. What is on the menu? It does not even matter! Who is invited? All are welcome! It is an illustration of God's love for us that He has already prepared a place at the table. Our nametag is one with the most exquisite calligraphy you have ever seen. The kingdom of God has the finest banquet table of all time, and our invitation was sent long ago. Did you get yours? Are you too busy to join him at the table? Are there other more important things on your calendar? The thrilling part is that, unlike a typical invitation, this invite never goes away, nor expires. Go ahead and RSVP. Join the table and feast with Jesus. Like Applebee's, it is a veritable all-you-can-eat, but so much more satisfying!

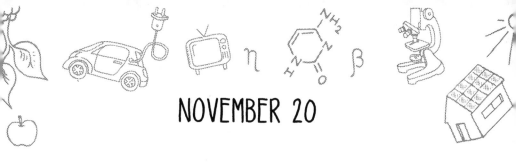

NOVEMBER 20

The Black Sox

1 Kings 3:9

On November 20, 1866, Kenesaw Mountain Landis was born in Millville, Ohio. He was a federal judge for most of his life, but also served as the first Commissioner of Major League Baseball from 1920 until he died in 1944. He was named for a mountain next to the town where I grew up in Marietta, Georgia. It was where his father was injured during the Civil War. When we had kids, I thought about suggesting it, but surely it would have been voted down by my wonderful wife. I digress.

What's His story? As he was more commonly known, K-Mount, or Commissioner Landis, oversaw one of baseball's biggest scandals, the Black Sox Scandal. It was called such because the 1919 Chicago White Sox intentionally lost The World Series for a financial payday. The scandal cast such a dark cloud over baseball, the team ended up with the Black Sox nickname. They thought that by losing, they could help some unsavory folks collect on bets. They were all caught, and Landis oversaw the expulsion and penalization of many players. His wisdom and courage remind us of King Solomon. 1 Kings 3:9 shows just how wise he was. Solomon could have asked God for anything, but instead, he asked for something we should pray for daily. He said to God, "So give your servant a discerning heart to govern your people and to distinguish between right and wrong." Solomon was asking for God to work through him, not for God to just give him something temporal. The power of wisdom and discernment is incredible when it is done for God's glory and in praising Him, not us. How are you on your wisdom and discernment? Could it use a bit more God and a little less of us?

NOVEMBER 21

He Is All Around Us

Mark 4:9

On November 21, 2007, the film *August Rush* was released. It is a story of a boy who thought he was orphaned, but the story proved otherwise. He was the son of a couple of talented musicians, and his story showed the musical influence that was passed on to him, and his quest to find his parents. It is a feel-good, happy ending kind of film with lots of musical artistry along the way.

What's His story? One of the songs from the movie and the movie soundtrack is entitled *August's Rhapsody*. It is supposedly a piece the young boy wrote. At the end of the song, he eloquently reminds us, "The music is all around us. All you have to do is listen." I believe the Holy Spirit is the same way. He is all around us and in us, desiring a deep relationship with us. All we have to do is listen. Why do we find ourselves too distracted or too involved in something else to listen? Think of the beautiful, soulful music we could make together. In Mark 4:9, Jesus is reminding us to listen when he says, "He who has ears to hear, let him hear." Jesus sent the Holy Spirit for us to hear. Some ways to show we are listening is through prayer, love, and other actions. We cannot treat it like background music wafting into the air. No, it must be like the magnificent performance of *August's Rhapsody* in the middle of Central Park, in where else but New York City! When we listen to Jesus and the Holy Spirit and truly hear, then our tune and our lives are changed. Are you listening? He is all around us. When we seek God, we can find Him in everything. Where have you seen or heard God lately?

NOVEMBER 22

Crawling for God

Ephesians 3:14

On November 22, 1978, Hans Mullikin reached the White House in Washington, D.C., having crawled on his hands and knees from Marshall, Texas. He covered a distance of over 1600 miles, and it took eighteen months of off-and-on crawling to do it. Hans typically covered four to five miles a day with some pretty stout kneepads. He encountered one snake, lots of curious onlookers, and plenty of roadkill.

What's His story? Mullikin believed that the United States, as a nation, needed to return to God. Crawling on his hands and knees all the way to Washington, D.C., was his way of raising awareness. He believed that, as a nation, we needed to restore God's rightful place in our lives by bowing before the most high and honoring His sovereignty. Along the way, he pulled a cart that said, "Pray, America." Not much has changed since 1978. We, as a nation, still need God more than ever. In Ephesians 3:14, Paul writes, "For this reason I kneel before the Father." Paul is preaching to the Gentiles, inviting them to receive the message, and he gives the church in Ephesus a summary of why he kneels before God. Paul calls himself less than the least of God's people, yet God's grace was given to him! We are no different. We can approach God with freedom and confidence as Paul writes, but we must also adopt the proper posture to honor God's rightful place. Mullikin's crawl for God was meant to heighten an awareness that we need to get back on our knees and bring God back to that proper place in our lives. Are you on your knees today? You do not necessarily have to crawl past Arkansas armadillo roadkill to understand it. God is the Almighty, and we kneel in honor of His glory!

NOVEMBER 23

Life in Christ

John 10:10

On November 23, 1936, the first issue of *Life* magazine was published. On its cover was the Fort Peck Dam Spillway, located in Montana on the Missouri River. I will be honest, I had no idea the Missouri River flowed through Montana! *Life* magazine was full of beautiful, moving, sometimes horrific, and always historical pictures. It is said that while *Time* magazine delivered the news, *Life* magazine showed it!

What's His story? *Life* changed the way people absorbed the news. By seeing it, they reacted differently. What about you? When you listen to the news on the radio, do you respond differently than watching the news on television? The title of the magazine itself played into that. *Life* revealed life. Jesus does the same for us. In John 10:10, He says, "I have come that they may have life and have it to the full." In the Greek language, life can be translated three different ways. One is bios, meaning physical, which is where we get biology. Another is psuche, which refers to mind and emotion. This is where we get psychology. Lastly is zoe, which is the Greek word for life eternal, or the divine life Jesus is referring to in John. Life is a word that you can pronounce and let it linger, extending the "f" sound for emphasis. I have heard many a pastor do this and always wondered why. I believe it is to remind us of the offer that Jesus makes to us as the Good Shepherd in this passage from John. Life in Christ is so much more than we can imagine ourselves. Just like the magazine by the same name, life comes to life in such a different way when we are alive in Christ! Have you subscribed to it?

NOVEMBER 24

Winning Friends & Influencing People for Jesus

Luke 2:52

On November 24, 1888, American author and motivational lecturer, Dale Carnegie, was born in Maryville, Missouri. Carnegie was famous for his writings and speeches on leadership, salesmanship, self-improvement, corporate training, and public speaking. His ideas and objectives are still used today by individuals and companies alike.

What's His story? While the ultimate motivational speaker was Jesus, Mr. Carnegie might have been there after Jesus left the stage. Carnegie's most famous work was entitled *How to Win Friends and Influence People*. Published in 1936, it described techniques to handle people, including ways to make people like you, ways to bring people to your way of thinking, and how to be a leader. Avoiding conflict is a recurrent theme in the book. Paul obviously did not read the book! He knew that to be a Christian would not always win friends and influence people, but it was necessary to live for Christ. The book of Proverbs is probably the best example of winning friends and influencing people while avoiding unnecessary conflict! Interestingly, Carnegie's book is really about servant leadership and putting others ahead of your own needs. We know from Luke 2:52 that Jesus sets the example that we should follow. It says, "And Jesus grew in wisdom and stature, and in favor with God and men." It does not mean men and God. The order of those two is significant. When we first seek favor in God and through God, our influence over others is precious, pure, and holy. Just add the words "for Jesus" at the end of the book title, and you have got it right! The new title should be *How to Win Friends and Influence People for Jesus!* Is this the one you are reading?

NOVEMBER 25

Tres Leches

Joel 3:18

On November 25, 1884, John Meyenberg of St. Louis, Missouri, received a patent for evaporated milk. You have used this milk that comes in a can if you ever made a pumpkin pie in the fall. Evaporated milk is made from unsweetened, fresh, homogenized (meaning the fat molecules stay together instead of separating as cream) milk that is then heated to reduce, or concentrate until 60% of the liquid is removed. Vitamin D is added, and then it is canned!

What's His story? Now that you have the science behind it, you may (or may not) have a deeper appreciation for evaporated milk. The neat thing about evaporated milk is that it is in more than just pie recipes. Have you ever had that wonderful Mexican dessert known as Tres Leches? It means "three milks" and includes heavy cream, condensed milk, and evaporated milk. To me, it sounds like the Trinity of the Father, Son, and Holy Spirit. Each adds a flavor and purpose of its own. Each is also necessary to the completeness of the end product. The water removal process in evaporated milk creates a more luxurious, richer taste. It concentrates the flavor. Throughout the New Testament, we see examples of nourishing milk as a metaphor for God's word and purity. In the Old Testament, Joel 3:18 harkens back for us to remember a restored land flowing with milk, wine, and water. It was a vision representing the beauty of God's provision for us as His people. The land was so fruitful that milk flowed forth everywhere! No longer will you look upon those cans of evaporated milk on the bottom shelf with disdain! They epitomize one of the necessary components of God's love.

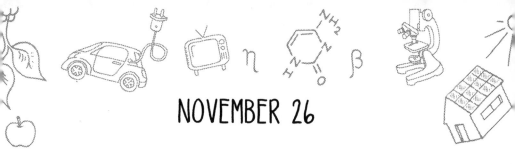

NOVEMBER 26

Curiosity Didn't Kill the Cat

Exodus 3:2-3

On November 26, 2011, the Mars Science Laboratory rover Curiosity was launched on a rocket from Kennedy Space Center in Florida bound for the Red Planet, Mars. The most elaborate planetary vehicle ever built, it was due for a long journey, landing on Mars August 5, 2012. I thought flights to Australia were long.

What's His story? At night if you find yourself in a dark place on a clear night, Mars is a planet that is sometimes easy to spot, with its characteristic orange glow. Imagine growing up believing that you would be responsible for launching a vehicle that would land on Mars one day. There are brilliant scientists who thought exactly that, and we should all be grateful to them. As for the rest of us, we can aspire to live in the fullness of the name of the rover, Curiosity. There is that saying about cats and the natural proclivity to risk one of their nine lives for the sake of curiosity, and they think it is worth it. Even Moses was curious! Look at Exodus 3:2-3. The angel of the Lord appeared to Moses in the form of flames burning in a bush, yet the fire did not consume it. Moses says, "I will go over and see this strange sight – why the bush does not burn up." Of course, you will, Moses! I would have too. Our sense of curiosity allows God to reveal His glory to us in His time and His way. Look at Proverbs 25:2-3. It is God's prerogative to satisfy our curiosity as He sees fit. That does not mean we need to stop searching! Are you launching your own Curiosity rover today? Are you filled with hopeful expectation for what God will reveal?

NOVEMBER 27

City of Steel

1 Kings 8:51

On November 27, 1758, the city of Pittsburgh, Pennsylvania, was founded. Pittsburgh sits at the confluence of the Allegheny, the Monongahela, and the Ohio rivers, thus its "Three Rivers" nickname. It is also known as the "City of Bridges" for its 446 (wow!) bridges. But it is best known as the "Steel City," related to the 300+ steel-related businesses found there.

What's His story? Since we have already reflected on the biblical importance of Jesus as our bridge to God, let's talk steel! As you know, steel is used in a myriad of things, from buildings, ships, and trucks to safety pins. It is firm and resolute, just as we should be. But did you know how steel is made? To summarize, it is a complicated process in which iron ore from the ground is smelted in a blast furnace where impurities are removed, and carbon is added. No, smelted is no typo. The difference between melting and smelting is that melting converts a solid substance to a liquid, whereas smelting converts an ore to its purest form. Now we are getting somewhere! 1 Kings 8:51 reminds us of this purification process as it says, "for they are your people and your inheritance, whom you brought out of Egypt, out of that iron-melting furnace." In this passage, Solomon has reminded the people of the toil and bitter bondage of Egypt as hot and oppressive as a smelting furnace. Just like a smelting furnace removes impurities from iron ore to give steel its firm and unrelenting strength, God has given His people power through their tribulations. It was a lesson and reminder for the Israelites as it is for us today. God delivers us, purifying us in ways we may not understand, but in the end, strengthening us with resolve and fortitude to become not just a city of steel, but also a people of steel! Maybe you are not a Steelers fan, but will you allow God to purify and mold you into something great?

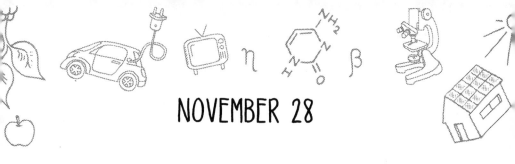

NOVEMBER 28

Not a Team of One

Joshua 1:5

On November 28, 1929, Chicago Cardinals fullback Ernie Nevers set a National Football League record for most points scored in a football game. The Cardinals beat the Chicago Bears 40-6, and Nevers scored every single point! He went on to do the same thing in their next game, scoring all 19 points himself. That included extra points, which he kicked!

What's His story? Well, this guy was obviously a talented player and lived up to his nickname, "The Big Dog." Yes, he is in the National Football League Hall of Fame. When you look at Nevers record-setting accomplishment scoring all points, you initially think, that is pretty impressive, and it is. For most of us, the reality is that we do not have to do it all on our own. The first chapter of Joshua is our reminder. As the handoff took place from Moses to Joshua (see what we did there?), the Lord says in Joshua 1:5, "No one will be able to stand up against you all the days of your life. As I was with Moses, so I will be with you; I will never leave you nor forsake you." He repeats it in Joshua 1:9 as he asks Joshua to have courage. While Ernie Nevers was able to score points on his own, we realize that we must rely on our Lord to win this game of life. Spoiler alert here - the game has already been won! We can rest assured that, like a trusted teammate, He will never leave our side. Is it hard to believe He is always with you? Why or why not? Are you playing on the same team as the Lord today? Sometimes, it is a tough question to answer.

NOVEMBER 29

Core Strength

Psalm 18:32

On November 29, 1965, a student from Berry College in Rome, Georgia, broke the world record for consecutive sit-ups. Dale Cummings did 14,118 in roughly twelve hours. He ended up eight pounds lighter than when he started. I am not sure about you, but the record is not in danger from me, and I prefer other methods of weight loss. By the way, the current record is 133,896 by Brazilian Edmar Freitas.

What's His story? While there might be mixed opinions over the benefit of sit-ups, they have always been a part of our lives. Whether it was a grade school assessment, a piece of a thirty-day challenge, or a resolution, sit-ups are an easy way for us to get up off the couch and get active. I really despise them! However, the point of a sit-up is to strengthen your core. When we say core, we are really talking about the groups of muscles responsible for several different things, such as posture, breathing, initiating, and sustaining movement. These are all vital activities when it comes to hula hooping! Having a strong core can also be a reference to your inner strength, buried deep within your body's muscles, all the way to your soul. God's power is always more than physical strength. God's strength gives us what we need to meet challenges. Psalm 18:32 says, "It is God who arms me with strength and makes my way perfect." By perfect, we are not talking about six-pack abs that Cummings and Freitas may have had. Instead, we are talking about the perfection of the way God has set out before us. His plan is perfect, and strengthening our core God strength through prayer, daily devotionals, and worship is our exercise routine to build soul strength! Are you headed to the God gym today?

NOVEMBER 30

I Am Third

Matthew 6:33

On November 30, 1971, the movie *Brian's Song* was released on ABC. This tear-jerker of a film is a true story of love. It is about a friendship between Chicago Bears football players Gale Sayers and Brian Piccolo.

What's His story? The movie is based on Sayers' account of his friendship with Piccolo in his book title, *I Am Third*. The bond between men of different races is unexpected during a time of heightened racial strife in the United States. Still, their budding relationship spurs each other on in brotherly love for one another, transcending any differences in skin color. If you have not read the book or watched the movie, I will not spoil it for you, but suffice to say, Sayers' realization is that love is an action. Further, he learns that love is full of sacrifice and knows his own place, as the book title reveals. You see, Sayers' credo was this, "The Lord is first, my friends are second, and I am third." In the Bible, Matthew 6:33 reinforces this for us as it says, "But seek first his kingdom and his righteousness, and all these things will be given to you as well." We must put God first, seeking His counsel in all things before anything else. Is this our pattern, or do we sometimes act irrationally expedient in perceived control? How often does a misplaced priority order counteract the goodness God has in store for us? Sayers had the right order. In doing so, his eyes were opened to a friendship that impacted his life in a way that can only be attributed to the goodness of God. Who is the subject of your song, and how is God revealing His splendor in that relationship?

DECEMBER 1

Hearing & Receiving

Galatians 3:2

On December 1, 1923, in Kansas City, Missouri, William Fouts House was born. He became a doctor and medical researcher who created the cochlear implant. In other words, he helped people hear again.

What's His story? Did you know that depending on which version of the Bible you have, the word "listen" is found 347 times? Many of the instances have to do with hearing God through scripture or hearing His voice. The specific phrase "hear the Word of the Lord" occurs thirty-two times in the NIV. In Mark 4:9, the Lord warned, "He who has an ear, let him hear," and again in Mark 4:23, "if anyone has ears to hear, let him hear." In Galatians 3:2, it says, "Did you receive the Spirit by observing the law, or by believing what you heard?" To truly hear Jesus' words is to believe them. It is to put them to use and to change your life because of them. To hear, and then be transformed, is to allow your light for Christ. It will most certainly let those around you know that what you hear is divine and something to behold. Do not forget, you also need to put those words into action. Obeying is essential, and we receive the Spirit by hearing and doing. Paul reminded the Galatians of this, and we could use this reminder today as well. Do you believe you gain the Spirit by obeying rules? Or is it because you are actively listening to how God is using the Spirit within you and acting in obedience to Him?

DECEMBER 2

Brushstrokes by God

Luke 12:7

On December 2, 1859, French painter Georges Seurat was born in Paris, France. He was a post-Impressionism painter famous for creating a new technique of painting known as Pointillism. This technique involved many tiny brushstrokes, creating dots or points. When combined, the dots form a complete picture. His most famous work, *Sunday Afternoon on the Island of La Grande Jatte*, is an excellent example of this technique.

What's His story? Pointillism allowed Seurat and other artists to create massive compositions through tiny dots of vivid colors that were too small to distinguish when looking at the entire work from across the room. Every dot is necessary to see the complete picture when you took a few steps away from the canvas. The effect highlights the importance of each individual dot and each pigment of paint. Can we compare the body of the church to this technique? How many times do you feel too small to make a difference? We often think of ourselves as inconsequential or unimportant in the whole scheme of things. We say to ourselves, "I am not that big of a deal, or I do not matter to God." That is far from the truth. Seurat's Pointillism works needed each and every contribution on the canvas to make sense when viewed from afar. God seeks our engagement and involvement in the canvas of His creation. However, one very distinct difference is that God does not need us. No, He actually WANTS us to contribute to His masterpiece of creation! As Seurat painted each tiny dot in intentional concert with the rest of them to create the fullness of work, God knows you by name and knows how your individual talents and spiritual gifts can contribute. As Luke 12:7 says, "Indeed the very hairs of your head are numbered." The same goes for you who have the Mr. Clean look! You are important as an individual to God, and you have true worth in His eyes. We are all necessary for the complete work He is creating. Are you a part of the canvas? Allow God to paint with you through the Holy Spirit and be a part of His magnificent artwork!

DECEMBER 3

By the Light of a Neon Moon

2 Corinthians 4:6

On December 3, 1910, French inventor George Claude first demonstrated his invention, the neon sign, at the Paris Auto Show in Paris, France. A neon sign works by taking neon gas under low pressure and adding electricity to ionize neon atoms until they gain enough energy to become excited. When an atom returns to a lower energy state, it releases a photon to create the light you see!

What's His story? If you have ever driven through Atlanta, Georgia, you may have seen one of the best neon signs. Near Grady Hospital sits Big Bethel African Methodist Episcopal church. On its steeple is a two-line bright blue neon sign that simply says, "Jesus Saves"! Above, you learned that light is released when the neon atom returns to a lower energy state. You may be thinking that it is counterintuitive, but consider yourself as a neon atom. You might attend church, participate in a bible study, or hear a sermon podcast. These are all ways to encounter God's spirit, allowing yourself to gain energy and become excited for Christ. You might even buzz around spreading joy! When you leave or go out into the world after becoming charged, your bright neon light is then ready and able to shine out in the darkness! If it is quiet enough, you may even hear that light humming we associate with neon lights. 2 Corinthians 4:6 gives us the reason we should do this, "For God, who said, "Let light shine out of darkness," made his light shine in our hearts to give us the light of the knowledge of God's glory displayed in the face of Christ." Wow! Not only do gaudy neon lights stand up to that passage of scripture, but they are also a reminder of our opportunity to light up the world around us with a message of hope! Are you excited and giving off your light?

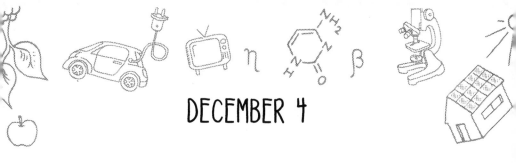

DECEMBER 4

Good Will Flying

1 Timothy 6:17

On December 4, 1991, with Captain Mark Pyle at the controls, the Boeing 727-200 *Clipper Goodwill* completed its flight from Barbados and touched down in Miami, Florida. This event officially ended the flight operations of Pan American World Airways, also known as Pan Am Airlines. Pan Am operated for sixty-four years, from 1927 to 1991, and had names for its planes, such as *Clipper Defender, Clipper Beacon Light,* and *Clipper Fortune.*

What's His story? Each plane was called a clipper because Pan Am rightfully considered each aircraft to be a clipper, or ship, of the sky. For the last one to be named *Clipper Goodwill* is fitting and suitable. With this name, surely plenty of goodwill missions took place. We do not know all of their stories, but the Bible is full of goodwill stories. In terms of everyday living and how we can demonstrate goodwill towards all, following God's example, 1 Timothy 6:17 is a great one. It says, "Command those who are rich in this present world not to be arrogant nor to put their hope in wealth which is so uncertain, but to put their hope in God, who richly provides us with everything for our enjoyment." Simply put, our hope should be placed in God. Doing so allows us to act in good faith, and with goodwill toward others through good works and generosity. Reflecting the goodness of God is how we land the plane of goodwill, showing that everything does flow from God. Are you flying with that approach, or do you need to reset your navigation to point towards God?

DECEMBER 5

The Swiss Army Attacks!

1 Thessalonians 3:12

On December 5, 1985, the Swiss Army accidentally attacked the neighboring country of Liechtenstein. During a military exercise, they shot a few missiles into the Liechtenstein forests, and the explosives started a few forest fires. I would hate to be the commander in charge of explaining that one. Reading this, you may have just realized that the Swiss are really not neutral all the time and carry more than just pocketknives and chocolate!

What's His story? Would you say this faux pas, committed by the Swiss Army, is an example of being a bad neighbor? I guess it depends on the apology that followed, and perhaps making each Swiss soldier wear a Smokey Bear t-shirt that says, "Only You Can Prevent Forest Fires." While we are not typically shooting missiles at our neighbors, there are other ways we can be bad neighbors. We are all guilty, whether it is rooted in neglect, avoidance, or anger. 1 Thessalonians 3:12 is our reminder of how to be a good neighbor everywhere we go, discussing the importance of having an overflowing love for one another. When our love overflows for each other, looking past all obstacles or blocks, we are the neighbors God intended us to be. We become each other's confidants, navigating hardship and blessings as a unit, instead of in isolation. Human nature craves connection and community. The words of this passage lead us to a place where we are cutting a neighbor's lawn, picking up their newspapers, and greeting one another with a smile. Now move beyond your immediate neighborhood, and let the overflowing love of Christ sends missiles of grace into your community. It will ignite the Spirit within the recipient, spreading Christian love everywhere. You can tell them the Swiss Army made you do it. Where is your aim today?

DECEMBER 6

Book of Knowledge

James 1:22-25

On December 6, 1768, the first edition of Encyclopedia Britannica was published. I still remember using these growing up, before the Internet, where maps, facts, and figures were at your fingertips. Quite honestly, it probably planted the seed for this book. Door-to-door Encyclopedia Britannica salesman, wherever you are, I want to say thank you!

What's His story? The Bible is the best encyclopedia out there. It is full of people, events, cultures, buildings, maps, history, and a list that is endless. The glorious thing about the Bible is the life application we gain from the scripture found within the pages. This is something no encyclopedia contains, but if you have been tracking along with this devotional book throughout, significant and mundane events in history still have the fingerprints of God. Each moment in time lets us learn about His goodness and discover ways to apply the principles we find. The "mirror" verse we find in James 1:22-25 is a great way to illustrate the importance of applying biblical learning to our lives. Read it! The first part tells us not to merely listen to the word, but do what it says. It would be like reading about how to take the subway, but walking instead. It could be done, but why would you? The next part of the passage compares seeing yourself in a mirror and then walking away, forgetting what you looked like. It is another reminder to let the scripture you read settle on your soul and guide you daily. Reading scripture, praying about it, and then finding an outlet to spread His kingdom are ways we can communicate with God. Are you using your Encyclopedia God today?

DECEMBER 7

Basketball Jesus

Matthew 10:27

On December 7, 1956, Larry Joe Bird was born in West Baden Springs, Indiana. Larry Bird was one of the greatest basketball players of all time. Bird had such a talent on the court, it was as if he had eyes in the back of his head.

What's His story? To some, Larry Bird was known as "Larry Legend" or the "Hick from French Lick." He was someone I can recall from that era in the 1980s and 1990s who could effectively pull off a mullet, a mustache, and super-short shorts simultaneously. He was also known to some as "Basketball Jesus." Why? Perhaps it was his tendency to make assists, in which he helped other players score points, or maybe it was the countless ways in which he persevered. I believe it was because basketball just seemed to come easy for him, as if he could do it in his sleep. As Christians, we should want our profession of spreading the Gospel to come as naturally. When people ask why we smile, or why we push on, our instinct should not be to search our brains for an appropriate response. Our knee-jerk reaction should be as lightning fast as a Larry Bird pass. Our answer should be resolute and firm, reacting instinctively with words that stamp us as a disciple of Christ. Bird was not shy about exhibiting his talent. Nor should we be shy about the good news of the Gospel! In Matthew 10:27, Jesus says, "What I tell you in the dark, speak in the daylight; what is whispered in your ear, proclaim from the roofs." In other words, preach brothers and sisters in Christ!! Preach so that others may know His name and His mighty works. We may not all be a Larry Bird of faith, but we sure can persevere as he did. Are you in the game today? Why not?

DECEMBER 8

Cold Heavy Metal

Job 28:24

On December 8, 2014, the band Metallica performed at the Argentine Carlini Station in Antarctica, thus becoming the first band to perform a concert on all seven continents! I have so many questions. Were they wearing parkas? Who was in the audience? Was there crowd surfing? And that is just a start.

What's His story? I know what you are thinking. Metallica? Put that aside for just a second. In Job 28:24, we find: "For He views the ends of the earth and sees everything under the heavens." To hit all seven continents, you are reaching the ends of the earth, but this short verse abundantly illustrates that God knows and sees all. His knowledge is unlimited, and His power is infinite. Even in the darkest, coldest corners of the world, God is present. His light shines and reigns above everything else, and nothing is hidden from Him. God is with us all the time. Even at a gig in the far reaches of the planet, delivered by a controversial heavy metal band, He is present. I encourage you to read up on the history of the group, their backgrounds, and how religion plays a vital role in their lyrics and music. There is no need to visit all seven continents to experience God's presence. You can do it right where you are! How will you seek it today?

DECEMBER 9

Coffee Table Book About Coffee Tables

Romans 1:20

On December 9, 1993, on the television sitcom *Seinfeld*, the character Kramer came up with an idea to write a coffee table book about coffee tables. His book even had little fold-out wooden legs to make it look like an actual coffee table.

What's His story? Sometimes the obvious is right under our nose. Yet, other times we have to stretch and search. While clearly comedic since it was, after all, on Seinfeld, Kramer's book is an example of the obvious. In that regard, it is much like God. However, we regularly take the latter path, acting like God is so hard to find. Why do we make it so difficult to see God in action in our lives? In Romans 1:20, Paul sums it up well in his letter to the church in Rome. In this passage, Paul describes God's wrath in a manner in which God has been made plain to us, yet we still suppress the truth of His word. We see God's hand in our lives, but somehow we attribute it to our own actions. Romans 1:20 says, "For since the creation of the world God's invisible qualities – his eternal power and divine nature – have been clearly seen, being understood from what has been made, so that men are without excuse." There is no denying the power of God in our lives, or in the world for that matter. We are continuously reminded. Would it take more than a coffee table book about coffee tables to convince you that the obvious power of our Lord is worth the sacrifice? Let God reveal his divine nature to you, and be open to the obvious that can be so magnificent!

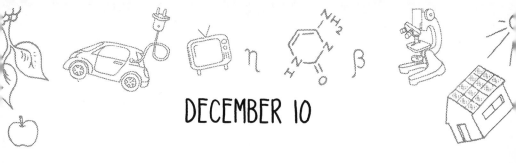

DECEMBER 10

Why We Work

Colossians 3:23-24

On December 10, 1901, the first Nobel Prizes were awarded. You have already read about the man for which the prize is named, and the irony of his inventions. On this day in 1901, the first prize was shared between Swiss Jean Henry Dunant, founder of the Red Cross, and Frenchman Frederic Passy, founder of the French Peace Society.

What's His story? The Nobel Prizes are awarded to more than just peacemakers. They are awarded to those individuals or groups that have excelled in their various fields. The prestigious award recipients include people like Albert Einstein, Teddy Roosevelt, Nelson Mandela, Ernest Hemingway, Marie Curie, and a host of others. To observe talent in one's field is to watch grit and doggedness lead to recognition, although many of them would tell you that was not the driver. They might say it was for the sake of humanity. But even if you are not an aspiring Nobel Prize nominee, Colossians 3:23-24 puts perspective on our vocations, no matter what it is. The scripture says, "Whatever you do, work at it with all your heart, as working for the Lord, not for men, since you know that you will receive an inheritance from the Lord as a reward. It is the Lord Christ you are serving." Some days, especially Mondays, when it is hard to rise from the bed, just remember who you are genuinely working for when you head to your office. Work takes many forms, with some clearly defined, and others open-ended. It all leads back to God. For it is He who should be glorified! Is this the attitude you have today? What would you need to change to make it better? What is stopping you? There is a prize even greater than a Nobel Prize waiting for you!

DECEMBER 11

Swamp Land Discovery

2 Corinthians 4:18

On December 11, 2000, United States President Bill Clinton signed legislation launching an official restoration and revitalization of the Florida Everglades. This thirty-year project was created to return this pristine and unique area of South Florida back to its natural state. Over the prior years, man-made water diversions and pollution had wrecked the "River of Grass."

What's His story? While you may not be fond of alligators, you must agree that there is a unique beauty in the Everglades. Seeing the beauty from the air in the daytime flying into Miami is one thing, but at night the stark darkness so close to a metropolitan area is striking. The Everglades was almost passed over as a National Park. No one in Congress wanted to vote for it. It was not until a few men from the Corps of Engineers saw it from the air during a blimp ride that they understood its beauty. They were expecting beauty like the other National Parks out west, like Yosemite and Yellowstone. 2 Corinthians 4:18 reminds us, "So we fix our eyes not on what is seen, but on what is unseen. For what is seen is temporary, but what is unseen is eternal." In the Everglades, plenty of wildlife can be found above the marshy surface of the water. But, if you were to look just below the murky tannin-filled water, you would see a brand new world and ecosystem teeming with life. The same is true for us. When we look beyond the immediacy of our anguish and pain in this life, we are finally able to gain a glimpse into the place God promises us where there is no suffering and no pain. It is easy to get bogged down in the drama of the surface of our life. Instead, let's look at things from Heaven's perspective! There is hidden beauty in the here and now, but the world revealed to us through scripture is so much more spectacular! Are you missing the forest for the cypress trees, so to speak?

DECEMBER 12

Christmas Flower Diplomacy

Luke 6:35

On December 12, 1851, Joel Roberts Poinsett died in Stateburg, South Carolina. Poinsett was a physician and a United States diplomat. Five United States Presidents called on him for diplomacy activities. He was also an avid horticulturist. Those are not related, you say?

What's His story? In 1825, while Poinsett was ambassador to Mexico for President John Quincy Adams, he brought clippings of a very distinctive plant back with him. It was a Mexican plant with leaves of deep green, but the ones highest on the plant turned a beautiful deep red very late in the calendar year, coinciding with the Christmas colors of red and green. You guessed it! Interestingly, it took four years to earn his fame tied to the plant he brought back from Mexico. Friends of Poinsett displayed the plant at a flower show in Philadelphia, and the name stuck. The poinsettia was born. When we look at his career, Poinsett clearly followed the pathway of Luke 6:35. It says when we love our enemies and expect nothing in return, our reward is great. His diplomacy skills were excellent and, while he was a deft negotiator, he also did not expect anything in return to highlight his personal accomplishments. Even with the plant, he got great joy out of giving away clippings of the poinsettias he brought back from Mexico. You might have a neighbor like him! Poinsett's name is forever bound to a plant we embrace at the most joyous and festive time of year! His reward is much more than just a plant, but that is our reminder today of what a great diplomat and peacemaker Poinsett was. Are you loving freely with no expectations? You may not end up with a plant being named for you, but your reward could be Heavenly!

DECEMBER 13

High Fidelity

Psalm 150:1-6

On December 13, 1759, the first music store was opened in Philadelphia, Pennsylvania, by Michael Hillegas. In addition to instruments, this music store in Philly had all kinds of sheet music available, including ballads, hymns, carols, and probably just a few tunes that were sung in the taverns. Oh, dear!

What's His story? God can be found in music, and music can lead us to God. It is an exciting and tightly cohesive relationship. Music can take you to a completely different place and allow you to remove all barriers and obstacles toward pure and unbridled worship. Do you have a favorite worship song or one that just seems to bring you closer to God? Psalm 150:1-6 gives us the imagery of how that first music store must have looked. There were trumpets, harps, lyres, tambourines, strings, flutes, cymbals, and dancing. I know you know the only thing that was missing, and that was more cowbell. I suppose you cannot have everything. Does music allow you to praise God and sing to Him? It does not matter if you have musical talent or not, praise for God is simply enhanced by the music. Music is God's gift to us. I would argue that it is a gift that gets used every single day. Are you singing with God today? What would it take to get you on the same sheet of music as God?

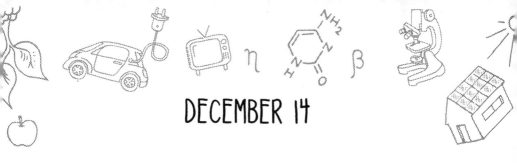

DECEMBER 14

Thicker Than Water

Colossians 1:13-14

On December 14, 1863, United States President Abraham Lincoln issued a pardon to Emilie Todd Helm. She was the half-sister of Lincoln's wife, Mary, who was the widow of Confederate general Benjamin Helm. This was the first pardon under Lincoln's Proclamation of Amnesty and Reclamation aimed at rebuilding and renewing a united country.

What's His story? Sure, Emilie had some inside pull, and Lincoln clearly knew the phrase, "happy wife, happy life." More importantly, he knew the power of love and forgiveness. It did not matter if it was his own family or throughout a nation torn by a tragic civil war; this was an opportunity he could not refuse. Lincoln probably knew Psalm 103:12 as it says, "As far as the east is from the west, so far has he removed our transgressions from us." In this case, it was from the north is to the south, but the point remains. God's grace and forgiveness have no bounds, especially familial ones! Colossians 1:13-14 then asserts what happens when we love and forgive as it says, "For he has rescued us from the dominion of darkness and brought us into the kingdom of the Son he loves, in whom we have redemption, the forgiveness of sins." When we forgive as God forgives us through the sacrifice of Christ, we are literally transported from a place of darkness and hopelessness into the kingdom of Jesus! Why would we even think of choosing anything else? Lincoln caught a lot of flack for this pardon, but his example set forth is another reminder of how we can act in Christlike love. Where does forgiveness need to start with you? Is it in your family or with someone else important to you?

DECEMBER 15

Laughter Is the Best Medicine

Genesis 21:6

On December 15, 1933, actor and screenwriter Tim Conway was born. If you are familiar with the *Carol Burnett Show*, Conway was a regular. The show was full of fun and entertaining skits, so much so that Tim and the other stars of the show were often cracking themselves up with laughter!

What's His story? I believe that laughter comes from a joy that evolves deep within, and manifests as an outward expression of happiness. It is a gift from God. It helps us cope with the sadness of everyday life. It really can be the best medicine. Do you ever find yourself in a full-on belly laugh, and suddenly, tension and tightness are entirely gone? In the Bible, you can see that even God has a sense of humor. In Genesis 21:6, we find Sarah laughing at the notion that she was going to have a child at ninety years old! God simply asks, "Why is that funny?" I am not sure why that strikes me as comedic, but it reveals God is searching our hearts. I believe that it also reveals Him as our Father in a way that conveys relatability endearingly. It is that story and a silly *Carol Burnett Show* skit that can make us smile and realize that God created us in His image to have a happy and joyful heart. Laughter is such a powerful tool for dealing with daily struggles. How do you find laughter and joy today? What can you do to make laughter contagious?

DECEMBER 16

Immortal Beloved

Psalm 146:1-4

On December 16, 1770, in the city of Bonn, Germany, one of the world's finest pianists and composers, Ludwig Van Beethoven was born. While the date is disputed, most historians agree on December 16th. Beethoven began playing the piano at a young age and performed his first recital at age seven. A few of his famous works are *Moonlight Sonata* and *Symphony No. 5*. You may know it as the "dah, dah, dah, dum" symphony. Of all of the works of music he composed, he only composed one opera, *Fidelio*.

What's His story? Beethoven was instrumental in connecting the Classical and Romantic ages of music. He bridged them through his magnificent works, many of which were later finished while he was almost completely deaf! He started losing his hearing around age twenty-six. Later in life, he went so far as to saw off the legs of his piano, and laid on the floor as he pounded the keys to "hear" the notes! Psalm 146:1-4 best describes Beethoven as it says, "Praise the Lord. Praise the Lord. O my soul. I will praise the Lord all my life. I will sing praise to my God as long as I live." He lived with his impairment and made the most of it. He continued to work with passion because he believed the opposite was inexcusable. How often do we bail out of genuine and pure praise for God, because of some deep-rooted resentment towards something we perceive as a malady or handicap? The lesson Beethoven sets out before us, and the words of Psalm 146 give us the sheet of music we should follow. We have an opportunity each day to compose our own symphony of praise to God. Do you take advantage of it, and do so with passion, or are you in the audience, watching and waiting?

DECEMBER 17

On Wings of Eagles

Isaiah 40:31

On December 17, 1903, Ohio brothers Wilbur and Orville Wright piloted the first powered airplane twenty feet into the air, for twelve seconds, and 120 feet from a hill along the beach in Kitty Hawk, North Carolina. They decided Orville would fly first using a coin toss!

What's His story? When the brothers were young, a homemade helicopter made with cork, bamboo, paper, and a rubber band instilled their passion for aviation. Their father, who was a bishop in the church, brought it home and shared it with them. In the family of a church leader, I am sure the Wright brothers heard the verse from Isaiah 40:31, "but those who hope in the Lord will renew their strength. They will soar on wings like eagles; they will run and grow weary, they will walk and not be faint." It is one of my favorites, and it sums up the story of the *Wright Flyer* like no other. Hoping in the Lord is not wishing. Rather, it is a result of faith. It is the expectation that God will show up and lift you the same way the rushing wind somehow lifts an aircraft or eagle into the air. I will spare you the scientific explanation, for once. But, if we accept God's provision for our life, amazing things can happen. When we allow ourselves to be guided by a deep-seated trust, then our life is transformed into a source of courage, innovation, and passion for God and his kingdom. Orville once took his elderly father for the only flight his dad ever experienced. His dad purportedly cried out, "higher, Orville, higher!" Like a jubilant kid on a swing set, joy flowed as they soared like eagles. No doubt, the verse might have been in his head. Did you know that two pieces from the *Wright Flyer* were tucked into his spacesuit when Neil Armstrong walked on the moon? The fragments were a piece of fabric from the wing and a chunk of wood from the propeller! Today, are you soaring with God?

DECEMBER 18

You're a Mean One

Ecclesiastes 5:20

On December 18, 1966, the television cartoon *How the Grinch Stole Christmas* first aired. It is a depiction of the mean green Grinch who tried to steal the joy and packages from the Whos in Whoville. He did this with his trusty, yet oblivious companion, Max the Dog. The Grinch dressed up as Santa and swept into town on Christmas Eve, stealing everything associated with Christmas. Or so he thought he did.

What's His story? The Grinch did not take the size of the hearts in Whoville into account, or the true meaning of Christmas. When Christmas arrived, he "puzzled and puzzled till his puzzler was sore. Then the Grinch thought of something he hadn't before. Maybe Christmas, he thought...does not come from a store. Maybe Christmas, perhaps...means a little bit more!" Ecclesiastes 5:8-20 is an excellent passage for the Grinch. He would soon learn that greed and love of money and things are empty and meaningless. The latter verses in this passage remind us that by finding satisfaction in our toil, we come to accept and enjoy the lot from God as a gift of God. Ecclesiastes 5:20 says, "He seldom reflects on the days of his life because God keeps him occupied with gladness of heart." That should be our one true vocation, to find gladness in our hearts. How often do we believe that we can find happiness and joy through material things? We may not be dressed up as Santa stealing roast beast, but we sometimes take the same approach when focusing on riches instead of God. It almost sounds like that old adage of "time flies when you're having fun." Fun is a life lived for God, focusing on the giver, not the possession! Are you a Grinch today? Can a position of humility and thankfulness change you?

DECEMBER 19

Curling for Jesus

Isaiah 45:2

On December 19, 1881, the first indoor curling club was opened in Boston, Massachusetts. The sport of curling came to Boston in the 1800s and is a game played on ice. The indoor club allowed it to be played all year long, just as they eat chowda and lobsta all year long in Boston.

What's His story? Have you ever watched curling? I was first exposed to it watching the Winter Olympics. Curling is a sport, almost like shuffleboard, where two teams of four players each slide a forty-pound granite stone down a sheet of ice toward a target at the other end of the rink known as the house. The player releasing the stone in a rather picturesque posture can make it turn, or curl towards the house. Two other players sweep the ice vigorously back and forth as the stone glides down the ice. It is their guidance that puts the stone in the house. You have probably never thought of God as one of those sweepers, but he certainly performs the same task for us. Just as they guide the stone to the house, God guides us. He probably does not have to do it as vigorously as the sweepers in curling, but He probably feels that way as we stray from the path. Isaiah 45:2 reminds us that God goes out before us on that path. He levels the mountains, breaks down gates, and cuts the bars. Why? Because He loves us! This passage from Isaiah is where God anointed a Gentile, Cyrus, for a particular task. No matter who you are, God's pathway of reassurance is available to everyone. Will you let God guide you to the house? We sometimes act like huge immovable chunks of granite, but with a leveled and smooth sheet of ice and God sweeping the pathway for us, we can make it to the house! But first, who, or what, is going to start you down the ice?

DECEMBER 20

What a Wonderful Life, Indeed!

Matthew 13:32

On December 20, 1946, the film *It's a Wonderful Life* starring Jimmy Stewart and directed by Frank Capra made its debut at the Globe Theater. It is a blissful Christmas classic. You can probably find it on television right now if you are reading this book as a daily devotional.

What's His story? The film is about a man named George Bailey, a struggling businessman facing a financial crisis. He believes he has no other option but to commit suicide. However, he is saved by a guardian angel named Clarence, who is trying to earn his wings. Clarence takes Bailey on a tour of his hometown, showing him how it would appear if Bailey were never born and never made an impact. Bailey quickly realizes things are not good, and as small and inconsequential as he thought he was, he did make a positive impact. We are the same way. We believe that our small acts of kindness, while helpful, do not amount to much, or our prayers are wrong, and God does not answer them. We should stop to realize that the Creator, who gave us the universe, wants a deep personal relationship with each one of us, and that He does care about our needs, and hears every word, spoken and unspoken. Whatever we do contributes to God's kingdom. I want you to envision the mustard seed mentioned in Matthew 13:32. The verse starts out, "Though it is the smallest of all your seeds." Have you ever seen a mustard seed? It truly is tiny, but it is a lot like us. Even our smallest contribution can grow into the largest and most effectual thing to benefit His kingdom. Kind words, an encouraging letter, or prayer you think are unimportant can allow the Holy Spirit to work through us. God knows the impact it has or will have on someone or something, and that is all that should matter. Have you ever thought about what your world would look like without you in it?

DECEMBER 21

God Is Up, Down, and Across

Micah 4:12

On December 21, 1913, the first crossword puzzle was published in the *New York World* newspaper. It was in a diamond shape and called Word-Cross. Arthur Wynne was responsible for it. Believe it or not, if you search on the *Reader's Digest* website, you may be able to find it online today and try to solve it!

What's His story? Some people love crosswords, and the challenge it presents. I have never been able to solve a *New York Times* crossword fully, but what are some tricks and tips you typically use to help solve crosswords? There are plenty of examples to follow: a theme, focus on the small words first, clues obey rules, do not jump to conclusions, wordplay is wonderful (e.g., European staff = pole), and lastly, practice makes a better solver. It is interesting how many of these might also help us understand God's message to us. We often feel like we are trying to solve the veritable crossword puzzle of life, harder than any Saturday version of the *Times* puzzle. But Micah 4:12 provides a proper perspective. We would like for all of the blanks to be filled in for us, but that is not God's intent. For if He revealed His purpose in everything, how much differently would you live your life? Thankfully, being open to how God reveals His purpose and plans makes us motivated to serve in joyful obedience, trusting His will and ways. God does not complete the puzzle the same way we do. And while we aim for the easy fill-in-the-blank answers, God assures us that through tips and tricks like prayer time, kindness, love, and peace we can solve even the hardest of life's puzzles. As a diligent solver, we can trust in a future with God as the master crossword creator. How can God help reduce complexity in your life? Does He already give you clues to help solve some of today's unsolvable puzzles?

DECEMBER 22

NUTS!

Philippians 1:6

On December 22, 1944, in the forest of Bastogne, Belgium, during World War II, the infamous "NUTS!" reply was delivered from the American Brigadier General Tony McAulliffe to the German Commander. This was the last major German offensive in the Battle of the Bulge, and four German soldiers had presented the Americans with an offer to surrender or be annihilated. McAulliffe replied, "NUTS!" Obviously, the Germans did not quite understand the response, but it served as a rallying cry for the soldiers of the 101st Airborne in that Belgium forest. The Americans ultimately held the line, and the victory at Bastogne became a turning point in the latter stages of the war.

What's His story? As Christians, we are offered plenty of opportunities to take the quick, easy, and unchallenging road. However, we sometimes take the tough road ahead and hope for results in justice and peace. The path that requires us to stand by our character, or commandments of our Lord, is not always the easiest. We can choose to just say "NUTS!" and stay the course that Christ has established for our lives. In Philippians 1:6, Paul reminds us of the purpose of being joyful in the Gospel. Paul, knowing what he is pointed toward, can then pray joyfully in the fact that Christ will bring it to completion when He comes again. Let us finish the good work that He started. Why quit early? Do not be weary, but continue to fight the good fight for Christ. When the enemy forces seem to have you surrounded, the best option is to tell them "NUTS!" and pray! Are you weary today? Or, are you charging onto the battlefield in the name of Christ?

DECEMBER 23

Love from God

1 John 4:7

On December 23, 1954, Dr. Joseph Murray, a surgeon at Boston's Peter Ben Brigham Hospital, performed the first categorically successful kidney transplant. It was completed between a pair of identical twins, Richard and Ronald Herrick. Evidently, the Red Ryder rifle that Richard had on his Christmas list was not acceptable to Ronald, so he gave Richard a kidney instead of a rifle. He also got it early.

What's His story? All joking aside, both of Richard's kidneys were failing, and he needed a miracle. Did you know that your amazing human body can survive with just one kidney? In Richard's case, he needed only one good one to replace his. Organ donation matches within families are usually a safe bet, but no one had transplanted a kidney with much success until this operation. As we often pray for God's hands to enable and equip the surgeon's hands, he did on this day! Richard went on to live another eight years after the transplant, and Ronald lived another fifty-six years! Ronald's kidney donation reminds us of the passage in 1 John 4:7, "Dear friends, let us love one another, for love comes from God. Everyone who loves has been born of God and knows God." We are commanded to love. Love is God. When we love those who love us it feels natural, but to love in the way Ronald did is supernatural and sacrificial! When we love one another in this manner, it is proof that we are of God. You may not have to share a kidney to show love, but one of the preeminent ways we can point to God's love working through us is wholly sharing it! How will you love naturally, supernaturally, and sacrificially today? That last one takes the most effort, but some might say, is the most rewarding.

DECEMBER 24

He Is Everywhere

Jeremiah 23:23-24

On December 24, 1974, American radio and television personality Ryan Seacrest was born in Dunwoody, Georgia. If you have watched television within the past decade, you have seen him. From morning talk shows to music competitions, and taking over for Dick Clark to ring in each new year at Times Square, he stays incredibly busy.

What's His story? When you look at all the things Mr. Seacrest is involved in, you start to believe that there has to be more than one copy of him, perhaps a hologram. The only real example of omnipresence in our life is God. As we approach the day of the Messiah's birth celebration, we have an opportunity to give thanks for how He is active and present in our lives today. Jeremiah 23:23-24 tells us in no uncertain terms about the omnipresence of God. The holidays can sometimes make us feel alone or desolate depending on our circumstances. This passage reminds us that we cannot hide from God, even if we think we can. As big as our God is, He is not far. He is near! Maybe you will celebrate a candlelit service at church tonight, or spend a quiet evening reflecting. Either way, you are not alone. God is near, and He wants a relationship with you! So if you have ever wondered how Ryan Seacrest can be everywhere at once, take it a step further and acknowledge the true meaning of omnipresence. God is in infinitely more places than Ryan Seacrest! Who thought you could use Mr. Seacrest for perspective on how wonderful, beautiful, and far-reaching God is, but it works. In the stillness or chaos of this particular eve, do you feel His presence?

DECEMBER 25

The Christmas Truce

Ephesians 2:17

On December 25, 1914, the historic Christmas Truce took place along the battle lines in World War I. Just after midnight, through the night and into Christmas dawn, German soldiers stopped firing their weapons and began singing Christmas carols. At first light, many crossed unarmed into no-man's land exchanging "Merry Christmas" greetings with men who were sworn enemies just hours before the truce.

What's His story? On this most beautiful day as we celebrate the birth of the Messiah, the Rescuer, and our Savior, we also acknowledge Him as the Prince of Peace. On the western and eastern fronts of battle, the power of His birth overcame brutal and horrific fighting. Ephesians 2:14-19 is an appropriate passage for today and in special remembrance of the Christmas Truce. In it, Paul is highlighting how Jesus broke down barriers. Although the passage is about Jew and Gentile, we could apply this today in any division in society that keeps us from Christ. The words, "he came and preached peace to you who were are away and peace to those who were near," emphasizes the fact that no matter who we are, we need Jesus. One of my favorite t-shirts I have seen says, "Y'all Need Jesus!" It is so true. We all need Jesus. We give thanks on this day to celebrate His birth, because of what He brings this world. He unites us through His birth. That was the case with the Christmas Truce, but even more so every single day through what He did on the cross! Today, as you celebrate Christmas, do so with the knowledge and understanding that Jesus gives you all of the power of the Holy Spirit to look beyond barriers to that place where we are united by peace. Are you at peace today? Not just relaxed in your new comfy slippers or pajamas, but do you have tranquility in your heart that can only come from Christ? Should you negotiate your own Christmas Truce? Merry Christmas!!

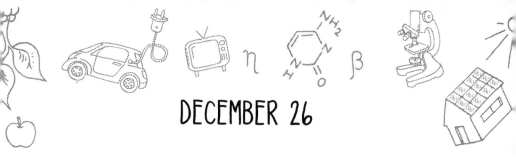

DECEMBER 26

The Cowcatcher Gospel

Mark 1:2-3

On December 26, 1791, English mathematician Charles Babbage was born in London, England. Also an inventor, he is credited with designing the first analytical digital calculator. He was an incredibly talented mathematics architect, and his calculators of the 1800s were astonishing when you think about the time during which they were created.

What's His story? Babbage excelled at all things math, including the invention of a type of speedometer. He even helped design the modern postal system in England. But, you will never guess something else he invented. This guy invented the cowcatcher! The cowcatcher is that plow or v-shaped attachment hooked on to the front of locomotives designed to clear any obstructions from the railway tracks, namely cows! Maybe it should have been called the cow pusher. Mark 1:2-8, ascribing the words of the prophet Isaiah, proclaims Jesus as the coming Messiah, but also presents us with the greatest cowcatcher of the Bible, John the Baptist. John has cleared the tracks and made way for Jesus similarly to how Christ clears the tracks of our life as He goes on ahead of us. John prepares the people for what is to come, so they can receive the message Jesus brings. Occasionally, the messenger is as striking as the message. As an uber-talented mathematician invented a tool to clear the tracks, this loud rebel named John, wearing camel hair and eating locusts, prepares the way for our Savior. No cow is going to block the message of my Jesus! What about you? Do you accept Christ as your own personal cowcatcher? Sure, that may be the craziest thing you have ever read, but think about it. Are you allowing Him to clear your paths for you to focus on His message? Cows be gone!

DECEMBER 27

What Time Is It?

Revelation 1:17-18

On December 27, 1947, the first episode of the children's television show, *Howdy Doody* aired on the NBC network. It starred human character Buffalo Bob, and marionette puppet Howdy Doody. Each show began with a question, "Say, kids, what time is it?" and the resounding response was, "It's Howdy Doody time!" It was a popular show during it is run from 1947 to 1960.

What's His story? Doody was a marionette puppet, which meant that he was controlled from above by a series of strings attached to his limbs and mouth. The operator can move the strings in a variety of ways to generate natural motion as if the marionette were alive. How often do we find the things of this world are controlling us as if we were the marionette puppets? What are the things or strings that control you? Is it fear, anger, or anxiety? Revelation 1:17 is a verse of reassurance that God is in control. When it says, "I fell at his feet as though dead," the imagery of a lifeless marionette comes to mind. But then Jesus says, "Do not be afraid. I am the First and the Last. I am the Living One; I was dead and behold I am alive for ever and ever!" This provides an image of that lifeless marionette coming to life once again! This time, it is because God is in control. When we finally relinquish control fully to Him, we can move beyond the fear, anxiety, or whatever else is attempting to control us. What is pulling your strings today? His favor is upon us, and we have no more reason to stay tied to something that has no power over us. What time is it? It is His time!

DECEMBER 28

Linked to Him

1 Corinthians 12:27

On December 28, 2002, the professional networking company, LinkedIn was founded in the Mountain View, California, living room of Reid Hoffman. Hoffman and a few others founded the company launched the website in May of 2003, to help employees and employers get connected online. You can share professional information such as resumes, schooling history, and other pertinent bits related to the workplace environment. See if you can find me on LinkedIn.

What's His story? The name of the company and its website tells the story. It is designed to "link" people together, and it does a pretty good job. Millions of people use it today. The business-oriented social-networking site connects people in a professional environment, allowing people to form meaningful and sometimes fruitful vocational connections. Hoffman felt that if members of the professional community were linked, they could explore and gain access to more professional opportunities. The same holds true for the Christian community. Reasonably it could be called CrossedIn. Because of Jesus' sacrifice, the words of 1 Corinthians 12:27 resound, "Now you are the body of Christ, and each one of you is a part of it." Even if you do not think you have an impressive resume, you really do. The only position you really need on there is - Child of God! We are a body of Christ, and the mission is the same as the professional networking site – connection in a meaningful way. God is asking you to link in with Him every day and form that relationship that surpasses all understanding. Once you do that, you can then link to others through love to spread His kingdom. Let your heart choose to sing His praise and join in as you are! How do you join? You can do this by accepting Christ as your Savior, going to Him in prayer, and reading His word! Are you ready to link to Him? #LinkedtoHim!

DECEMBER 29

Y or Y Not?

John 17:21

On December 29, 1851, Thomas Valentine Sullivan opened the first YMCA in America. It was located in Boston, Massachusetts. George Williams founded the original "Y" in 1844 in London, England.

What's His story? YMCA stands for Young Men's Christian Association, focusing on building Christ-like character that would spread throughout the communities. Williams founded the "Y" as a refuge of Bible study and prayer for young men seeking escape from the hazards of life on the streets. Today, although it is only referred to as the "Y," the Christian foundation remains. John 17:21 is the Bible verse the "Y" originally adopted as its motto. It says, "that all of them may be one, Father, just as you are in me and I am in you. May they also be in us so that the world may believe that you have sent me." A shortened name is no match for the power and might of our Lord and Savior. His presence and the impact of His word provided did two things. It became the cornerstone for this organization and emphasized the power of abiding in God. When we do so, and in community with others, the world will believe! As Jesus' prayer in the passage of John attests, we are the future believers He was referring to, but adding to our numbers daily in His name. Today, how are you showing it? Is it by building up others, or working together in community, or even lifting some weights or playing soccer at the local "Y?" Your opportunity and mine are everywhere! Are you ready? "Y" not?

DECEMBER 30

Your Canary in Life

John 14:16

On December 30, 1986, plans were introduced in England to phase out the use of canaries in coalmines. Yes, they were still using them. At some point, modern technology finally caught up to them and proved to be more capable, not to mention cleaner and quieter.

What's His story? The use of canaries in coal mines was established because the yellow-feathered creature was susceptible to some of the dangerous gases in the mines like carbon monoxide, which is odorless, colorless, and tasteless. The miner knew that if his canary friend stopped whistling or worse, keeled over, then danger was imminent. Who or what are your canaries today? What is it that gives you that sense that danger is near, and you should reverse course? We all should have a friend who fits this bill, but what about the Holy Spirit? In John 14:16, Jesus promises the Holy Spirit, referring to Him as the Counselor and the spirit of God himself! How do we enact our own canary in the coalmines of our life? Those dark, frightening, cold places full of danger are no match for Him. By faith, the Spirit guides and protects us. There is no phasing out the Spirit due to newer technology or a better way of doing things. He was, and is, and is to come. Do you accept The Counselor today? One thing is for sure. You cannot keep Him caged up, but He is a faithful companion.

DECEMBER 31

More Than Resolutions

Psalm 51:10-12

On December 31, 1904, the first New Year's Eve celebration was held in, yes, New York City! It took place at Times Square, which is the junction of 7th Avenue and Broadway. While this was the first official celebratory event of its kind ringing in 1905, the ball dropping did not start until 1907. In 1904, it was just a bunch of happy people and fireworks, but two years later, a 700-pound ball dropped. An immigrant ironworker named Jacob Starr had built it.

What's His story? As you finish this journey we shared together, today is an opportunity to reflect on this past year and the opportunity to seek, and find God! New Year's Eve celebrations are often filled with decision-making about what the resolution will be for the upcoming year. What new skills will we learn, how much weight will we lose, where will we visit, or what habit will we break? But, did you know that most resolutions fail? Why? The simple answer is because we choose not to include God as a part of it! Even losing weight can incorporate God when we realize that if we lose weight, maybe we have more energy, and with more energy, we can do more things for His kingdom like volunteering and caring for our community in need. Psalm 51:10-12 is the perfect way to end the current year and start the new one. This is the resolution to make. It begins with creating a clean slate, or a clean house ready to accept God, and finishes with a restoral of the joy of salvation, granting us a willing spirit! In other words, we can make the house ready, invite God in, and become transformed by His love, grace, and salvation. Maybe you have already decided on your resolution for next year. Whatever you choose, is God a part of it? Make it more than a resolution and ask God into your heart. Do not wait for a new year, either. Do it every single day, because just like every birth, every death, and every event mentioned in this book, you are a part of history. You are a part of HIS STORY!

ACKNOWLEDGEMENTS

I give Him the glory for this book. For so many things to fall into place was to see God moving through my life, my pen, and my words.

Special thanks to my sweet wife, Ruthie, for her love as I researched and wrote my first book. Writing a book to spread His kingdom has always been a dream, and she helped make it a reality. Ruthie, your loving support, encouragement, patience, stellar editing, feedback, and advice were given with your whole heart, and I am eternally grateful. You have been one of the most meaningful Christian influences in my life. You prodded me to listen to the Holy Spirit when I had my hands over my ears. It changed my life. Your wisdom, awareness, and perception are incredible and persistently helped me write this book. I love you! I give thanks to God for you!

Many thanks to Liz and Joey, and much love! All those car rides full of suggestions and contributions, as well as listening ears, made such an impact as I wrote. You lifted me up when I needed it and kept me going throughout. I love you both! I hope you both continue to write. You inspired me through your own writing. God is indeed working through you!

Love and thanksgiving to my Mom, also known as G-Mom. You and dad taught me to appreciate the creation around me and love others as God loves us. Your own beautiful writing and heavenly piano skill have always stirred and moved me! Love you! And for Karen, Allen, and Suz, who were continually instruments of love as only siblings can be, planting the seeds of scripture, music, history appreciation!

Thanks go out to my extended family, especially my in-laws, because your love and backing on this journey served as fuel and sustenance to keep going. The botanical discussions, in particular, continually highlighted the ability to find God in His creation!

To Steven and Kelly Brumbeloe, thank you for recognizing the stirring within me, and for fanning the flame that has awakened my heart and opened my eyes to the pathway God has lit before me. Allowing me to deliver a message was one of the most meaningful and impactful things on my Christian journey. You are special people!

Many thanks go out to John Freeland for the experience that gave me perspective on the presence of the Holy Spirit. Without that new posture, I do not believe the words would have flowed so freely. I often reflect on the notes I took back then, and how much I learned. You were right about what you said! And by the way, if you ever wondered, yes, I totally get your humor!

To the North Campus family, thank you for your readership and love. You were the guinea pigs for this endeavor and instilled in me the real sense of a church community and family. Sorry for all of those wordy, long, winding emails. They served as the launching pad for this book. Sometimes the outpouring of what is inside takes a while! You never complained and led me to a much deeper relationship with Christ. Thank you for being an outlet and such an appreciative audience.

To Vicki Watts, who taught me that Godly standards and leadership have a place at work and they should be embraced daily, and never sacrificed. Your faith and investment in me and my career transcended the cubicle to bolster me with a renewed sense of personal courage, allowing me to step into uncomfortable places full of confidence.

To Greg G., for the long texts and scripture discussions that stoked the fire of being a better writer, father, husband, and friend. Your Christian brotherhood is treasured!

To the folks at Younique, especially Dave Rhodes and Kelly Kannwischer, for helping me gain clarity in my life plan and how it can contribute to His kingdom. I will not forget the afternoon filling out my LifeCall, revealing my call to write. That Younique moment was a lot like that moment from the *Friends* episode where Ross was yelling, "Pivot!" Clarity can become absolute rocket-fuel for God when you are open to it.

To the Alford family, our Alfomerlot journeys and trivia nights full of conversation and laughter certainly come from a deep love and friendship. To break bread with you, and to share the majestic beauty of His creation as we traveled together influenced this book in many ways. The memories made are inextricably linked to the joy found in experiencing God's kingdom and community. You are special people. Love y'all!

There are so many more who contributed to this first book. Whether it was through regular texts of Christian brotherhood or super-early mornings at the gym lifting weights while planting seeds of theology. Some helped to lead student ministry groups, Friday morning men's Bible studies, or even small-group studies early on my Christian journey. You all made an impact. You were a vessel for Him, and I was the recipient. Thank you for being the Christian signposts placed along the pathway lit by my Savior.

Printed in the United States
By Bookmasters